New quality management for the nonprofit sector

Guido Cuyvers

Thomas More University College, Belgium

Series in Business and Finance

VERNON PRESS

www.vernonpress.com

In the Americas:
Vernon Press
1000 N West Street, Suite 1200
Wilmington, Delaware, 19801
United States

In the rest of the world:
Vernon Press
C/Sancti Espiritu 17,
Malaga, 29006
Spain

Series in Business and Finance

Library of Congress Control Number: 2023949178

ISBN: 979-8-8819-0012-0

Also available: 978-1-64889-806-8 [Hardback]; 978-1-64889-837-2 [PDF, E-Book]

Cover design by Vernon Press using elements designed by pch.vector / Freepik and Freepik.

For Rosita, Bart, and Katleen

Table of contents

List of figures

List of tables

About the author

Guido Cuyvers studied criminology, sexology, and philosophy at the Catholic University of Leuven (Belgium) and holds a doctorate in criminology with a dissertation on the secondary victimization of crime victims. During his professional life, he was a lecturer, researcher, and head of the social work department at Thomas More University, where he taught psychology, psychopathology, organizational science, and quality assurance. He was also affiliated with the teacher training program of the faculty of psychology and pedagogy at the Catholic University of Leuven.

Dr. Cuyvers has repeatedly been a member, chair, or secretary of assessment panels in higher education (universities and colleges). He has also coached many nonprofit organizations in their process of quality development, a theme on which he has published extensively.

Currently involved in civil society, policy concerning older adults, and research on the social participation of older people in society, Dr. Cuyvers is committed to the Vlaamse Ouderenraad (Flemish Council of Older Adults) as a board member and independent expert as well as chairman of the council's Participation and Inclusion Committee. He is Belgium's representative on the Administrative Council of Age Platform Europe.

Dr. Cuyvers publishes extensively on all types of social themes. He is strongly involved in the problems that socially vulnerable groups in society experience, such as human trafficking and slavery, the unequal position of patients in health care, and the difficulties that aging people experience in asserting control over their own lives. His great passion continues to be publishing and teaching about these themes.

Preface

Because of the influence of various developments in society, quality has long been the central concern of the nonprofit sector. Partly due to government intervention and increasing competition, all parts of organizations in the nonprofit sector are obliged to work systematically on their quality. Quality has become necessary. However, as more people gain experience with quality assessments, visitations, and accreditations, criticism also grows. This is related to the way in which quality is assessed and the criteria used. In this book, I will take a critical look at this phenomenon. Many questions remain unanswered, and contradictions remain unresolved. Moreover, it is a major challenge to motivate everyone in an organization to think and work in the same direction. In short, there is still work to be done.

When I became interested in the theme of quality in the mid-1980s, what was then called *quality assurance* was still relatively unknown in the nonprofit sector. Initially, there was also a great deal of resistance because the quality was considered something typical for the profit sector and, therefore, not applicable to the nonprofit sector. Gradually, interest grew, partly because governments also began to recognize the importance of quality assurance. Since then, the practice of quality assurance has evolved greatly. Unfortunately, the dimension of control has received too much attention in recent years, often to the exclusion of the other aspects. The social context has also evolved greatly since the 1980s. We live in a society in which standardization, control, and measurement have become increasingly important. The focus has been transformed too much into manageable quality, and quality assurance has quietly taken on the role of controller. It seems like Big Brother really is watching us more. These evolutions and my growing insights made it clear that a different and new way of thinking about quality was needed.

I have several goals with this book. To begin with, I want to place the quality issue even more clearly in the current social context and hold it up to the light of critical thinking that has taken place in the meantime. I hope to achieve a balanced assessment of the risks and added value of striving for quality in an organization.

Subsequently, I want to broaden the traditional view of quality and quality assurance to a vision and approach that is compatible with and supportive of the mission of organizations in the nonprofit sector. Incidentally, I will speak of quality development rather than quality care. The term "quality development" is used in the hope of inspiring people to look differently at quality and at how their organization deals with it. Words create worlds, according to David Cooperrider. The question is not simply, "What is quality?" It is also, "How can we work on quality improvement in a systematic way?" My answer to this book is "quality development."

A third goal is to provide nonprofit organizations with methodologies and instruments that can lead to permanent quality development. I consider a methodology in this book to be a strategy or framework of ideas about how to proceed in developing quality. An instrument is a concrete tool that employees in an organization can use to perform their tasks in a high-quality manner. The description of an instrument often takes the form of a step-by-step plan.

I have organized this book into two parts. In the first part, I discuss the fundamentals of the concept of quality and the process of quality development in depth. I am convinced that a good understanding of the underlying concepts is at least as important as a thorough understanding of the methods. Consequently, an organization must meet several conditions so that working on quality does not result in sterile compliance with rules and procedures. This requires a constructive-critical attitude toward the entire quality process. I will also thoroughly clarify my own premises in this section, both the clarification of concepts and awareness of underlying trends-so that the readers can develop their own vision. In the first chapter, I focus on both the meaning of quality and its added value, as well as some of the pitfalls that often obscure thinking about quality and quality development. In the second chapter, I critically examine what visions are in force about quality, their underlying assumptions, and what the consequences are. In the third chapter, I discuss in detail the starting points for my vision of quality development. I close the first part with a discussion of what is needed to develop quality integrally.

The second part of this book focuses on practice. First, I describe the basic methodologies that support our vision of quality development. Quality development requires an empirical approach from organizations. "Facts and figures" is a commonly used slogan. A critical approach is also right here. It is about much more than collecting numbers. It is about how an organization can prove, in a reliable and credible manner, how it develops its quality and systematically checks it so that it does not depend on chance. In the sixth chapter, I therefore discuss aspects of measurement. In the seventh chapter, I review the important quality models that are currently in vogue. They form the framework for the many efforts that organizations make to continuously improve their quality. In the eight chapter, I discuss a series of techniques used in the different stages of quality development. Finally, I conclude this book with summarizing the core ideas to approach quality from a new perspective.

Part 1.
The fundamentals of quality development

Chapter 1

Quality

Quality is not an act; it is a habit.

— Aristotle

In this chapter, I discuss what quality can mean for organizations in the nonprofit sector. I am looking for a contemporary and idiosyncratic approach to and interpretation of quality in that sector. I do not allow myself to be limited to the notion of manageable quality, as is customary in the profit sector. The specificity of the nonprofit sector can be characterized as a set of relational practices that develop between the client, service provider, and other stakeholders. The result is that not all relationships or processes are manageable, externally controllable, or objectively measurable. In this quest for a correct definition of quality in the nonprofit sector, I not only propose a definition but also explain several pitfalls in thinking about quality. In addition, I seek to justify why quality is important and should receive the attention of all those involved in the nonprofit sector.

1.1. What is quality?

A clear definition of quality is a natural requirement that the reader may expect from a book on this theme. Rightly so, but defining quality is a perilous task. It is a bit like the concept of intelligence in psychology. To date, there is no consensus among psychologists on the exact meaning of that term. Yet, they have been working with tests that claim to measure intelligence for many decades. Therefore, even without a precise definition, it is possible to work with intelligence in practice. The same is true of quality, which is being seriously evaluated in both the profit and nonprofit sectors. For this reason, we can ask ourselves how important a correct description of quality really is. In the preface, I stated that this book should also be able to prove its worth in practice. I, therefore, cannot let this cup pass me by.

1.1.1. A definition is not without consequences

In our experience with various nonprofit sectors, I have repeatedly found that a definition of quality is not without consequences. Some practitioners have given up on attempting a definition because they have disagreed with the definitions (or supposed definitions) used.

As a result, they were not motivated further to think about the possible significance of quality development to their sector or to take part in quality improvement projects in their own organizations. Others reacted with such closed minds that they were no longer able to explore the possibilities for quality development. Still, others respond to the term quality with mostly scornful remarks. While negative reactions are part of reality, many professionals engage constructively. They feel called upon to give the best of themselves in the quest for quality. In any case, it is important that all those involved—I will refer to them as the stakeholders—have a nuanced view of quality right from the start. A clear description can help with this. In addition, the way in which the stakeholders experience the implementation and practice of integrated quality development contributes to its success.

1.1.2. A container concept?

Our experience is that quality usually functions as a container concept—anyone can put in it whatever they want. Moreover, stakeholders too easily assume that they are all using the same definition when they talk about quality. This obscures the concept more than it clarifies it. Let us look at some examples. Some reject the idea of quality because, according to them, it has to do mainly with measurability, which they feel cannot be the essence of the quality of education or care; others see quality as a value-free, highly objective concept, while the core processes in the nonprofit sector are not neutral but always value-laden. Still, others think that quality should only be related to efficiency and that in the nonprofit sector, content should come first. Still, others reject the concept because it refers too much to the product and too little to the process. Hence, there is a great deal of criticism, which, unfortunately, all too often stems from an approach to quality that is too narrow. Under that approach, quality can be described in one characteristic, such as customer satisfaction, the extent to which a service meets the customer's wishes, the characteristics of the result, and so on.

1.1.3. What about customer satisfaction?

Let us zoom in on the emphasis on customer satisfaction. An example is the description by management guru Peter Drucker (2014, p. 244):

> *"Quality in a product or service is not what the supplier puts into it. It is what the customer gets out of it and is willing to pay for it. This is incompetence. Customers only pay for what is useful to them and provides them with value. Nothing else is quality."*

Some nonprofit administrators find it hard to accept this strong emphasis on customer focus on the grounds that an organization in the nonprofit sector should not simply respond to the consumerist attitude of its customers. If the client were the only criterion, such criticism would be justified. In our view, customer focus is an essential but limited criterion. Of course, a nonprofit organization should not be blindly guided by client expectations; there are other factors that must come into play, as I will explain later in the chapter. Others in the nonprofit sector fear that giving clients a bigger voice will lead, for example, to healthcare providers too easily putting their money where their mouths are and giving in to the client's will. Here, too, evaluation by clients is important, but it is still only one dimension in achieving quality development. An organization also has a mission or a project driven by values, which helps determine its goals. Consistently achieving these goals and being accountable for them is, therefore, also a dimension of quality development.

1.1.4. Characteristics of quality

Before proposing a nonprofit-specific description of quality, I indicate in advance some characteristics that a definition of quality must respect. To begin with, quality is not a static characteristic that is fixed once and for all in an organization. On the contrary, quality is fluid or flexible. What quality is depends on the zeitgeist and the context in which it is defined. Our time, for example, makes different demands on the quality of education than did the postwar period. Today's empowered patient has different expectations and even sets different requirements for the relationship with doctors and nurses. The services provided by governmental officials now must deal with citizens who are much more critical than in the 1950s. Westerners have different requirements for water quality than people in Third World countries that suffer from water shortages. People often have radically different views on quality of life. Ideological, cultural, religious, and philosophical views, among others, play a role in this, which is reflected, for example, in discussions about the end of life. A timeless, generally accepted definition of quality is, therefore, impossible.

Subsequently, quality always relates to a dimension of a complex process. It can be about the quality of the process, the characteristics of the product or result, the satisfaction of customers and other stakeholders, which can be quite different, the meaningfulness of the vision and the project itself, and so on. A proper description should indicate these nuances.

Third, quality is also relative because it depends on the methods and instruments used by experts to map quality. The profit sector strives for standardization of processes and products. To this end, it has calibrated measuring instruments that pretend to show facts objectively—that is, regardless of human input and interpretation. Such standardization and objectivity are neither possible nor desirable in the nonprofit sector. That is not possible because the core of what happens between people cannot be measured. I will have more on that later. Such striving is also undesirable because standardization would ignore the unique experiences and feelings that take place in the relational practices between people. The critical reader will wonder, "Is there nothing to say about it? Is accountability impossible?" In our approach to quality development, it is the stories and experiences of the stakeholders that are necessary for identifying the core of the quality development process. They clarify how stakeholders perceive or experience the quality of both processes and results. Unlike numbers, stories enable deeper insight. The trick is to distill "the general in its diversity" from the unique stories. This requires quality and great expertise from those who must assess the quality of an organization.

Naturally, figures may also have a place in the accountability process and in the management of quality development itself. I clarify this explicitly in Chapter 6: To measure is to know. In the nonprofit sector, however, figures are a limited way to find out how quality is achieved and how it will be pursued in the future. I will also clarify later why no measurement or evaluation can guarantee the quality of the future organization. Because figures, in the form of so-called indicators, have an odium of objectivity, some authorities value them more than a narrative approach, or often, even exclusively. Therefore, an assessment of quality can consist of both a goal and a subjective aspect.

A fourth characteristic concerns the degree of quality. Quality is not an absolute or measureless given. For example, an organization may be excellent, which means that it gets the highest score on all standards that an assessor uses. Or that the organization is leading other similar organizations. Or that the stakeholders, both clients and employees, show extraordinary enthusiasm. Applying a yardstick, and thus assigning scores to core processes and results in the nonprofit sector, can only be a subjective undertaking. This often leads to discussions about the quality of the assessors. Quality can also mean that the organization simply meets the requirements of some assessment framework.

A fifth characteristic of quality is that it is always formulated from a certain perspective. For example, the perspective of the assessor who wants to figure out the actual quality, or that of stakeholders who have certain expectations about and perceptions of quality, or that of the management of an organization, or that of the government that imposes standards. These different perspectives determine how different parties evaluate quality. The assessment of quality can, therefore, differ from different perspectives. For example, when clients choose a service, school, or hospital, they often claim to do so based on quality. Yet that is not the objective quality, but the quality as expressed, for example, in the name, the success stories, and the gossip—

the image of the organization. However, that quality may differ radically from that assessed by a panel. Another example is that learning processes can demand strenuous effort from students, which the students experience subjectively as unpleasant. Teachers and the school board, however, may consider these efforts necessary and justified to guarantee the quality of their graduates. It is, therefore, useful to distinguish between expected, actual, imposed, and perceived quality, as I clarify in Figure 1.1.

Figure 1.1. Perspectives on quality

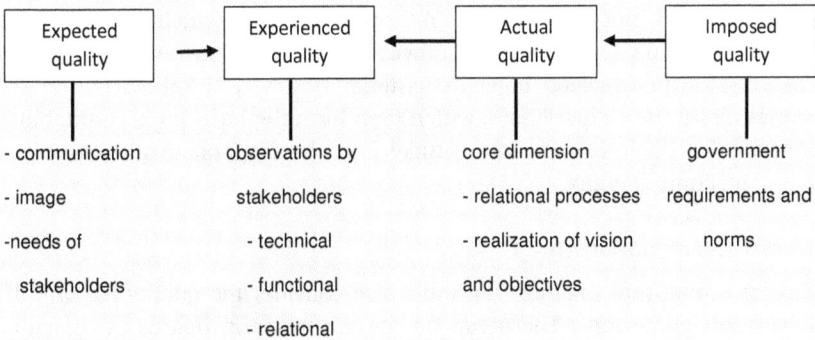

Expected quality		Experienced quality		Actual quality		Imposed quality
- communication		observations by		core dimension		government
- image		stakeholders		- relational processes		requirements and
-needs of		- technical		- realization of vision		norms
stakeholders		- functional		and objectives		
		- relational				

Expectations

Quality means different things to different parties. For the organization itself, management, and employees, quality may primarily have to do with the extent to which it succeeds in realizing its vision and goals through its core processes. Not all stakeholders approach quality that way. For example, clients have expectations about the quality of contacts, communication with employees, atmosphere, and material infrastructure. Employees may have different expectations when they think about quality. Expectations may or may not be realistic. In addition, they differ according to the category of stakeholders. Incidentally, the expectations of all stakeholders will not necessarily coincide with the goals set by the organization itself.

Experience

Different stakeholders perceive quality differently, partly based on the different expectations they have. The perception of quality is colored by three dimensions. First, the stakeholders experience several characteristics of the nonprofit sector, such as reliability, expertise, and punctuality. In short, a few technical aspects. Subsequently, their experience is partly determined by the extent to which the process and the results meet their needs, the so-called functional quality. Finally, the way in which relationships develop between the organization and the stakeholders also plays a key role in the perception of quality. The experience of that relational dimension is often more important than the other facets and the actual quality of the results. Because this is a subjective experience dimension, the experienced quality does not necessarily say much about the actual quality.

Facts

Based on facts, an evaluation, whether internal or external, leads to a certain judgment about quality. This evaluation is often based too strongly, sometimes very one-sidedly, on what can be measured and determined empirically. However, this is not enough in the nonprofit sector, in which the core of the operation has to do with relational processes. These are much more difficult to "measure" with so-called objective criteria. However, stakeholders can tell stories about their experiences, which then form the basis for accountability. This requires different skills and attitudes from the assessors than an approach based on controllability.

Norms and requirements

Finally, a nonprofit organization must also consider the quality required by inspection authorities. These can be the government, boards of directors, umbrella bodies, accreditation bodies, and so on. Their approach often consists of examining the extent to which an organization complies with the imposed indicators. The quality requirements they set are often not in line with the expectations of other stakeholders, such as employees and clients. Moreover, the opinion of the inspecting body can differ radically from the quality experienced by the client.

Our definition of quality in the nonprofit sector

With the above considerations in mind, I define quality as follows:

> *The extent to which an organization achieves its objectives—which are always formulated in a certain time and in a certain context—as reflected in a systematic way of working, in a result, and in a degree of appreciation by the stakeholders.*

This description deserves further clarification and nuance.

1.2. Facets of quality

Quality has to do with the qualities or characteristics of both the product and the process. Applied to the nonprofit sector, quality, therefore, has to do with the characteristics of the process as well as the characteristics of the results.

Process and results are driven by the goals that an organization wants to achieve to realize its vision or project. When formulating these goals, the organization considers the input of many stakeholders. Quality, then, also has to do with assessing the extent to which goals have been achieved. On the one hand, this can be done using empirical criteria, the so-called indicators (more about this in Chapter 6). Quality is always a process or a result for someone. The perception of quality is, therefore, an important dimension in addition to objective measurability.

We must be careful not to view the realization of that quality as a linear process. First, we cannot set a vision and goals once and for all. Vision and goals must be developed anew every time the actors or the social circumstances change. Subsequently, that development itself is not a simple top-down process in which the top of an organization decides which goals the others must achieve. Due to the value-related nature of vision and goals, it is important that the various actors in the organization be involved. Finally, the organization is a dynamic entity in which people, their commitment, and their positions change and in which micropolitical processes take place. This means that the quality of an organization cannot be fixed once and for all.

Figure 1.2. Factors in the realization of quality

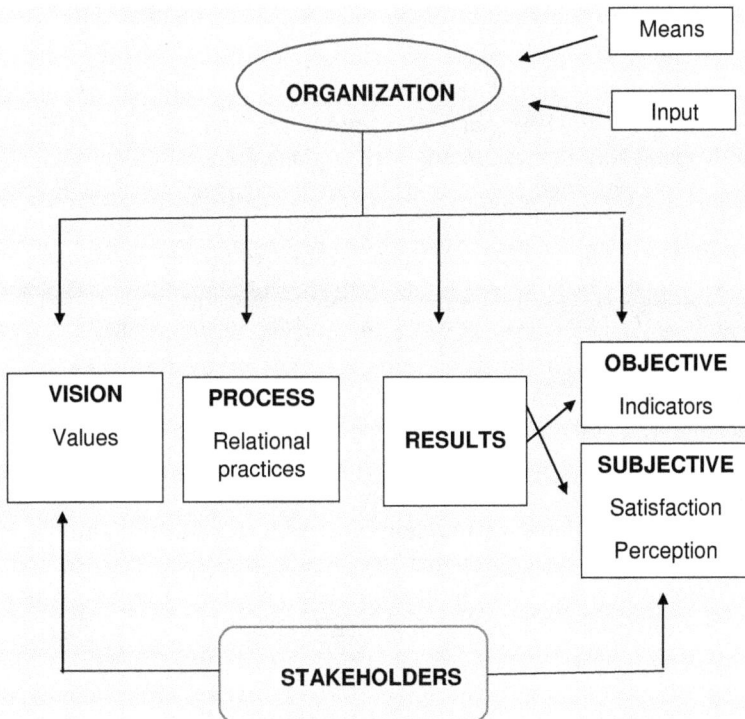

The essence of a process in the nonprofit sector, namely the relationships between people who develop their identities and personalities in the process, is difficult to fit into a traditional control-oriented concept of quality. In Figure 1.2, I combine the essential elements schematically and offer a brief explanation.

1.2.1. Who is involved?

Before an organization can assess its quality, it must know where it wants to go and what type of quality it wants to achieve. To this end, the organization formulates its vision and its project and translates these into goals. These goals are extremely important for the nonprofit sector. I will, therefore, return to this in more detail in Chapter 4. This important process of developing a vision and setting goals does not take place in a vacuum. The organization must consider or at least listen to the requirements, needs, and expectations of many stakeholders.

First, there is the government, which gives a mandate to certain organizations in the public sector to supply services. It attaches certain organizational and substantive conditions and requirements to this. For example, the standards that healthcare, education, and other services must follow are described in protocols, which are ideally set up together in the professional field. Developments in science and technology also influence visions and goals. Partly because of competition, organizations must be up to date and adapted to these new developments.

In addition to external stakeholders, there are internal stakeholders: management, staff, clients, and their entourages who have expectations and wishes, along with interest groups such as trade unions. The question can be raised here as to whether and to what extent clients are justified in claiming services, assistance, or education. Naturally, their needs and expectations must be given attention, for example, when it comes to the organizational context and the way in which the employees in the organization relate to the clients. I prefer the term "optimal customer focus" to "maximum customer focus."

Each organization is also faced with the task of formulating a unique project based on its values and shaping its realization in its own way. Let us take education as an example. Bull (1990) argued that an educational organization should play a pioneering role in society. It must be a source of innovation and development, and therefore, it must do more than supply customer-oriented services. An educational organization must be a social institution that fulfills individual and social educational needs in a way that leads to the best development of both. Quality is, therefore, less a product of material conditions and more of a result of inspiration from beliefs and opinions.

That is why organizations must be able to form sufficient autonomous space within society, where other values, norms, and criteria apply than in society itself. This approach to quality means, of course, that tensions can arise between the various actors involved in quality. I give an example. Healthcare providers within a health facility may be focused on quality development, while management and support services are more concerned about achieving standards and respecting procedures. Those who examine, from the perspective of society, how the organization deals with the resources that society makes available will, from that accountability perspective, mainly focus on the extent to which the organization realizes the set standards.

1.2.2. Process and result (output)

Another factor of quality has to do with the characteristics of both the process and the results. Initially, quality assurance focused strongly on the output, the product, or the result. Gradually, the process itself has also been recognized as a dimension. For quality in the nonprofit sector, it is certainly necessary to include both the process and the output in the quality definition. I repeat that the core of the process in the nonprofit sector, namely the relational event, can be described in terms of goals, but at the same time, it is the least technically manageable and steerable; moreover, it is difficult to put into objective indicators.

Output can be measured by the extent to which an organization achieves its set goals. I have already said that many different stakeholders have their own requirements. They are often complementary and sometimes contradictory. In conclusion, we must consider the extent to which the organization takes the various parties into account and does not unilaterally, for example, respond only to an overly consumeristic attitude of some clients or react too submissively to the expectations of the economy. The output dimension alone is insufficient. For example, a school could ensure that its students were capable of university education through a strict selection policy and a very one-sided project. The output would then probably meet the requirements of higher education. However, the process could take a heavy social and human toll. A quality that is defined unilaterally based on the efficiency requirement ignores the quality of the process: how students are guided toward the realization of the school's goals, what atmosphere prevails in the contact between civil servants and citizens, and how communication takes place between doctors and paramedics and their patients.

Finally, this nuance. How and to what extent an organization can realize its vision and goals partly depends on the resources made available to it for this purpose. The organization itself is not always responsible for this. In addition to purely material resources, we should also mention the context in which an organization operates, such as the social class of the average patient, the intake characteristics of students, and the composition of the population.

1.3. Pitfalls

Several lines of thought about quality and the way in which organizations and actors in the nonprofit world give substance to quality have led to many justified critical remarks. Based on our desire to give the road to quality formulated above every chance, I outline several pitfalls that can tarnish quality thinking and thereby discredit quality development.

1.3.1. Controllability

De Dijn (1991) pointed out the risk that while quality management leads to greater efficiency and purposefulness, it often overshoots its goal. He believed that integral quality assurance—he did not yet use the term "quality development"—was an expression of the modern pursuit of controllability, controlling not only nature but also human life itself, collectively and individually. On the other hand, a correct understanding of quality, both organizational and interpersonal, implies that we cannot organize everything. If quality management is understood as perfect control of the process, it is counterproductive, according to De Dijn (2002, 2007). That illusion of manageability then requires more energy than it yields—more organization, more administration, and more technology in the professional approach. Moreover, it threatens to be at the expense of interpersonal connection and solidarity. As a result, people become lonely in the process (Bouckaert,1999; Bouckaert & Zsolnai, 2007).

The above considerations force us to make the following statement: An integrated approach to quality implies that the process of supplying services in nonprofit organizations cannot be understood and controlled in its entirety. The specificity of the nonprofit sector has to do, among other things, with relational practices. These are relationships in which people are held accountable for their responsibility to others and in which they can develop their identities. In relational practices, the unique human qualities of the stakeholders play a key role. This is a process that escapes objectively measurable effectiveness. This does not alter the fact that all kinds of development and assessment processes can supply an added value for the nonprofit sector: They must realize and monitor the organizational context in which the core processes can fully develop. However, at a time when the nonprofit sector is constantly questioned and criticized about its effectiveness, there is a significant risk that the concern for quality will get bogged down in the role of accomplice to results thinking. It may be seen from the foregoing that I consider traditional quality management primarily to be a creator of conditions for relational core processes. Wanting to control those core processes objectively and demonstrably is then only an empty illusion.

Still, recent developments in quality control, such as audits, visitations, and accreditation—imposed by the government and boards of directors—force organizations to arrive at a kind of level determination of quality based on so-called "objectifiable indicators." This raises many questions. For example, what is the minimum or sufficient level of quality that an organization must achieve to receive a positive assessment? While I recognize the importance of external quality control, I must remain alert to its disastrous side effects (namely that efforts to reach the required minimum leave the organization breathless) so that there is no longer room for critical reflection.

1.3.2. Objectivity

A statement by a top politician makes it clear that a critical approach to quality is necessary. He said that some of his liberal friends sent their children to Catholic or Protestant schools not because of their philosophy of life but because of the quality of the education. That statement creates the illusion that quality has nothing to do with values but everything to do with objective control of processes and goal orientation. Quality could then be a kind of measurable perfection.

Philosophers' criticism of such a concept of quality forces me to think about what I intend by quality management, especially in the nonprofit sector. In critical voices and articles about the approach to quality (in education, for example), there is a concern over uncritically placing young people in a performance-oriented, economic, and competitive society. The critical discussion about what makes a life of high quality should certainly be held in the nonprofit sector, and that cannot be a value-free discussion. Choosing solidarity, equal opportunities, human development, independence, sustainability, respect for people and nature, and social self-sufficiency—in short, choosing what makes life humane and of high quality—requires a clear commitment to values. Quality development must, therefore, be more than goal-oriented. As important as targeting is, it must be supplemented with what Bouckaert (1999) calls "meaningful quality assurance." Care, services, and education do not take place in a vacuum. Quality development must, therefore, also pay attention to the connection between people (for example, to the relational processes between doctor and patient, care-provider and client, and teacher and student). To work in a qualitative manner in government, in education, or in health and welfare must, therefore, also include a reflection on the basic principles of society. In a climate in which the concept of quality management threatens to become a decisive factor, substantive discussion is more than necessary.

1.3.3. Efficiency

Efficiency is usually another criterion for assessing the quality of an organization. This might be functional in the manufacturing industry, but when used indiscriminately, it might kill quality in the nonprofit sector. To be clear, by efficiency, I mean that the greatest possible result is achieved with the smallest possible effort or at least with an extremely balanced deployment of resources. In other words, it means achieving a lot with few resources within a brief time. I must distinguish this from effectiveness, however. That term stands for achieving the set goal. So, someone can be effective but not very efficient: He achieves the goal, but it takes a long time, and it costs a lot. When efficiency becomes the dominant criterion in the nonprofit sector, we are in big trouble. The core processes are often unpredictable and cannot be calculated in advance in terms of time and resources. Of course, one can expect organizations to manage resources carefully—which is not necessarily the same as efficiently—but always in proportion to the effectiveness of the realization of the value-driven goals of the organization. The tendency of the government to rely heavily on procedures and protocols that are evidence-based may promote efficiency but not necessarily effectiveness in terms of quality, meaningful care, services, or education. Some authors also point out that this one-sided pursuit of efficiency must be framed within a neoliberal ideology in which economic norms suppress other values (Verhaeghe, 2012, 2023; Achterhuis, 2010).

1.4. Why is quality important?

Why should quality be key in a nonprofit organization? In the past, there was hardly any explicit mention of quality assurance or quality development, and yet good business was done. I can list many good reasons for an organization to invest in quality.

1.4.1. Relational process

The most important argument concerns the core of good service and care provision: the relational process in which people who are responsible for each other create the space in which identity and personality can develop. That process is so fundamental to the person and to society that, for that reason alone, the pursuit of the best possible quality must be at the heart of every action of individuals, groups, and structures in the nonprofit sector.

1.4.2. Context

Furthermore, the current context in which the nonprofit sector must operate ensures an emphasis on quality. Every organization competes with comparable organizations. An organization rarely has a monopoly position and must, therefore, function within a complex social context. Quality appears to be, much more than ideology, a criterion clients use to choose an organization. Usually, it is about subjectively experienced quality and not about an objective standard. For example, it is more the name and image of an organization that plays a role and less the thorough knowledge of that organization. In any case, an organization must deal with articulate customers who compare organizations. Unfortunately, for too many overarching or executive stakeholders, the quality control dimension with the goal of control is too prominent. So far, they have paid too little attention to the development dimension.

1.4.3. Social responsibility

Civil society organizes the nonprofit sector. Society often makes resources—in fact, taxpayers' money—available through governments and links that support requirements. Naturally, society asks organizations to account for how they have used those resources. Because of its claim on public resources, an organization has a duty to deliver the best possible quality to society and to account for itself. This again raises the question: What quality? What autonomous space may an organization form in which other values, norms, and criteria apply than in society itself? For example, higher and university educational institutions have gradually acquired a position in which they can determine and develop values, norms, content, and working methods autonomously from the government. The principles of self-responsibility and self-evaluation are established right there. In secondary and primary education, government intervention is still much stronger for the time being.

1.4.4. Job satisfaction

An integrated approach to quality development offers opportunities to optimize the job satisfaction and motivation of employees in the nonprofit sector. If this approach is successful, it will lead to a better organizational context in which cooperation and support are important barriers against phenomena such as burnout and cynicism. Moreover, an optimal organizational context and a positive culture offer employees many more opportunities to continue to develop as a person in their work.

1.4.5. The costs

The relationship between quality and cost is often misinterpreted. I then hear statements such as, "We cannot afford to invest in quality development because we do not even have sufficient resources for our core processes." This comment suggests that quality and care or service are different things that can be separated. Yet, distinguishing between quality and service is not acceptable. Quality must be an essential and inalienable characteristic of all services, care, and education. All processes in the nonprofit sector must be of high quality. Therefore, I regard the costs of quality as a necessary part of the costs of services, care, and education.

The question, then, is, what are the extra costs of quality? Let us be clear: Investing in quality costs a lot financially, organizationally, and psychologically. However, ignoring quality costs much more in the long run. The investment in quality will eventually pay for itself through, for example, lower costs due to errors. Numerous mistakes are made in organizations, usually with major consequences. For example, what waste of quality does a school have if too many students skip school at an early age? How should the turnover figures of clients in a care organization be interpreted? How expensive is an authoritarian hospital policy that demotivates nursing staff? Errors and shortcomings cost an organization a lot financially, humanly, and in terms of efficiency. Therefore, let us zoom in on the issue of costs using the PEF model. This model (Prevention – Evaluate – Errors) maps out the most important costs (Moullin, 2002, 2007):

- Prevention costs. These costs refer to efforts to avoid inferior quality or defects in advance. This means, for example, more attention to the organization of the service, training of employees, development of a quality system, time for training in quality development, and writing procedures.

  Evaluation and measurement costs. These costs relate to more monitoring of the way services are delivered to clients, research into the quality of the work delivered, and measuring client satisfaction. Of course, it would be ideal if these forms of in-process evaluation were performed by the service providers themselves, and not separated from the process.

- Internal error costs. These costs relate to the rectification or correction of errors resulting from the fact that the service has not been performed correctly but without this having a direct impact on the satisfaction of the client. For example, a group loses time during a case discussion because essential information about the client is missing. To prevent such problems, it may be necessary, for example, to invest more in the further training of employees. Such a lack of quality causes problems for staff, including stress, tension, negative emotions, and dissatisfaction.

- External error costs. These costs occur when the client or patient finds shortcomings in the service. They are often difficult to rectify, and they have important consequences for the attitude of the client toward the service provider. For example, poor planning of consultations can lead to long waiting times for clients, because of which, several clients will drop out. An incorrect approach to the care process, a wrong diagnosis, or a late intervention are examples of factors that may lead the client into even greater problems. Such problems can damage the image of the organization and result in a loss of clients.

Figure 1.3. Effect of quality development on costs

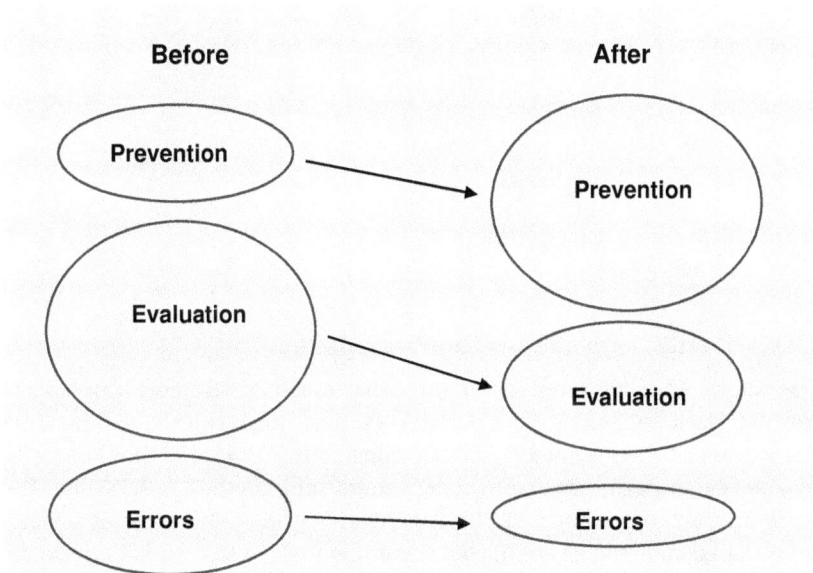

Source: Adapted from Moullin (2002)

The PEF model states that quality development increases prevention costs in every case. At the same time, it leads to a reduction in error costs and evaluation costs, as shown in Figure 1.3.

Finally, I can integrate all of these arguments in favor of quality development in a diagram (see Figure 1.4) (Ovreteit, 1990, 2009).

Figure 1.4. Effects of the reduction of failure costs

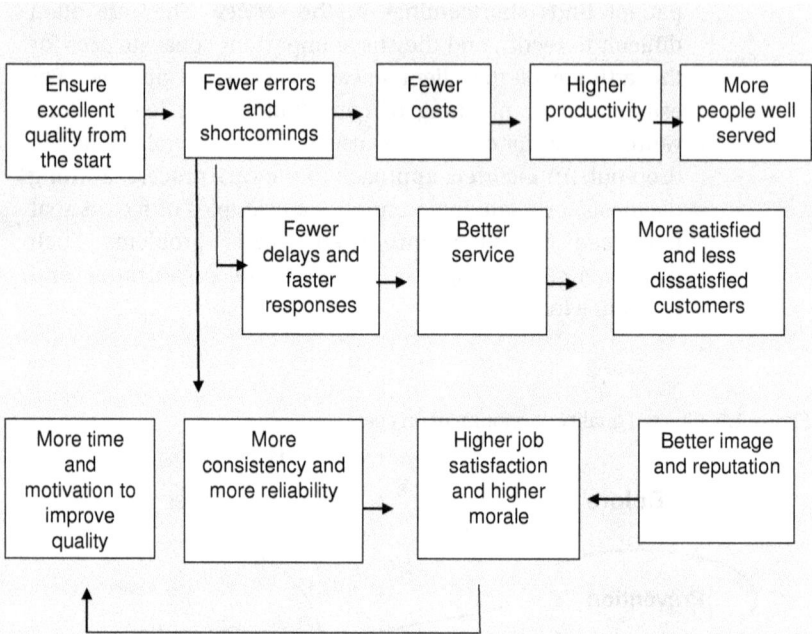

Source: Adapted from Ovreteit, 1990

1.4.6. Self-critical dynamics and internal reflection

The nature of the nonprofit sector advocates integrating the core processes of care, services, education, and culture, etc., in quality development. That process must be redesigned repeatedly, considering new social developments, new needs and expectations of stakeholders, and new insights. Neither the goals nor the course itself can be definitively decided. Moreover, it is not a process that can only be conducted according to fixed standards because the actors in the process are constantly faced with the challenge of working together—in interaction with each other—to realize the goals of the nonprofit sector. The process cannot, therefore, be captured in standards or strict, predictable procedures. Traditional quality assurance aimed at control is, therefore, not sufficient.

The concern for quality, if properly integrated into an organization, means that stakeholders continue to be stimulated to critically examine their own actions and the functioning of the organization on a regular basis. This does not necessarily have to be in response to an imminent visitation or inspection. Ideally, the organization develops its own system that guarantees internal reflection and critical questioning. In this way, the organization can adjust during the process and does not have to wait for an external assessment to indicate pain points or shortcomings. When an organization systematically integrates quality into its operations, there is a good chance that it will remain alert to new developments in its sector. Self-evaluation then becomes a stimulus for innovation.

Finally: What is really important?

- The specific nature of the nonprofit sector (i.e., processes based on relational practices), requires its own approach to quality, which may differ from quality assurance in the profit sector.

- Relational practices cannot be (fully) captured in so-called objective figures.

- Quality is the necessary stimulus to motivate people as an organization to give the best of themselves for the realization of the goals of the organization.

- Indicators such as objectivity, manageability, and efficiency are not able to adequately assess quality in the nonprofit sector.

- The pursuit of quality must be supported by all stakeholders in an organization and is not the privilege of experts.

Chapter 2

Worrying about quality management, a critical reflection

A neoliberal organization invariably creates an unproductive top layer whose main function is to support itself through the control of others.

— Paul Verhaeghe (2012)

A reaction that people often give when they are confronted with quality management projects in their organization is, "Some outsiders pretend that we have not delivered quality until now, while we have not tried anything else in our lives." Of course, most professionals have long been concerned about quality. This is clear in the way they interact with clients, the continuous training, and so on. Their concern for the process is real but often is still an individual matter. There are major differences in what quality can mean for someone and how an organization or professional wants to realize it. Just as there is no single definition of quality, there is no uniform way of approaching quality in an organization. This is why I first give a rough sketch of diversity in the way of working on quality. I then clarify the background of certain practices. Finally, we highlight several consequences of an overly one-sided approach to quality.

2.1. Setting

Based on Table 2.1, I briefly outline the evolution of thinking about quality in general. Different organizations are at various stages.

Table 2.1. Types of approaches to quality

	Quality control	Quality assurance	Quality building	Quality development
Control	Top-down	Top-down norms are imposed	Top-down	Dialogical organization – self-managing ability of teams
Focus on	Individual	Individual	Team	Relational practices

Dealing with errors	No errors – sanctions	No errors – adjustment	Errors can be discussed as a source of learning	Errors are learning opportunities for the entire organization
Involved people	Interns	Interns – accountability to third parties	Attention to external relations	External parties are seen as partners
Judgment	Measurements of results with hard criteria	Measurement of processes with hard criteria	More than measuring with hard criteria	Quality is a culture that is developed with attention to criteria
Responsible	Controller	Quality expert	Quality Coordinator	Everyone takes part in the whole

2.1.1. From quality control to quality assurance

Initially, working on quality received explicit attention, especially in the profit sector, first as pure quality control and from the 1970s in the form of total quality management. While the nonprofit sector gradually evolved in that direction from the success of quality assurance, people quickly experienced the traditional profit approach as oppressive. The development of quality models, especially EFQM, which proposed an integrated approach that was also useful for the nonprofit sector, means that specific instruments have also been developed for the nonprofit sector with which that sector can feel reasonably comfortable. This created more room for soft shape management with attention to motivation and learning as an organization as well. This resulted in more focus on the process of the development of the organization, although still very much dominated by the top and quality managers.

2.1.2. Quality building

The term quality assurance is too static because he suggests that it is about controlling what exists with stable norms. If taken too narrowly, the weakness of quality assurance is that it once again results in a one-sided emphasis on rules and procedures. As a result, it has failed to deliver on its first promise to innovate traditional management approaches (Staut, 2000). It obviously makes no sense to burden the nonprofit sector with a system that could eventually lead to even more cramping. I choose to call the phase after quality assurance the phase of "quality building." There is still management from above, but the teams are given a more significant role. Moreover, learning from mistakes is central here. External stakeholders are also receiving more attention in the development of quality.

2.1.3. Quality Development

A further step in this evolution consists of the consistent involvement of all levels of the organization and external stakeholders in the development of a vision for the organization and its realization. The ability and experience of all stakeholders is fully recognized and given space. This is accompanied by a different relationship between the management of the organization and the stakeholders.

Quality development is now everyone's business. The conviction prevails that working on quality is not only, and not primarily, a matter of procedures, criteria, and protocols but, above all, relational practices. Quality development should ultimately be a concrete way of working that ensures that the quality, both process and content, can continuously increase during the interaction between the different actors.

That is why we resolutely opt for the term quality development to emphasize the dynamics and the relational dimension. After all, in the nonprofit sector, there is little that is fixed once and for all, and that can be immortalized in rules, standards, and procedures. Nevertheless, I want to guard against a one-sided and, therefore, unrealistic approach. I accept that the concern of complying with formal quality criteria can also be a necessary element of quality development. Measures based on indicators may have a place, provided they are not the sole or main measure in the assessment process. Each organization must give shape to its pursuit of quality in its own way. Quality is, therefore, in any case, tailor-made and embedded in a specific context. Next to the care dimension is the development dimension (see also Figure 2.1). It is based on self-management by organizations. Moreover, it permanently challenges organizations to keep reflecting on their vision of care, services, education, and the process itself. This requires continuous learning and innovation on both an individual and collective level. When an organization reaches that stage, one can speak of a quality culture.

The government and many clients in the nonprofit sector still attach too much one-sided importance to facts and figures. By formulating indicators, they try to map out both the process and the results in a measurable way. That is an illusion. What is more, this approach threatens to reduce the concern for quality to a desire for control, resulting in strict management. However, such an approach hardly contributes to the quality of the nonprofit sector, of the interactions between client and healthcare provider, patient and doctor, student and teacher. Moreover, too much control leaves no room for the development dimension.

Figure 2.1. Quality development process

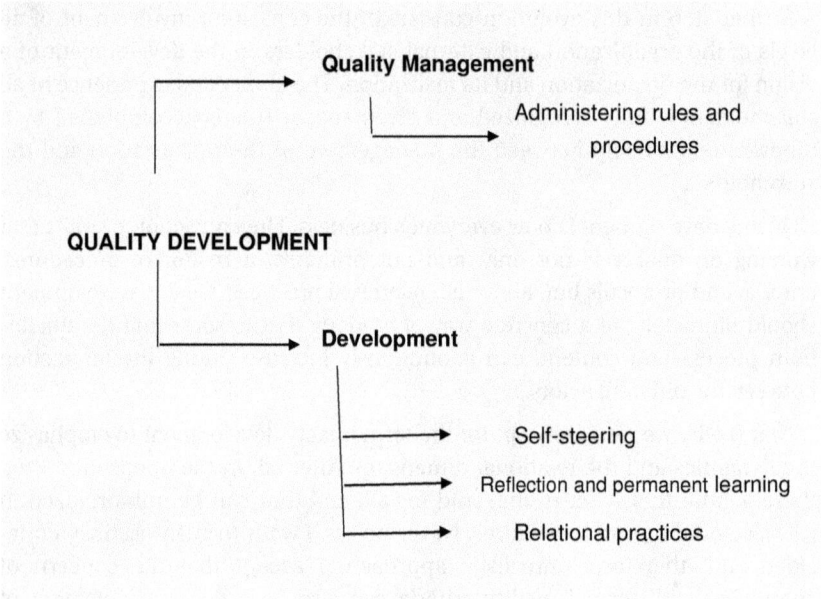

Quality Management

Administering rules and procedures

QUALITY DEVELOPMENT

Development

Self-steering

Reflection and permanent learning

Relational practices

Consistent quality development embedded in a real quality culture is still not the case in many organizations. There are reasons for this, which are not always immediately obvious. Consequently, in this chapter, I first want to look for the backgrounds that play a role in how an organization approaches quality. Only then will I zoom in on the quality development that I advocate in this book.

2.2. Background

To understand why an organization is concerned with quality in a specific way, it is not enough to listen to formal communication on the topic. Unspoken opinions always play a role; perhaps the key players in the organization are not even aware of them. That is why it is useful to look for the underlying visions behind the practices. Of course, I can only discuss them briefly in the context of this book. For those who wish to delve further into various aspects of the topic, I refer to additional literature in the notes.

2.2.1. Vision of society

Every organization works in a specific social context and consciously or unconsciously adopts views on how society can best function. These are the so-called ideologies. Their importance is that if you believe in a certain vision of society, you allow it to determine your behavior. In quality thinking, the predominant ideology currently seems to be neoliberalism. Let's briefly explain it.

Neoliberalism is primarily an economic theory that focuses on the role of the corporate world in society. At the same time, it questions the role of government and the organization of society. The opinion is that it is not the government but intelligent entrepreneurs that determine the prosperity of a society. Competition, not cooperation, drives people to get the best out of themselves. The government should not interfere with this. The free market will regulate itself. As a result, competition in the business world drives better products at more competitive prices. Competition drives the pursuit of efficiency, achieving the greatest possible return with the least possible effort. Educational institutions must then, for example, produce competent people who are useful to the economy. People should take responsibility for their own lives and not be pampered by the government. You get what you deserve. Those who are better (i.e., more competent and efficient) and who work harder earn more. Competition drives up quality. Efficiency, then, is one of the underlying criteria in assessing the quality of an organization.

The reasoning is that the best way to assess efficiency is to measure it with hard, objective criteria. Whether something is worthwhile must be proved with data. This is reflected in the type of evidence-based thinking that first flourished in healthcare and later in social work. Something is worthwhile only if its results can be proved. In short, what cannot be measured is not important. Various authors have warned of the disastrous consequences of this evolution in thinking for the core processes of education, care, services, culture, and for the solidarity and cohesion of society (Verhaeghe, 2023; Achterhuis, 2010; Beekman, 2016; Biebricher, 2017).

2.2.2. Organizational vision

Quality thinking and acting is also fed by the way stakeholders view organizations. Too often, managers' approach to quality betrays a mechanistic vision of organizations. This mechanistic thinking approaches an organization more in terms of stable machinery than in terms of cooperation between people. Anyone who thinks this way is usually convinced that shortages or weaknesses can be tackled through technical interventions and that systematic tinkering with shortages will ultimately boost the quality of an entire organization. This mechanistic approach focuses on structures rather than processes. That is why stability is paramount. In this book, I contrast this with an organic vision of organizations.

To do justice to the diversity in the visions of organizations, I propose a simple typology. To keep things clear, I use two criteria to classify visions of organizations, realizing that each typology also implies a simplification of reality. Our aim is to show how the vision of an organization decides quality thinking. The first criterion is the dynamics of an organization. Some see an organization mainly as a structure with a division of roles and procedures. Others emphasize that an organization is primarily a dynamic event, a kind of construction site, where nothing is fixed forever because neither the internal history nor the context is predictable. The second criterion is the type of direction given to the organization. On one hand, there are people who still view an organization in a highly individualistic and top-down way. There is management from above in a kind of waterfall system based on a strong, result-oriented mindset. If everyone takes up their own piece well, the result is guaranteed. The other approach sees an organization rather as a community of people who together develop the organization in the function of collective values. In this way, I arrive at four visions of an organization, as illustrated in the following figure.

Figure 2.2. Visions of organizations

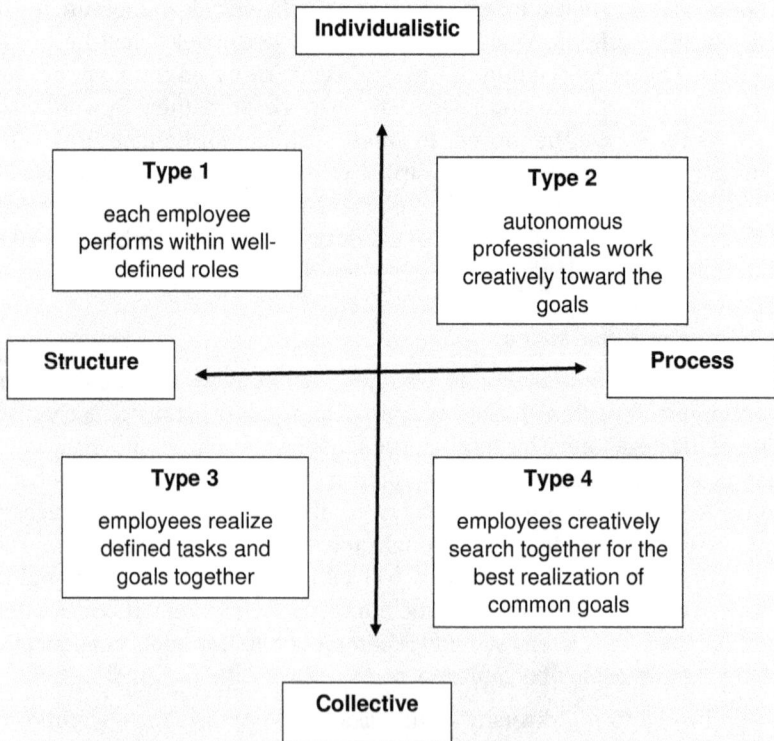

Individualistic

Type 1

each employee performs within well-defined roles

Type 2

autonomous professionals work creatively toward the goals

Structure

Process

Type 3

employees realize defined tasks and goals together

Type 4

employees creatively search together for the best realization of common goals

Collective

Let's briefly outline the consequences of quality thinking.

In type 1, quality is measured solely based on the product or the result. The process is not relevant. Criteria that the result must meet are imposed without the participation of the employees in the organization. It is not about the stories; it is about the numbers. Efficiency and objectivity are the key factors here. Unfortunately, this is still often the way the government looks at and assesses organizations. In fact, it is not much more than a form of quality control, which contributes little to the development of quality itself.

In type 2, the realization dawns that the result itself is related to the processes used to arrive at the result. Even though criteria and results are still the final assessment material, processes receive attention and are able to adjust the course. If each employee completes their own piece, it will help the whole. This vision forms the basis of the quality assurance approach.

In type 3, the organization is still approached as a structure, but it is much more about achieving collective goals. The classical education system is an example of this, as are religious organizations and most civil society organizations. For example, most civil society organizations involve volunteers and give them a voice, but always within the framework of the existing structure. The realization prevails that achieving collective goals is only possible if members and employees are involved as much as possible. For quality thinking, the story is now important. The strength of an organization is clear, then, from the fact that the members know and can tell the collective story of the organization with its collective values.

In type 4, an organization is seen as a construction site that never needs to have a definitive form, which can be further built upon if the context or circumstances make sense. The Sagrada Familia in Barcelona could serve as a symbol of the process-based organization as a construction site. The Sagrada Familia is the biggest unfinished Roman Catholic church in the world. Its construction started in 1882 and is still not completed. It is situated in the hearth of Barcelona, Spain, and is the most visited and most famous attraction in the city. It is important that all stakeholders take part in the development of the organization and in pursuing its goals. This creates a quality culture that could be the ultimate form of quality development.

The vision of an organization goes hand in hand with a vision of leadership. I will discuss this theme in detail later. Here, I want to point out, however, that a mechanistic view of organizations runs the risk of narrowing true leadership to simple management in order to control reality. Solving quality problems then means eliminating causes with the proper set of instruments. In contrast, if we assume that quality development is primarily about people's attitudes and relationships—about communication and meaning, then formal management thinking falls short. Too many managers lack the communication and relationship skills to truly inspire and motivate their employees. I, therefore, conclude that working on quality is too often reduced to the standardization of processes by this type of management. This is a form of a top-down approach in which the top believes itself to be the expert. In our approach, the challenge is to realize joint involvement in which employees at various levels are given and take responsibility for creating meaning (Cuyvers, 2019).

2.2.3. Vision of people and motivation

Ultimately, behind every approach, there is also a human image, a vision of what motivates people. According to De Dijn (2017), it will come as no surprise that behind the approach to quality control, there is a deterministic view. He is convinced that people's behavior can be controlled and influenced from the outside. It comes down to supplying the right incentives, and then the effect will follow automatically. People must be guided in this view, conditioned, if possible, because they are unable or unwilling to take responsibility on their own. Moreover, people are not just reliable. Things go wrong without oversight. That control then claims to be objective. This is based on the conviction that human actions are measurable, stable, and standardizable. Such an approach ignores man as a signifier. The result is that quality control is reduced to a matter of good rules and procedures and, above all, of controlling phenomena. It is too easily or too naively assumed that such procedures will almost automatically lead to results.

The quality management approach recognizes the added value of involving employees in the performance of tasks. This approach does not consider the policy of the organization. People march when a carrot is held out to them. That carrot means, in this case, having a say in technical issues that can improve quality. Yet here, too, faith in numbers and facts predominates over trust in people's stories. The systematic measurement, adjustment, and empirical demonstration of results do not yet require the involvement of employees and other stakeholders in the policy of the organization. Ultimately, it is still a form of denial of self-responsibility. Here, too, the conviction prevails that without measuring and checking, things will go wrong.

In the third type of vision, the belief that people can commit themselves to collective values breaks through. People no longer act purely instrumentally, under a system of conditioning and reward, but also based on self-chosen commitments. They must, however, act within the existing framework of the organization. These organizations often still react uncertainly to structural changes that are necessary in changing contexts and circumstances.

Only in the fourth vision is there room for a comprehensive approach to man. People not only commit themselves, but they are also able and competent to take co-responsibility for the development of the organization. In this vision, trust in people is crucial. Moreover, it is not only about internal stakeholders, our own members, and employees but also external stakeholders who are recognized as partners. These partners are also considered essential for the development of quality and of the organization as a whole.

2.2.4. View of measurement and objectivity

The consequence of a deterministic view of man and of a mechanistic view of organizations is the practice of measurement and control with a strong belief in the objectivity of human behavior. This theme is so important that I discuss it in detail in Chapter 6: To measure is to know.

Here, I would like to point out that measuring is often wrongly still reduced to a quantitative approach in which figures are the only salvation. I cannot deny that figures can have limited value in quality development. However, to gain in-depth insight into the way in which an organization works on quality, figures are certainly not enough. The stories of all stakeholders are meaningful and perhaps more enlightening. I therefore advocate putting the measurement culture into perspective and supplementing it with a narrative approach. It is, incidentally, very short-sighted to only use figures objectively. Figures are usually just rough results that still need to be interpreted. For example, if the success rates of two higher education programs are placed side by side, not much is clear yet. It is possible that one program selects very strongly at the gate and admits only the best students, while the other program wants to give everyone opportunities and invests heavily in the supervision of weaker students. A lower pass rate can hide an excellent-quality culture. Many subjective factors play a role in the interpretation of grades, such as the experience of the assessors or their underlying pedagogical views.

2.3. Consequences

After examining the underlying and usually unspoken visions, I dare say that the exaggerated belief in control is typical of a culture of distrust. This is very problematic in the nonprofit sector. Anyone who does not believe in people's self-responsibility, who has a strongly deterministic and authoritarian view of what goes on in organizations, usually also shows distrust and disbelief in people's positive possibilities. Such individuals then short-sightedly cling to an illusion —namely, that quality is best achieved through control and measurements. What is not sufficiently emphasized is that such a culture of distrust requires a lot of effort and resources. Such a culture also carries many risks, such as the demotivation of employees, mediocre quality, and a weak culture. I will now list several consequences of a one-sided approach to quality in the nonprofit sector.

2.3.1. Moral displeasure

An authoritarian system ensures that employees feel that they cannot practice their profession in the way they would like to do. Vanlaere and Burggraeve (2018) speak of "moral distress" or "moral dissatisfaction." This can be the case, for example, if nurses are put under such time pressure that they can only supply basic care and have no time to invest more qualitatively in the patient as a person.

The link with quality care is that they must measure and register so much that there is no time left for the actions they find useful—for example, having an encouraging conversation with the patient. The compulsion to tackle everything more efficiently to meet imposed quality indicators causes a great deal of stress and less job satisfaction. The result can be that people become demotivated. According to Vanlaere and Burggraeve (2018), no longer being able to do what you think you must do as a professional to do your job properly, as well as the feeling of falling short, affects the heart of a professional's identity.

Another important consideration is that paper procedures and protocols generally leave no room for professional reflection. Additionally, honest reflection could be evidence of failure and insufficient professionalism. An open discussion of problems and failures, however, is precisely a condition for learning as an individual and as an organization and for permanent quality improvement. More about that later.

The way governments and accrediting bodies organize quality accountability entails the risk that quality becomes a paper reality that is far removed from what takes place in an organization. Moreover, this government approach appears to lead to regrettable practices such as window dressing, cooking the books, concealing shortages, and forcing staff to prepare for a visitation from a formal assessment body. In other words, the figures to which some people attach so much importance do not guarantee a realistic representation of reality.

Finally, many professionals in the nonprofit sector seem to have the predominant feeling that little attention is given to the professional as a person in formal quality activities (Vandenberghe, 2014). There is usually little room left for their professional dreams, their inspiration, and their enthusiasm. They therefore experience the formal part of registration and assessment/ accreditation as alienating.

2.3.2. Culture of risk avoidance

When the pressure of control and the oversimplified evaluation of figures are dominant in an organization, employees are held accountable for the results achieved, and then only as those results appear from the figures. The consequence is that employees no longer dare to take risks and only focus on achieving the figures. This leads to standardization and kills the creative search for solutions to unfamiliar problems. Employees prefer the certainty of figures to the risk of being criticized. Naturally, in every work situation in the nonprofit sector, unpredictable situations occur that do not fit within the prescribed protocols and that require a creative approach. If employees no longer dare to respond to such situations for fear of reprimands, the organization will lose a great deal of quality. Expert thinking, namely, leaving too much to the so-called experts (in this case, the quality coordinators), leads to employees who no longer dare to take responsibility for situations that are not in the booklet. Ultimately, the clients or patients will quickly feel that they are not receiving an adequate qualitative response to their needs and requirements.

2.3.3. Burden

Employees often complain about the extra burden that everything related to quality imposes on them. They do not experience quality as an added value for themselves but as a burden that makes it more difficult to perform their core tasks to a high standard. For the organization, the quality requirements imposed by governments also mean an added burden for which they are not compensated: because more employees must deal with reporting to the government in the context of accountability, fewer employees are available for core tasks, so the general workload increases. The financial costs of assessments and accreditations and their preparation are high for large organizations. So, if organizations and employees start to groan under the bureaucratic burden of quality accountability, the conclusion must be that the system is unreasonable. Policymakers bear great responsibility in this regard.

After these critical reflections, I want to continue with an inspiring story that I strongly believe in myself and from which I have gained positive experiences in my professional life. It outlines a valuable way of dealing with quality tailored to nonprofit organizations.

Finally: What is really important?

- The way organizations deal with quality hides underlying and often unspoken visions (visions of society, people, organizations, and measurement).

- The dominance of figures and control in the quest for quality is counterproductive because it undermines the motivation and creativity of employees.

- Quality development integrates figures and stories, people and resources based on a belief in the self-reliance of all stakeholders.

Chapter 3

Quality development: Our principles

When I dream alone, it is just a dream.
When we dream together, it is the beginning of reality.
When we work together, following our dream,
it is the creation of heaven on earth.

— Dom Helder Camara

Now that it is clear how I look at quality, I would like to describe what is needed to achieve that quality. I resolutely opt for the term "quality development." This term implies a specific vision of the role quality can play in an organization. That is why I want to clarify our starting points in this chapter. Quality development must be relational, appreciative, and value-driven. The supervision of quality development must also supply space for people's stories and meanings. Consequently, I see an organization as an innovative construction site, where all stakeholders work with creativity on the ever-changing future.

3.1. Relational practices

I propose a constructivist approach opposite to the traditional approach to quality assurance. I regard quality development as a dynamic process that never ends, in which people realize the goals of their organization together by giving the best of themselves. In that development process, relational practices are of crucial importance. Relational practice is an interactive project that requires commitment from all those involved, and that also has consequences for all (Bouwen, 2016).

Viewing quality development as a relational practice is an innovative approach to organizations, which, according to Wheatley (1994), must be holistic. That is, we must understand organizations as systems and prioritize relationships. It is, therefore, pointless to steer the development process with strict rules and procedures. Every organization is different, unique, and, to a certain extent, completely different from other organizations, with its own relationships with the world around it. Moreover, the boundaries of an organization are no longer fixed. Modern organizations are members of multiple, often temporary, networks with other organizations. The emphasis should also be on the opportunities for learning and innovation that every organization has within itself.

The quality of relational practice depends on three factors: meaning creation, participation, and knowledge development. I clarify each of these characteristics for quality development.

3.1.1. The Creation of Meaning

In relational practices, such as quality development, language plays a significant role in achieving commonality. An example of this is exchanging experiences to learn from them. In this exchange, understanding the meaning of what people say is extremely important. Only by this method can the interlocutors figure out how others experience shared experiences in a unique way. Without this willingness to listen, we too easily assume that the other person means what we think he means. There is more: meanings are not fixed once and for all. In communication, people constantly formulate and reformulate their definitions of issues. From a social constructivist perspective, problems are not mere facts to be simply discovered and discussed. Problems are constructed during the continuous interaction between the involved stakeholders (Gergen, 1983; Misra & Prakash, 2012). This has consequences for quality development.

In quality development, each party, often implicitly, has its own vision of quality. This is in line with one's own place and position in the organization and is fed by one's own, specific experiences. For some, quality is doing one's own work as well as possible; for others, it means accurately following the procedures. For the director, it means to have correct figures at his disposal; for a head of department, that relationships with and between employees are optimal. And for others, it means that the client is satisfied. It is not easy, but because of these different visions, experiences, and expectations, it is necessary to arrive at a common vision of quality. An organization should invest sufficient time and energy in dialogue between all stakeholders and in clarifying what quality means for each of them. In the end, everyone should strive for at least the same organizational goals.

It is also useful to find out how the various partners position themselves. For example, if a quality manager presents himself as the expert in the field of quality, who understands more and therefore has better insight than the employees, a difference in power arises. This can lead to the average employee minimizing their own experiential expertise and, at the same time, distancing themselves from quality development. Expert thinking creates distance and a lack of commitment.

To achieve a solution in which everyone benefits, major differences in competencies, interests, and social power must first be recognized and, if possible, adjusted in relation to each other. The different identities of managers, quality managers, employees, and clients must be recognized in their specific character and in their participation in the joint activity. Everyone must find their role in the various meetings, with the aim of achieving excellent quality. The recurring dialogue between parties who are equal and who accept the power of discussion is a precondition for arriving at a relational practice.

Such dialogue may not lead to absolute truth, but it does lead to a well-founded consensus at a certain time in a certain context. It is this dialogue that must form the basis of the pursuit of quality. Consider an example of how this can work in practice.

As a result of the development of a self-evaluation report, employees are asked to contribute based on their area of competence. The draft version is sent to all employees with the request to take part in small groups in a so-called dialogue round. In the first round, everyone can make comments, formulate suggestions, and criticize. A revised version is written using this data. This forms the basis for scoring. The results of that scoring are again discussed in small groups to arrive at priorities. The final priorities are then set up with the entire group, which are then included in the policy plan.

Of course, meanings are not fixed in a person once and for all. As a group becomes more familiar with quality development, as it becomes more of a group, and as quality is approached more integrally, employees can change their views and meanings and reformulate their judgments. That is why it is so important that the results of measurements be considered during consensus discussions. In these conversations, the partners clarify their scores and arguments, which often leads to new insights. It is, therefore, important that modern techniques, such as online scoring, be approached with the necessary critical sense. Without the meaning-enlightening conversation, they can quickly degenerate into fetishes that feed a false sense of understanding reality.

Meanings cannot simply be deduced from scores and measurement results. These are just the raw materials to be made meaningful during consultation with stakeholders. A negative score for satisfaction must be substantively clarified. This is only possible in a dialogue with the client or employees. For example, what does a score of 6 (on a ten-point scale) mean on a satisfaction survey? Regardless of the atmosphere in the group, without comparison with previous years or with the score of other groups, an interpretation is risky. In a group of twenty-five employees, three employees systematically gave the lowest possible score on all items. One employee was frustrated because he had not received a permanent appointment, the second had missed a promotion, and the third was not accepted by the group. The excellent group scores of the others were dragged down by these three people. Especially in the nonprofit sector, the problem of measurability and working based on facts and figures is a source of much discussion. On the other hand, it is, of course, true that meaning can only be meaningfully clarified based on experiences and facts.

In relational practices, communication and social skills are essential. Too often, however, some policymakers see investments in strengthening relational practices as a lack of efficiency. It should all be much faster and simpler, is the slogan. In our experience, involving everyone in the organization in the development of quality is the major challenge. This is made more difficult if efficiency is the leading criterion.

3.1.2. Participation

Failures of projects meant to improve quality have a lot to do with poor or even absent employee participation. If we want to stimulate quality development as a relational practice, the participation of everyone in all phases of quality development is necessary.

Interactive participation is a collection of working methods in which people contribute to the development and implementation of projects through discussions and a joint search for solutions (Bouwen & Tallieu, 2004). True participation involves employees at every stage of the process. Joint decision-making implies that interested parties may not only mediate in the planning but may also bear partial responsibility for the implementation and adjustment of the decisions.

Leaders must be adapted to this interactive participation. They must stimulate the realization that all stakeholders are building quality together. The empowerment of everyone in the organization is, therefore, an important condition for interactive participation. It is not enough for employees to have a say in the matter. They should also be given real powers for those matters in which they are competent. Managing projects together means being able to make decisions in one's own area of competence, implement them, and adjust where necessary.

3.1.3. Knowledge development

The process of knowledge building is essential in a relational practice. I can distinguish two different forms of conversations (Bouwen & Tallieu, 2004): knowledge-as-substance conversations and knowledge-as-participation conversations (Brown, 2002). The knowledge-as-substance metaphor sees knowledge as a substance or content, something that can be moved from one container or mind to another. The knowledge-as-participation metaphor emphasizes that knowledge is formed in the interaction between different actors who enter a form of cooperation. Knowledge building, knowledge development, and knowledge sharing are essential relational processes in quality development. People create knowledge by engaging in joint actions and in sharing and exchanging practical experiences (community of practice) (Wenger, 1998). In this view, quality development is a partnership for exchanging experiences since different actors are involved. It is not known in advance, and certainly not once and for all, what the wishes of the stakeholders are. For example, the wishes of clients change, and the visions of managers are partly determined by instructions from the government and by developments in the field. Every piece of knowledge has both a substantial and a relational aspect. Knowledge is always about something, but at the same time, it constructs the relationship between the parties involved (Bouwen, Craps & De Wulf, 2005).

In the process of quality development, experts, practitioners, managers, and employees must be willing and able to exchange their knowledge and experience openly with respect for each other's expertise. Everyone must, therefore, have access to the necessary information. A form of one-way traffic in which employees sometimes must supply information upwards or to quality service is obviously insufficient. It is essential that the various levels exchange information, not only about satisfaction, but also about experiences, problems, solutions, and especially processes. When parties in an organization work with a knowledge-as-participation concept, the relationships between them receive full attention.

The expert knowledge of quality experts and the experiential knowledge of employees are complementary and succeed each other in the cycle of quality development. Existing power differences become less important when all parties share their competencies. Drucker (1980) found that the best way to predict the future is to create it yourself. People create their futures, and so do organizations.

People construct and build up their knowledge together. Organizations are also socially constructed realities. Therefore, if we want to understand an organization and its quality, it is necessary to involve as many people as possible in giving meaning. Organizations are, therefore, not objects that exist separately from humans. They are continuous dialogues between all stakeholders, as well as between thinking and doing. The way in which these dialogues are or are not conducted decides the viability of the organization and also guides the attitude of the stakeholders toward future events.

3.2. Appreciative approach

Anyone who participates in quality development runs the risk of encountering resistance from colleagues and even from management. Even after a long period, when colleagues can be expected to know the quality system sufficiently, a kind of listlessness for quality can set in. One of the reasons is that quality is often (and in practice often appears to be) identified with assessment, criticism, weakness, and shortcomings. Confrontation with the negative demotivates people and drains their energy. Confrontation with shortages and inadequacies is especially frustrating when people feel that they cannot change the causes. Lists of problems do not motivate. People must be able to get energy from somewhere to sustain the efforts needed to work to a high standard. The classical problem-solving approach starts from an analysis of the problem and is rooted in traditional methods of organizational change. Unfortunately, this threatens to paralyze rather than inspire an organization. It is, therefore, no coincidence that many quality development projects bleed out and come to a standstill due to a lack of energy.

In contrast to the traditional approach, I opt for an appreciative approach. It starts with the strengths and possibilities of the organization. It can also be a lever for quality development, fueled by enthusiasm for an inspiring future and not by the disappointment of shortages. Of course, the appreciative approach also starts from a specific vision of the organization, which it sees as a center of human connection. Relationships only really come to life in an organization when there is an appreciative eye. That is, people are willing to see the best in each other. They share their dreams and take care of each other in an appreciative way. Together, they are committed to not only creating a new but a better world. If everyone in the organization gets a voice, a process is created that makes the organization vital (Cooperrider, 2000; Cooperrider & Whitney, 2017). Cooperrider, the founding father of the appreciative approach, formulated the following propositions:

1. In every society, organization, or group, there is always something going well.

2. What we focus on becomes reality.

3. Reality is created repeatedly, and there are always many realities.

4. Asking questions about the organization or group always affects that organization or group.

5. When people are on their way to a new, unknown future, they have more confidence and feel better if they can carry parts of their (familiar) past with them.

6. If we carry parts of our past into the future, it must be the best of our past.

7. It is important that differences be appreciated.

8. The language we use helps create our reality.

3.2.1. Pillars of the appreciative approach

To understand how the appreciative approach works in practice, an understanding of its foundational principles is necessary. Cooperrider and Whitney (2005) base the appreciative approach on the following five principles.

The constructionist principle

Drucker once stated in his book New Society (1993): "The best way to predict the future is to create it yourself." People create their future, and so do organizations. The constructionist principle states that knowing and acting are closely intertwined. Here, it implies that there is no knowledge outside of man but that people construct and build up their knowledge together. Organizations are also socially constructed realities. Therefore, if we want to understand an organization and its quality, it is necessary to involve as many people as possible in giving meaning. Organizations are, therefore, not objects that exist separately from humans. An organization is a continuous dialogue between all stakeholders and between thinking and doing. The way in which the dialogue is or is not conducted decides the viability of the organization and at the same time guides the attitude of stakeholders towards future events.

The principle of simultaneity

Research, assessment, and self-evaluation, on the one hand, and quality development, on the other, are not independent phases but take place simultaneously. Investigating something already means an intervention at the same time. We are already changing organizations by asking questions about it. "The seeds of change are implicit in the very first questions we ask" (Cooperrider, Ludema & Barrett, 2001, p. 189). The things people in an organization think and talk about, the things they discover and learn, the things that feed the dialogue, and the images of the future are already present in the first questions people ask. That is why asking questions is one of the most powerful interventions of a person responsible for quality development. The questions we ask help us decide what we will find and are the basis for the future we build. That is why questions about success stories are the basis for positive goals and powerful dynamics. Focusing too tightly on shortcomings and negative experiences leads to these problematic themes dominating thinking and acting. It is also important that the themes should appear from the success stories of the organization, and because they are rooted in the past, they gain credibility and are grounded in the organization's own reality.

The poetic principle

Of Cooperrider (2000) is the statement that words create worlds. He uses the metaphor here that organizations are like an open book or a poem. The story of an organization is constantly shaped by many authors. The past, present, and future are inexhaustible sources of learning, inspiration, and interpretation, just as a good poem or text from the Bible lends itself to many interpretations. All employees can be co-authors of the development of the organization and, therefore, also of quality development. This principle also expresses the organizing ability of language. An organization is created by the people who are part of it. Language is like a brush that someone uses to map the world. In telling stories about the organization, people co-create their organization. For example, if a meeting is referred to as 'a battle between leaders', there is a good chance that the employees will also behave in that image during such a meeting.

The anticipatory principle

The most important material for quality development is the collective imagination and discussion of the future of the organization. A powerful proposition in the appreciative approach is that the image of the future guides current behavior. The image of the future is a powerful mobilizer, and a positive image leads to better performance. That phenomenon, the Pygmalion effect, has been abundantly proved in performance situations, such as in education and sports. If a student is convinced that the teacher considers him an intelligent student, he will perform better as a result. It also appears that students and sports people who receive feedback about their positive performance perform much better than those who receive feedback about their shortcomings. That is why it is so important in organizations that stakeholders learn to look to the future from experiences of success. Moreover, conducting a dialogue about that future together is a major step in realizing it.

The positive principle

Simply put, experience shows that true development needs a great deal of positive affectivity, such as hope, inspiration, and the shared joy of doing things together. As more positive questions are asked from the outset to orient business professionals towards development, the effort to take part in it will be stronger and last longer. Drucker (1980) states that we learn from our failures but that we grow through our successes. Trust is of foremost importance in an organization. This attitude leads to a virtuous circle: Trust leads to more effort, leading to better results, a better atmosphere, and better cooperation (while distrust leads to less ambition, fewer positive results, and greater fear of failure). If we understand an organization as a stakeholder dialogue, then a positive basic attitude, coupled with confidence in the future, is an important engine for development.

3.2.2. Difference from a traditional approach

Traditional quality assurance starts with a problem-solving approach. It is based on the conviction that quality is a problem that must be solved. The appreciative approach, on the other hand, sees quality development as a challenge that can mobilize the energy of everyone in the organization. I compare both approaches in Table 3.1 (after Cooperrider, 2000).

Table 3.1. Comparison of the problem-solving and the appreciative approaches

PROBLEM-SOLVING APPROACH	APPRECIATIVE APPROACH
• Identification of the problem from a felt need • Analysis of the causes • Analysis of the viable solutions • Action planning – treatment of the problem	• Appreciation of the best that one has • Imagined view of what the organization can become • Dialogue throughout the organization about how the organization should be – Implementation of desired changes
Basic Belief: The organization is a problem that needs to be solved.	*Basic belief:* The organization is a mystery that needs to be unlocked.
Deficit Thinking	**Thinking from the power of people**

Source: Adapted from Cooperrider & Whitney (2005).

An organization that identifies certain shortcomings because of an incident, a complaint, or an evaluation usually asks itself, "What are we doing wrong?" From an appreciative approach, the question is different: "What can we do to have more satisfied clients?" Working on quality development, therefore, means making a choice between analyzing problems and gaining insight into causes. It also means looking for situations in which clients were very satisfied (and, from there, identifying the circumstances that make it possible to stimulate satisfaction). In the end, the problem-solving approach thinks in terms of deficits (so-called deficit thinking), which takes energy away from people rather than creating it.

3.2.3. What can an appreciative approach mean for quality development?

The appreciative approach can relate to different dimensions of quality development.

Desire to belong to the best organizations

Several quality models use a phase system. This supplies the incentive to continue to develop the quality of one's own organization to the highest level. To realize that ambition and belief in one's own strengths and possibilities is of vital importance. An appreciative approach will inevitably lead an organization to be aware of its strengths and possibilities to become more ambitious, transcend mediocrity, and desire to belong to the leading group. Thinking from the perspective of problems and weaknesses, on the other hand, leads at most to the desire to eliminate shortcomings without stimulating the ambition to be exceptionally good. Incidentally, where would members of an organization get the motivation and energy to work themselves into the leading group when they are burdened with deficits and a negative self-image?

Empowering people

In an appreciative approach, the input and contribution of everyone is essential. Quality development is a book to which everyone contributes. This contrasts with an expert approach in which quality managers are forced to know everything about quality and are therefore able to adjust situations if necessary. The problem with this is that the employees in an organization, on the one hand, hardly feel involved in quality development and, on the other hand, also shift the responsibility to the experts. This expert approach usually unintentionally gives the other employees the impression that they are not experts in the field. Incidentally, it is also necessary from the point of view of a quality model such as the EFQM that managers empower their employees and involve them in the quality policy. In addition, all stakeholders must be involved in policy development in an authentic way.

Shared ownership and commitment

Shared ownership is important in an appreciative approach. In our conception of quality development, I have also made it clear that quality development should fundamentally be a permanent collective project because it is about much more than techniques. The essence is about relationships between people that must be built up and renewed repeatedly. As I clarified in the earlier section, the meanings associated with quality (e.g., because of self-evaluations) must be created together if leaders want everyone in the organization to commit to future developments.

I discuss the concrete practice of the appreciative approach in the next chapter. Nevertheless, I can state here that the appreciative approach is receiving more and more attention in organizations.

For example, the NVAO (the Dutch-Flemish Accreditation Organization) expressly states that it is taking an appreciative turn in its approach (Franssen, 2001). The quality assessment of a higher education institution is based on an appreciative attitude. This translates into a focus on "success factors" (on what is going well and why) without being blind to what could be improved through changes. The context of the institution and the chosen model (both for education policy and management) are always the starting point. Within the assessment, special attention will be paid to what is going well, with a focus on embedding and stimulating well-running processes within the institution. The review committee also examines where (elements within) the education policy can still be strengthened, deepened, or intensified (NVAO, 2018).

3.3. Value driven

Striving for quality is often identified with a strong focus on results. If leaders want quality development to really lead to a sustainable quality culture, result orientation is not enough. Quality development requires that the organization be inspired by values and act accordingly. Any organization that consciously thinks about and is concerned with its place and role in society starts from a value perspective, whether or not explicitly stated. Such a perspective holds the basic values that should guide the behavior of the members of the organization. Examples are integrity, independence, customer focus, freedom, justice, fairness, and trust. Values are, therefore, about the ethical dimension of an organization and reflect what the organization believes in. For nonprofits, the value perspective is typically quite complex. Some organizations start from an ideology—think of political parties, pillar organizations, or religious and philosophical groups. Other organizations have a broad social goal in mind. Examples include environmental organizations, movements that strive for a fair distribution of goods or solidarity, and so on.

Values are abstract facts that have yet to become concrete norms, rules of conduct, or guidelines that must direct the behavior of people in the organization. For example, if safety is a value, "you shall not run a red light" can become a norm. The values of an organization are ideally reflected in its organizational culture, in its working methods, and in the behavior of each employee. They evolve with the growth and priorities of the organization. If trust is a value, then the organization cannot send a doctor to inspect employees on their first day of illness. When the concrete behavior of people in the organization is not in line with its values, there is a problem.

An example. The Flemish government states that it strives for a value-driven organization with the values of openness, decisiveness, trust, and agility. It wants to be an open and agile organization that proactively anticipates the evolutions and needs in society. Together with all stakeholders, the government of Flanders is working on sustainable services based on trust and in the public interest. I reproduce here some parts of that statement (https://overheid.vlaanderen.be/visie-en-aanpak-waarden-actie):

Openness

- We have an eye for what is going on in society.

- We collaborate with all relevant actors within and outside the government and put our data, information, knowledge, and skills at the service of society.

Vigour

- We take well-considered decisions with respect for all stakeholders, which we implement resolutely.

- We seize opportunities and take bold, proper actions to supply innovative solutions.

- 360° confidence.

- We act ethically and are honest and loyal to the public interest.

- We give and earn trust.

- We stimulate these qualities in our own organization and in society.

- We are authentic and do what we say we will do. Clarity and exemplary employment practices make us credible.

Value-driven actions improve the quality of that service.

To this end, the government of Flanders wants to achieve the following goals:

1. Senior civil servants show support for the values. Management exudes the values in its leadership.

2. All entities of the Flemish government include the values. Each manager translates the values into the policy of his organization. For example, the values are used as a criterion and touchstone when making decisions.

3. Every staff member knows the four values, can explain them, and can apply them. Each employee also finds something of themselves in the values. The values are visible in the organization's daily operations and the cooperation between its employees. Employees hold each other accountable for their values.

4. The politically responsible policymakers support the values and help propagate them.

5. The values are visible in interactions between employees, customers, and partners. The citizen recognizes the Flemish government as a value-driven organization: open, flexible, reliable, and decisive.

Value-driven quality development has an important but often misunderstood purpose. First, it functions as a touchstone for the organization. When making important decisions, it is helpful to ask yourself if the upcoming decision is in line with the organization's values. Values also orient the actions of people within an organization, assuming, of course, that they know those values. It is then the compass that keeps the organization aligned. In addition, an organization's value drive also forms a counterweight to a purely instrumental approach to quality, which presents quality as a purely objective, neutral matter.

Thinking and working around quality is the ideal opportunity for an organization whose "why" and values become explicit. Alderliesten (2017) speaks of valuable quality management as a meaningful process. Quality development can then (re)activate the moral horizon of the organization. Stories can play a significant role in clarifying values. That is why I advocate—in addition to the empirical quantitative approach that is based on numbers—for creating much more space for the narrative, telling stories about what makes a quality organization.

3.4. Room for a narrative approach

In addition to the numerical accountability, in our vision of quality development, there must be room for a narrative approach: the stories of the stakeholders tell a lot in depth about how the organization deals with quality. The meanings that people give to what they experience in the organization also become clear through the stories. It is our belief that the core of the processes in the nonprofit sector, that what goes on in relational practices, cannot be measured with numbers. Quality cannot be reduced to meeting several indicators that can be evaluated quantitatively. They may, of course, deserve a relative place in the whole of an accountability process. But even then, the figures have yet to make sense; they must be interpreted. The organization must be able to present a coherent and shared story. That should clarify how the organization is developing toward its dreams and goals. The story must be credible if it is to convince the accountability process. Telling positive experiences about what goes well is essential to arriving at an appreciative approach and is, therefore, a necessary phase in the development approach—it forces the organization to consciously make explicit what it wants to achieve. Such an approach can also be valuable in assessment visits. Of course, this requires that the assessment committee adopt an appreciative attitude and give space to the stories with the right questions. These stories make it possible to analyze the successes and the strategies that an organization uses for this (VAN DE WETERING, 2008).

3.5. Development as a construction site

If we do not approach organizations as fixed structures but organically as dynamic networks, it becomes clear that quality development does not usually proceed in a linear fashion. Linear development assumes that the organization realizes increasingly better quality and, at a certain moment, stabilizes at the peak. The reality is that internal and external evolution forces the organization to re-orient itself to the future and to align its operations accordingly. The ultimate highest quality can never be achieved once and for all. Employees change; society evolves and makes different demands on the organization. The network in which the organization moves grows and shrinks and grows again. I, therefore, prefer to view quality development as a construction site rather than a finished building. As an example, I can use the Sagrada Familia, the magnificent basilica designed by Antoni Gaudí in Barcelona that is still in construction after more than a century. While the church will not be finished for many decades, the building process itself is beautiful.

3.6. Towards a sustainable future through innovation and creativity

It follows from the foregoing that quality development requires a willingness to innovate. This requires creativity to constantly take on new challenges. Where the terms quality care and the associated quality assurance suggest a commitment to safety and stability, the term quality development fits better in a dynamic approach. Of course, this does not mean that an organization floats on the waves like a rudderless ship to an unknown destination. In this context, sustainability means that the organization cherishes the good things and is open to situations that can optimize its quality. At the same time, the perspective of a sustainable future implies that the organization is always aware of the consequences of its actions and of its responsibility to society.

This requires that values as an ethical dimension continue to receive explicit attention in quality development.

3.7. Our definition of quality development

For us, quality development is the royal road to the quality of an organization. Consistent with our principles, I describe quality development as:

"Quality development is the whole of relational practices in which all stakeholders of an organization are constantly looking for the best in the organization in order to realize the dream and goals of their organization in the best possible way with the use of their talents."

Finally: What is really important?

- The core of quality revolves around relational practices, about what happens between people.

- The positive that is present in every organization must form the basis of quality development.

- Stories and meanings must be given a necessary place within a process of accountability.

- Values must form the backbone of quality development.

Chapter 4

Integral quality development

First, we shape our structures and then our structures shape us.

— Winston Churchill

In the earlier chapters, I have tried to put things in order. I have clarified what I mean by quality and quality development. I also took a critical look at the backgrounds of several approaches to quality. In this chapter, I analyze what is needed to integrally develop quality to achieve a quality culture. That is quite a lot. To this end, I successively discuss the need for a quality policy, the role of stakeholders, the meaning of a quality culture, the aspects of micropolitics, the processes, and the need for awareness and quality development as a form of continuous learning.

4.1. A quality policy

Knowing what you want to achieve should logically be the starting point of any action. This applies even more to the pursuit of quality. Figure 4.1 schematizes those goals and the road to get there (Pupius, 2005).

What do we want to achieve with quality-oriented work? This must be clearly formulated so that all stakeholders are well informed. In doing so, the organization's leaders must be aware of its values. They decide what is possible and what is not possible. Values form the basis of the organization's mission. Within the framework of a mission, leaders of an organization want to achieve several things, which requires a plan with long-term goals. These goals must be translated into initiatives to which individual employees can contribute. The confidence and hope that the vision can be realized is as important as the vision itself. Without hope, people lose their enthusiasm, energy, dedication, and persistence. Positive change requires a great deal of positive energy. Appreciative leaders inspire by ensuring that the vision is supported by a clear future-directed path and a collective sense of efficacy. They do this by engaging all stakeholders in the vision development process.

Figure 4.1. Policy and goals

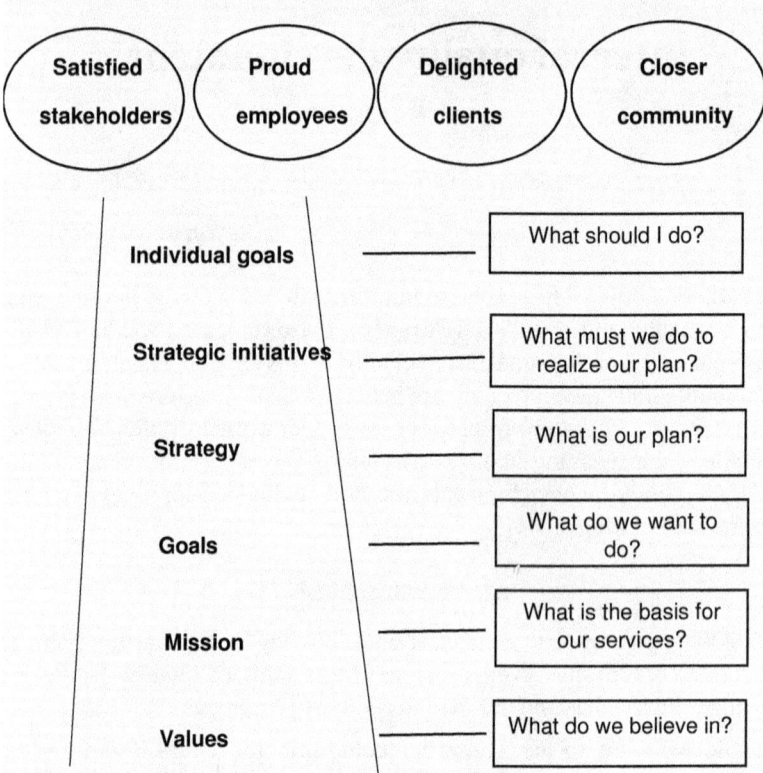

Source: Adapted from Pupius (2005)

An essential dimension of a quality policy is anchoring. Once the quality is under development, achievements must also be secured. During or immediately after the implementation of the plans, managers must take measures to avoid wasting the efforts that have been made. That would be disastrous for the motivation of the stakeholders involved. Hence, it is necessary to keep everyone's energy and motivation. In the long term, changes must become ingrained in the entire organization, in its daily processes, and, ultimately, in the culture.

During development, it is a great challenge to continuously refine the original plan for change without creating a whole new change process. There is little point in stubbornly sticking to the first options if internal or external circumstances require adjustment. It is more important to respond flexibly to the constant changes in the environment and in the organization itself. It is an art to avoid giving employees the impression that there is only chaos and that managers do not know what they want. Everyone in the organization must be aware of the broad outlines of the change project. From there, one can see that the broad outlines are the framework for the minor adjustments. Effective communication between managers and employees is important in this respect. Leaders must constantly ask themselves how their messages are coming across to employees in order to avoid a gap between their intentions and employees' understanding.

If the policy is to supply a solid basis for quality development, solid support is needed. To this end, it is necessary that quality development not be narrowed down to a department or quality manager. Of course, there must be people who do all sorts of preparatory search and analysis work. However, this information must be made useful to the organization. For example, the interpretation of data is ideally a collective process, and so are the decisions to be made based on the facts. The focus should, therefore, be on communicating the facts. Consequently, it is not sufficient for many people in the organization to supply information in order to update files. Experience shows that real development needs a great deal of positive affectivity, including things like hope, inspiration, and a shared enjoyment of what is done together. As more positive questions are asked from the outset to steer development, the effort to cooperate will be stronger and last longer. We already know from Drucker (1980) that success is important for growth. Trust is of immense importance in an organization. Trust and distrust can both lead to circles—the first virtuous, the second vicious. Trust leads to more effort, better results, a better atmosphere, better cooperation, and so on. Distrust leads to less ambition, poor results, and a greater fear of failure. Understanding an organization as a stakeholder dialogue with a positive basic attitude, coupled with confidence in the future, is an important driver for quality development.

Every organization needs a compass, a set of instruments that helps it find the right path to its goals. Facts and figures, analyses, and the resulting self-assessment reports fulfill that vital function but do not in themselves lead to quality improvement. They are necessary, also in an appreciative approach, but insufficient in themselves. Many measures taken by the government or a board of directors can weigh so heavily on an organization that they exhaust all its energy and thus stifle quality. Moreover, these measures often stem from a certain, sometimes rigid, way of thinking that does injustice to the specificity of an organization's quality system. Subsequently, such instruments are often unable to map the specificity of the processes involved in the nonprofit. They therefore supply information about the preconditions (infrastructure, policy) but not about the core itself. Again, we need this compass, but without the motivation and dynamism I explained in the earlier chapters, it will not necessarily move an organization closer to its goals. That is why I advocate the development of process indicators in addition to all kinds of result-oriented indicators. These are documentation points of collaborative, relational practices. Examples of indicators that try to capture the dynamics of the processes can, for instance, be the extent to which everyone participates in the discussion about the meaning of benchmarking data, the strength of the collaboration, and the way in which the PDCA cycle (Plan, Do, Check, Act) is realized by teams and by individuals in their relationships with clients. This attention to processes need not reduce attention to results or performance indicators. On the contrary, by better mapping and checking the processes, the conditions for achieving superior results are tightened. Finally, I argue for a balanced, well-chosen set of indicators. There is no point in wanting to measure everything or in wanting to measure everything too much. Everything depends on the goals that leadership wants to achieve. And what makes sense in this regard can be agreed upon.

4.2. Stakeholders

Quality can only develop if the various stakeholders in that process are given a voice and are willing and able to play their part in it. The quest for quality, therefore, should not become a matter for quality experts and management alone. That is why I zoom in here on the significance of stakeholders in quality development.

4.2.1. The Customers

Quality care is often mentioned in the same breath as customer friendliness. A narrow customer-centric approach is problematic for nonprofits because who is the customer? The term "customer" is immediately a problem. Most nonprofit industries use other terms such as client, patient, student, citizen, participant, and so on. Moreover, it has become clear that a simple description of the customer is not possible. These difficulties lead us to abandon the notion of customer and use the term "stakeholders." This insight enables us to focus on the various parties involved in the process. In addition to the client, there are parents or partners, the government, interest groups (such as trade unions, professional societies, and other organizations with which relationships are supported), and society in general.

Spontaneously, we might be tempted to see the customer as the most important stakeholder in the nonprofit sector. The question, however, is whether a strong focus on the customer is a good criterion for deciding quality. Can the client figure out autonomously what the best quality is for him? He may not opt for the best quality of service but for the organization that requires the least of him. Or he may not properly assess the scope of his choices. In education, for example, the question is how someone who is not yet familiar with the profession or study can make a meaningful assessment of the content, the basic competencies, and the final attainment levels of the educational system in question. In healthcare, it is well known that patients sometimes ask for (demand, according to some) medications that are irrelevant or even harmful. The client cannot be the only criterion for determining quality, neither of the processes nor of the results, autonomously, without supervision. Of course, this does not alter the fact that he must have an important voice in the chapter. That is why quality models, such as the EFQM (European Foundation for Quality Management), pay explicit attention to the extent to which an organization promotes cooperation and involves everyone in the quality process. The old Flemish saying, "if everyone sweeps in front of their own door, the whole street is clean," applies to quality development only to a limited extent. The fact that individual service providers all work hard and are quality-conscious is not enough to produce an integrated approach.

In any case, it is still especially important to be at least aware of the expectations of customers and also of other stakeholders, of course. Based on research by Parasuraman, Zeithamsi and Berry (1985), Morgan and Murgatroyd (1995) described what clients expect as to the quality of a service. The respondents in the study defined what quality meant to them using the ten criteria shown in Table 4.1 (Moullin, 2002, p. 18).

Table 4.1. Dimensions of service quality

Criterion	Good example	Bad example
Reliability	IT is always available at the desired time	Service employees do not call client back as agreed
Willingness	Quick response	Long queues
Ability	Staff performs tasks competently	Staff is insufficiently trained for the task in question
Accessibility	Easy to access the service; accessible to people in wheelchairs	Not enough parking
Courtesy	Polite and helpful staff	Patronizing behavior
Communication	Good explanation of diagnosis and treatment without jargon	Lack of information about what is going to happen

Credibility	Client feels he can trust staff	Client feels that staff is not giving him correct information
Security	Sense of personal security and confidentiality	Unsafe entrance at night
Presentation	Modern work and reception areas	Outdated equipment or poorly maintained premises
Understanding	Staff meets the needs of the client	Rules are rules; there are no exceptions

Sources: Adapted from Moullin (2002)

4.2.2. Leadership

Integral quality development requires stimulating leadership that believes in its employees and can motivate them. Leadership is the critical factor in the success and failure of quality development. How does management deal with resistance so that employees can still be motivated toward change and toward the quality project? Managing such projects is much more than a technical matter. It is a matter of motivating people to acquire a new mentality, a different attitude, and different behavior.

I distinguish between a leader and a manager. "Manager" has gradually become a broad term that is used in many senses. The term has also become established in the context of nonprofit organizations. I use the term here to clarify the distinction with the "leader." In this context, the manager is primarily an organizational expert. That explains how it is possible for managers to move from one business sector to another. Commercial sector managers are also employed in nonprofit sectors to help the organization compete. A leader has a different function in an organization and, therefore, needs different qualities. Leadership must realize three functions: to give direction, to coach and to motivate, and to support the team or organization materially. In other words, the leader must be a visionary, a coach, and a manager. This makes it clear that opposition between leaders and managers is not especially useful. A good leader must also be able to manage the organization; on the other hand, management is only one dimension of leadership.

Figure 4.2. The Functions of leadership

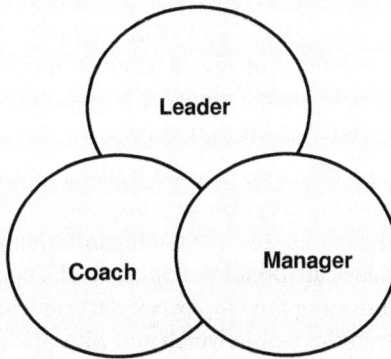

Source: Adapted from Francken (2011)

The leader, as a visionary, ensures that the organization develops a challenging future perspective that directs the behavior of the employees. Of course, the leader does not have to do this on his own. On the contrary, developing a shared vision requires that everyone, or as many employees as possible, be involved. The leader stimulates not only the "what" to do, through the organization's vision, but also the "how," through the organization's values. Inspiring leadership is synonymous with this. Leadership becomes inspiring when the leader also knows how to convey his vision to the employees so that they can also become enthusiastic about it. An inspiring leader is, therefore, a source of inspiration for the environment.

As a coach, the leader supports his employees in their personal development as an employee of the organization. Guiding employees toward better development, greater involvement in the organization, and better functioning is precisely the essence of coaching. It is a way of leadership that makes the employee reflect, think, and look for new opportunities. It is aimed at developing the self-management of a team and/or individual employees. Employees who work independently, take initiative, are critical of their performance, and respond proactively to an ever-changing environment are the organization's most important assets in a knowledge economy. This is expressed in aspects such as showing interest in the development process of an organization's people by motivating, giving feedback, and adjusting. And it adds something, namely having more options (coat racks) available, to let the employee take responsibility.

The leader as manager ensures that the material conditions for the functioning of the organization are realized and that this is done in a high-quality manner. A good leader is a manager, but not every manager is a leader. Management, then, is the total process of planning, decision-making, and managing all aspects of an activity or organization from start to finish. It is also sometimes expressed as follows: a manager is someone who does things right; a leader is someone who does the right things.

Another way of integrating the bases of good leadership is shown in Figure 4.3. Each of the three dimensions is necessary. Inspirational leadership refers to creating direction for the employees and the organization by ensuring that the mission, vision, and values are broadly supported. The appreciative aspect refers to coaching and motivating the employees. Servant leadership refers to creating space and opportunities within which and with which employees can achieve the goals of the organization.

Because the appreciative approach is one of the foundations of our vision for quality development, I further explore appreciative leadership. This is a leadership style that knows how to convert the human qualities (such as knowledge, experience, competencies, and skills) of all stakeholders into positive performance. This constructive approach typifies a shift from an individualistic and deficit-centered approach to relational practices.

Figure 4.3. What good leaders do

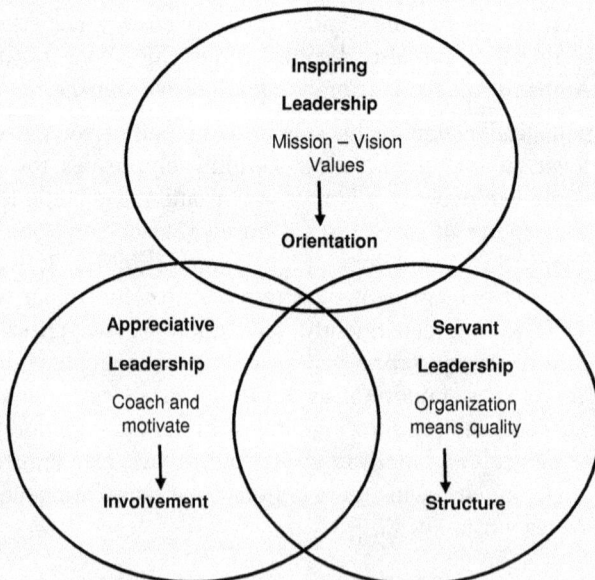

Appreciative leaders understand the importance of vision. But they also understand that inspiration is more than just vision. People need to share the vision; they also need to see the path forward and get the resources needed to get there. Therefore, they allow all kinds of stakeholder groups to take part in the discussions and in the decisions. Employees are, therefore, invited to create the future of the organization together.

Appreciative leaders recognize that executive involvement in quality development is a critical success factor. Without their active participation and involvement, the success of quality development is impossible.

However, involvement alone is not enough. Only when it is clear to everyone in the organization that management is also making an active effort to work in a high-quality way and to make quality possible will quality development receive the necessary support from the entire organization. Appreciative leaders inspire confidence in employees and other stakeholders. Charles Handy formulates the following seven principles of trust, which I briefly summarize here (cited in Haijtema, 2010, p. 59):

- Trust is not blind. In large organizations, small groups must exist so that people know each other and are not a number in a chaotic whole.

- In organizations, trust means belief in one's competence and commitment to the organization's goals.

- Confidence requires constant learning. Every individual must be able to innovate.

- Trust is like glass. Once broken, it is never the same again.

- Trust requires emotional bonding because it is not impersonal.

- Personal contact is necessary for trust. Visions are insufficient. A common commitment requires personal contact to feel that the involvement is real.

- You must live up to trust. Organizations that expect trust from employees must first show that they are worthy of this trust.

This emphasis on trust once again makes it clear that leadership is about relationships and reciprocity. The confidence of leaders in employees and in all stakeholders is essential, but also vice versa. Naturally, not all employees have the same competencies to autonomously fulfill the strict requirements that are set for self-management and self-responsibility in an organization. Appreciative leaders must also do justice to these employees; they must encourage and support them in using their strengths. De Vos (2016) introduced the term "pacemaker" in this context. In her view, pacemakers—for example, quality coordinators—are initiative-taking people with a clear goal in mind who can inspire others and supply clarity. In addition, they are strong in connecting people and interests. Steering without formal power but still guarding the common thread is their strength.

One of the core tasks of a leader is to motivate the employees towards the organizational goals. The leader faces a double challenge: on the one hand, he must deal with resistance in an effective way; on the other hand, he must create a commitment to the quality project. Every change project and a quality project is a good example of this, generates resistance among employees. It is possible that the employees have not understood the goals, background, or motives of a measure. They do not believe what is being said. They may be unable or unwilling to cooperate. They do not expect anything good from the measure. Finally, they may be convinced that they have no control over the change. Effective organizations are powerful and creative enough to recognize resistance and deal with it constructively. Resistance is a signal. That is why it is necessary to deal with this resistance in a constructive way, so that the problem can be solved optimally. At the very least, it forces leadership to think carefully about the desirability of the changes and especially about the underlying assumptions.

4.2.3. The employees

Quality development is not primarily a matter of technique but of mentality; in other words, of people. The employees of an organization are core stakeholders because they are responsible for the realization of the goals of the organization. That is why I want to clarify how an organization should earn the right to have good employees. Having good employees is not enough—how they interact with each other and with management is also crucial. Hence, some clarification of professional relations is in order.

4.2.3.1. Ensuring access to good employees

In many nonprofit organizations, care for staff is often still too limited to recruitment and selection. While these are important processes, they are not sufficient. The prompt selection of competent employees does not guarantee their commitment. I repeat, good employees must be earned by the organization. Therefore, managers must also consider other dimensions such as training, empowerment, support, rewards, and career planning. It is also necessary that the policy create the conditions for reliable, professional relations between employees. In Figure 4.4, I list the requirements that a good personnel policy must meet.

It is, of course, necessary that an organization have competent employees. To this end, a human relations policy is necessary. The starting point of any good policy must be understanding the current and future needs of the organization.

The human relations policy must focus on both the short and the long term. In addition, it must be clearly linked to the general policy of the organization. In every organization, the competencies of employees must be given attention. Usually, smaller organizations cannot afford financial extras, and progression to higher positions is not possible. To motivate and reward employees, management can look for and offer opportunities for them to further develop their skills. Being allowed to develop one's own personality at work can be a powerful motivator. To this end, it is first necessary that these competencies be mapped out. Training is then offered to further develop abilities and skills. Naturally, the development of these personal qualities must be geared to the needs of the organization.

Figure 4.4. Conditions for an effective personnel policy

Source: Adapted from Moullin (2002).

The empowerment of employees is an important asset in a modern human relations policy. I must conclude that many management boards have not yet learned much about this. By empowerment, I mean that employees are given responsibility and, at the same time, decision-making power for those areas in which they are competent. This not only concerns decisions that staff members are allowed to make in their relationships with clients but also powers concerning the resources needed to achieve operational goals in particular: money, information, material, knowledge, time, and technology. Subsequently, the employee is responsible for showing good stewardship of those resources. I know from motivational psychology that empowerment can be a powerful motivator. This goes beyond mere participation. It is about decision-making powers, both individually and as a team. To speak of a systematic empowerment policy, it is necessary for management to develop procedures for this in consultation with all those involved in the organization.

Accountability must also be linked to this empowerment. The employee who becomes a steward must also be accountable. In this context, it is important that individual goals be aligned with organizational goals and that clear agreements be made that should be discussed later in performance and assessment interviews. The relationship between the employee and the organization is mutual.

In addition to the space that the organization gives to the employees, the characteristics of the employees themselves are important. Their employability is especially relevant here. Employability means the extent to which employees are usable and useful for achieving organizational goals. Naturally, it is up to the organization to ensure that the knowledge, skills, and attitude of its employees match its needs.

It is clear from all this that it is necessary for employees to know what their added value is for the organization, what their responsibilities and authorities are, and which indicators can be used to evaluate these things. Employees must also be guided, coached, and judged on their contribution to the organizational goals.

Another dimension of good human relations policy is the support and appreciation of the personnel by management. The legal organization of the nonprofit sector does not leave much room for leadership. However, supporting and valuing employees does not primarily mean providing material rewards, which are legally only possible to a limited extent. A good personnel policy can mean that management explicitly looks for ways to show appreciation for the work of employees. In this context, the saying of the Bond Zonder Naam, a well-known Belgian charity organization, is significant: "Give people a feather, and they will grow wings." It is about paying attention to people and expressing appreciation.

A good personnel policy is reflected in the organizational structure. This is the way in which tasks are divided and coordinated in the organization. When employees do not clearly know what their duties entail, it creates a breeding ground for uncertainty and confusion. As a result, certain tasks will not be performed, or others will be performed twice. If people do not know exactly which tasks fall within their competence, they will also feel less or not involved in solving problems. The above shows that it is necessary to use clear job descriptions in which tasks, responsibilities, and authorities are written down. A clear division of tasks applies not only between individuals but also between departments and levels in an organization.

In addition to clarity in the division of tasks, clarity in decision-making powers is also of paramount importance. I have already mentioned that a participatory management style is necessary if you want to get and keep motivated employees. Not all decisions have to be made at the top. An integrated approach to quality requires that everyone be allowed to make decisions at their own level about matters in which they are experts. This naturally requires coordination as well as effective communication channels in all directions: top-down, bottom-up and horizontal. This does not alter the fact that the management must be able to keep an overview. Of course, the personnel policy also requires that goals be worked on from a vision.

4.2.3.2. Professional relationships

Research by Staessens (1991) shows that professional relationships between employees are an important condition for the success of an innovation. Important social definitions are developed in those interactions. According to Staessens, communication and cooperation between employees are two basic processes in developing and supporting an organizational culture. For example, due to the way employees communicate with each other about professional matters, standards can grow about what constitutes good service. At the same time, these interactions form an element of social control. In that communication, it becomes clear what is possible and what is not possible. In this way, newcomers in the organization are also socialized: they learn what the culture is. However, it is not self-evident that professional collegiality also exists in an organization. For this, it is necessary that professional functioning be made a common fact about which communication can take place. For that, there must be a professional interest in the work of colleagues. But interest alone is not enough: there must also be cooperation so that there is a joint responsibility for the results. In an organization, the employees build a project together that must be situated in a total event in which many stakeholders are involved.

Too many nonprofits act like a professional bureaucracy. This means that employees behave like autonomous professionals, which can hinder the development of peer standards. Teaching, treating patients, and conducting counseling interviews are solitary matters. The classroom, the consultation room, and the desk are the private domains of the employee. Due to the tradition of the profession, employees in the nonprofit sector are still too often used to bearing sole responsibility for an activity. The core of the assignment is still too often working individually and not collaborating with colleagues. If interactions do take place between employees, they are usually not very professionally oriented.

Quality development requires the resocialization of the employee because quality cannot be achieved without cooperation and professional communication. In quality development, the importance of team functioning should be dominant over the traditional autonomy of the employee. In this way, acting professionally can take on a new meaning. Staessens & Vandenberghe (2006, p. 77) speak of a "shared normative connection." Research confirms that there is a relationship between the quality of professional relationships between employees and the implementation of innovations. In effective organizations, a collegial atmosphere prevails, and cooperation and support are regarded as self-evident. This professional communication should lead to a shared commitment to quality development. By analogy, I agree with Staessens that quality development projects are most successful if employees communicate often with each other about professional matters. Through these interactions, they build a common language. Moullin (2002) summarizes several aspects of effective teams.

Task:

- Clear goals
- Performance standards
- Clear responsibilities
- Systematic approach

Team:

- Awareness of common goals
- Supportive climate
- Growth as a unit
- Sense of success

Individual:

- Accepted by leader and team

- Appreciated by the leader and team

- Makes contribution

- Personal growth

4.2.4. The external partners

The nonprofit organization is not isolated within society—it needs good partners to help achieve its goals. The identification of partners who can supply added value and the proper maintenance of relationships should not be left to chance but should take place in a systematic manner. Partners exist when there is reciprocity. This is expressed in helping each other to achieve goals, helping each other develop and improving processes, and creating added value for stakeholders through cooperation. The management of external partnerships is reflected in activities such as the following: identification of key partners and strategic partnerships in line with policy; structuring partnerships to create and maximize added value; ensuring cultural alignment and knowledge sharing with partner organizations; supporting joint development; and creating cooperation by working together to improve processes.

In addition, there are stakeholders who have a hierarchical relationship with the organization. This is first the government, which imposes rules that the organization must follow—sometimes to qualify for subsidies and sometimes to simply follow the requirements that apply to all organizations, such as accounting, safety, and infrastructure. In addition, there are umbrella organizations that serve as the organizing body of local organizations: the large umbrella organizations of socio-cultural associations, the organizing bodies of schools, and the large trade unions.

4.3. A culture of quality

Not every organization is ready for the introduction of integral quality development. The organizational culture plays a determining role. That is why I am going into it in a little more detail here.

Every organization has its own character that can be recognized by, among other things, the typical way employees do things. How do they communicate with each other? What rituals do they use? How do they manage conflict? That specific character must deal, on one hand, with the values and norms that the employees in that organization strive for and on the other hand, with the way in which they behave because of these norms. I can best describe that specific character with the concept of organizational culture: "a set of values and norms of the members of an organization related to what the organization wants to achieve and the resulting behavioral patterns." Culture is thus both a collective and a cognitive system. It is a collective system because it concerns the views that the members of an organization share with each other, not personal views. It is a cognitive system because it holds beliefs and knowledge. Schein & Schein (2016, p. 50) defines this as "a shared pattern of thinking, ideas, feelings, and values resulting from shared experiences and shared learning." In this sense, organizational culture is a social construction. The meaning of the elements of the organization is not fixed in advance but is the result of the interaction between the members of the organization. The person and the organization are active creators of social reality. Organizational culture is both the creator of human interactions and its outcome.

It is also necessary to clarify the distinction between organizational culture and organizational climate. Culture refers to the collective system of beliefs within an organization. Climate refers to the personal experience of that culture and, more specifically, to the extent to which the organization meets the personal expectations of the employees. Climate reflects the extent to which there is agreement between personal expectations and the prevailing culture; it is also a sign of the underlying culture.

Although an organizational culture is difficult to change in the short term, it is nevertheless an important condition. Introducing a quality development project is not useful under all circumstances. For example, if the culture is characterized by authoritarian manners in which there is no trust between management and employees, a quality development project will have few opportunities. Of course, from its position of power, the top can formally impose several decisions. However, such an approach is counterproductive for integral quality development. The culture must make it possible for employees to take part in the project with intrinsic motivation. If the existing culture does not allow that, there is a problem.

An organizational culture that supports the implementation of a change project should, therefore, have at least the following characteristics:

1. Relationships should be sufficiently open.

2. Everyone in the organization must think and act in a customer-oriented way.

3. The organization must be sufficiently innovative so that a radical change, such as a change project, is in line with an already existing mentality.

4. Everyone should take a positively critical attitude towards their own performance and that of the organization. Everyone must want to learn, improve, and discuss their own actions, whereby territorial behavior is out of the question.

That is a sore point for some organizations. Mintzberg (1992) described such organizations as professional bureaucracies. The autonomy and self-determination of the professional employees are central to this. Collaboration and openness are not self-evident. Some cultures have elements that promote quality, while others have elements that undermine the pursuit of quality. I briefly summarize those elements in table 4.2 (Maas, 2001).

Table 4.2. Characterizations of cultures

Principles of quality work	Undermining elements of culture
• prevention, initiative-taking behavior • long-term oriented • focused on stakeholder needs • process thinking is central • teamwork is key • open communication and feedback	• putting out fires, fixing mistakes, reactive • short-term oriented • focused on meeting specifications • thinking in relation to products and services functions centrally • each for himself • pigeonhole thinking, accusatory behavior

Source: Adapted from Maas (2001).

Cameron (1995) examined more than a hundred organizations that had used quality improvement or downsizing to improve their effectiveness. The results were clear. Successful changes and increased effectiveness depended on whether the change strategy was embedded in a culture change. When organizational changes occur independently of cultural changes, they are doomed to fail. Why is that? Quinn (1996) argues that when values, orientations, definitions, and goals do not change, organizations quickly revert to the old situation, no matter how much strategy and procedure have changed. Failed attempts then lead to frustration, cynicism, loss of confidence, and resistance to change among members of the organization.

Eleven steps to a quality service culture

I briefly describe several steps that are necessary to arrive at a service culture in which the customer is central (Moullin, 2002).

Clearly describe the mission and core values

Organizations often get too much information and are hardly aware of the core processes. That is why the mission or mission statement plays a key role. It reflects the raison d'être of the organization. It should also clearly define the core processes that reflect the basic needs of the relevant stakeholders. The mission also reflects the core values that should guide the behavior of everyone in the organization.

Know customers and other stakeholders

Through close contact and effective communication, an organization must understand the characteristics and needs of all stakeholders. I explore this point in Chapter 2. That understanding is necessary to identify their needs and expectations, but also to find out the extent to which the organization is meeting those needs and expectations and to find alternative, better ways to achieve this.

Formulate the vision of the organization

Just as the mission stands for the core processes, the vision should outline the future on which the organization builds. Such a vision expresses in a motivating way the goals that must be achieved in the future.

Define the moments of truth

"Moments of truth" are the contacts between the organization and its clients that make the difference for the client compared to other organizations. They decide how the customer values the service. It is necessary that the service be arranged in such a way that the customer receives the best—so that he has a higher appreciation for this organization than for other organizations. The difference is also often made in short contacts. Just think of the importance of a friendly welcome or a listening ear at the first contact.

Serve each other well

The quality that the client can expect starts with the way in which the employees in the organization serve each other. This mutual service contributes to a smooth organization that the client experiences with flawless service. Lack of mutual communication, competition, and conflict eventually lead to the client becoming the victim.

Create excellent service

Excellent quality does not just happen but is the result of careful planning and organization. To meet stakeholder needs, the organization must have well-spoken, well-trained employees. Employees must be knowledgeable and communicative, both in dealing with stakeholders and with colleagues. The satisfaction of stakeholders also depends on the extent to which they receive correct and understandable information at the same time.

Learn lessons from complaints

"Complaints are a gift" is the slogan of a quality manager because they offer opportunities to improve service. Complaints are an essential source of information for any organization. Most dissatisfied customers usually do not supply any information but simply stay away. It is, therefore, important to seek feedback from all stakeholders and then use it to improve the quality of service.

Stay in close contact with customers and other stakeholders

It is useful to involve clients and stakeholders in one way or another in the development of policy and certainly in the evaluation of the services. This does not mean that their wishes should be included in the policy unquestioningly. It is often necessary to clarify how their input can be useful to the organization while not harboring unrealistic expectations.

Plan and shape the service program

In this phase, the various ideas for quality improvement are processed into a service program that is leading in the field of quality and integrates all aspects of quality. The purpose of this book is precisely to contribute to that.

Set standards and standards

To ensure that the services provided to stakeholders meet the set standards, it is necessary to develop an evaluation policy with standards and criteria. These are not separate measurements but a systematic approach that can guarantee that quality does not lag but improves continuously.

Recognize and reward good service

Usually, employees receive direct feedback from clients about the excellent quality of their services. However, that is not enough. To guarantee that employees continue to supply quality service, it is also necessary that they receive support and recognition from management.

4.4. Micropolitics

The micropolitical perspective forms an illuminating and supplementary framework for an adequate understanding of reality in organizations (Kelchtermans, 2000, 2007). This perspective has an explicit eye for irrational processes, power and influence, and for conflicts and cooperation. The actions of people in an organization are determined by their interests. Such processes take place in every organization, both in cooperation and in conflict. An example of this is a group of employees within a department that follow a training session in quality thinking and discover new perspectives. They also want to convince colleagues of this and discuss it in team meetings. Moreover, they are already starting to take initiatives in their own fields. These are political actions to optimize the organization.

Micropolitics is a matter for everyone in an organization. For example, executives often appear to engage in micropolitical activities. They have every interest in continuing to control the organization. They have control over the information and its dissemination, over rewards, and over the working conditions of the employees. They have a lot to lose if they lose control. But the employees also have micropolitical skills. For example, through lobbying and coalition building, they can prevent the introduction of certain forms of quality assurance or make them ineffective. Their opposition can lead to significant changes in organizational policy. The distribution of power and influence in the organization is not strictly linked to positions in the organization. The development of micropolitical competences is fundamental for a successful career and for the necessary job satisfaction of employees. It is, therefore, important that learning how to deal with micropolitical realities forms part of the professional development of those responsible for quality development in nonprofit organizations. Working on quality development will, therefore, have to consider the visible or invisible interactions between individuals and groups of employees.

4.5. Processes

In practice, we sometimes find that processes are lost sight of due to a one-sided focus on results or an excessive emphasis on structures. In a developmental approach, the focus on the permanent improvement of the processes and their interdependence is essential because "If you play well, you will get the marbles automatically" (Hardjono & Bakker, 2006).

The main place of processes in quality models such as EFQM, which I explain in detail in section 6.1, is not a coincidence. Processes are sometimes called the heart of the organization. In the first place, processes make the connection between results and conditions (leadership, policy and strategy, employees, and resources). An organization realizes its goals through processes. Secondly, an organization's core competencies are embedded in its processes. The processes make the organization unique and supply a competitive advantage (Hardjono & Bakker, 2006). Until now, the problem in quality assurance has been that measurements are extremely focused on results, while we still have few procedures to measure processes.

4.5.1. Definition

What are processes? There are many definitions. In any case, they concern the following: a coherent, logical sequence of activities aimed at achieving a certain goal or result with which added value is realized.

Process management is then the design, management, assurance, evaluation, improvement, and development of processes so that they can connect seamlessly with a view to achieving the goals of the organization. The PDCA circle I discuss in Chapter 5 is a process management model. Processes often go wrong during the transition to another person, department, or agency. A patient in a hospital often goes through many departments (for example, during an examination) and uses many services that the hospital offers (meals, cleaning, preparing medication, relaxation). There is an increased risk of errors at intersections between these services and departments: information is not passed on or is passed on incorrectly or too late, which disrupts continuity. The intention is for process management to recognize these risks and take the necessary measures to reduce them (Brandt, 2003).

4.5.2. Process description

Since processes are becoming increasingly complex and must be able to change faster, it is also becoming increasingly important or necessary to have good and up-to-date process descriptions to support process management. Inventorying and describing processes in an organization is an important exercise for gaining insight into the various sub-processes that together must achieve the goals of the organization and their mutual relationships. Describing processes in the right way creates more insight, overview, and clarity, making them more manageable and able to be improved. Such a description can be graphically represented in a diagram—for example, a flowchart. In such a diagram, the different activities or steps in the process are outlined in chronological order. Subsequently, the description should also clarify aspects of the process (ZBC Consultants, 2006) according to the following questions:

- What needs to be done (the chain of successive actions and decisions, the process)?

- To what end should the process be performed (the process goal)?

- When is the process successful (mention of performance indicators)?

- Who conducts the action or decision, and who is responsible (process managers and process executors)?

- Which external and internal requirements and standards must be met?

- With which (auxiliary) resources is the process conducted (the input and output and supporting systems are important)?

- When should the process be performed?

- Where, and at what location, is the process being performed?

- For whom is the process intended (process customers)?

- A good process description must meet the following conditions:

  o be clear and supply insight to those involved.

  o be complete, correct and up to date.

  o be flexible and adaptable: a process description must be able to be easily and quickly adapted to new circumstances.

  o be efficient and effective: employees must have insight into their work and the contribution they make to the overall process or product; this allows them to make suggestions for improving the process.

  o be transferable and simple: new employees must be able to learn quickly.

There are several reasons why a process description is important. According to ZBC, it can primarily help to understand the dynamics of the organization (although such a description can, of course, only be a snapshot). If such an exercise is only done to standardize and record, it can lead to rigidity, because of which the organization may no longer be able to respond efficiently to changes in the environment. The description should, therefore, also clarify the dynamics of the processes in the context of continuous improvement. When an organization receives instructions from customers, the environment, or internal evaluation processes, it must be clear to which processes that information should be assigned.

Secondly, by mapping out the processes, an organization makes clear what its strengths are and what its core competencies are. This is essential information for external stakeholders. This makes clear to the internal organization which agreements have been made. Employees must know what the process entails and must know what contribution they make to the process and its products or results, and what this means directly or indirectly for the customer and the organization.

Naturally, this exercise also contributes to the continuity of the organization. The execution of the processes can be documented in such a way that it is no longer dependent on people. When someone disappears, the description provides the successor with the necessary information to conduct the process in the same way.

A clear description also supplies clarity about powers and about who manages which process steps. Moreover, a clear description assures that everyone is headed in the same direction. In this way, it becomes clear which methods must be followed to achieve the goals and thus contributes to a shared understanding of the work being conducted. To improve a process, those involved must be able to communicate about it, and a description of the existing process is a crucial tool in that regard.

4.5.3. Organization of the processes

Processes can be organized in diverse ways. A common classification is the division into primary, support, and management processes (Brandt, 2003). Primary processes are processes that result in a service or product. These processes have everything to do with the core goals of the organization, for example, care, services, education, activation, and information. The primary processes are aimed at the external customers of the organization. Those primary processes depend on a series of supporting processes in the organization, such as facilities management, economic management, recruitment, and so on. These processes are aimed at internal customers. The conditions in which the primary and supporting processes can run are made possible by the management or steering processes. They are the activities that are necessary to manage the organization and the processes. Examples of this include policy planning and the organization of satisfaction measurements.

Figure 4.5. Organization of the processes

Steering processes

  - Policy & strategy

  - Improvement

  - Internal and external communication

Primary processes

   - Selling

   - Planning

   - Operations

   - Aftercare

Supporting processes

   - Human Relations

   - IT

   - Quality Management

   - Finances

   - Environment

   - Support

Source: Adapted from Brandt (2003).

An ordering that integrates two levels was designed by Garvin (1998). As can be seen from Table 4.3, he integrates management processes on one hand and organizational processes on the other. His ordering concerns processes with which management shapes and directs the organization in such a way that the goals of the organization are achieved. Garvin distinguishes three categories:

Table 4.3. The effectivity of processes

Management processes	Organizational processes			
Management processes	Directional processes	Work processes	Behavioral processes	Change processes
		clear strategic and operational goals?	well-defined approaches to communication, decision-making, and learning	direction and way for change
	Negotiation processes	necessary agreements of the various departments	widespread acceptance of the preferred approach to communication, decision-making and learning	everyone in the organization is convinced that change is necessary and that the proposed changes are the right ones
	Monitoring and control processes	how does the performance match the plans?	the actual behavior corresponds to the desired approach to communication, decision-making, and learning	the critical milestones have been reached and the planned changes have been implemented

Source: Adapted from Hardjono &&Bakker (2006).

In addition to management processes, Garvin distinguishes organizational processes. Here, too, he uses three categories:

Work processes

These are a series of activities that transform an input into an output for an (internal or external) customer. On the one hand, there are the work processes with which the organization makes services and products available to external customers: care, education, services, information, and so on. Those are the operational processes. When the output is aimed at internal customers, Garvin speaks of administrative processes. Examples are planning, budgeting, measurement, and so on.

Behavioral Processes

These processes concern the action and interaction between the people in the organization. In concrete terms, this concerns decision-making processes, communication processes (in which the transfer of information is central), and organizational learning processes (which aim at attracting and developing new knowledge, as well as developing collective mental models).

Change processes

These concern how the organization changes over time. Changes arise and are fueled by an internal dynamic; other changes are deliberately started, planned, and directed.

4.6. Awareness

Many people react scornfully when confronted with quality development. What is all this fuss about, they wonder. Have they not been busy delivering quality their entire career? What can an integrated approach to quality development add to that besides sounding fashionable? Such expressions of resistance must be taken seriously. They hold a message and force managers to properly account for their quality project, preferably based on a promotional vision of quality. This resistance must be able to be addressed so that employees are prepared to go along. That is why awareness of the need for integral quality development in an organization is a necessary first step. This awareness can arise from external or internal factors.

4.6.1. External factors

Organizations in which autonomous professionals work are often referred to as professional bureaucracies. Mintzberg (1992) found that the professional who often works autonomously, for example, the civil servant in his office or the care provider with his client, has little motivation to engage in organizational processes. The professional considers the organization as something that serves him and not the other way around. This makes it more difficult for him to worry about organizational changes. The professional's own development comes first, and he does not want to invest a lot in new processes. An integrated approach to quality development requires the transcending of those individual concerns, however important they may be in themselves. Integral means that the employee also engages in a process of interdependence and cooperation.

The practice of organizations that started with integrated quality development shows that an external stimulus often functions as a lever to persuade professionals who work individually. That is why government initiatives are often necessary to function as incentives. Government involvement in, for example, education, healthcare, and welfare work has had such a lever function. The fact that something must be done because the government demands it is more convincing to some than the internal logic of quality philosophy.

Another powerful lever is the market-oriented approach of the nonprofit sector. Organizations are in a competitive position with respect to each other. A system that is financed based on the number of clients stimulates market-oriented thinking. Organizations have often put a lot of energy into marketing activities such as poster campaigns and leaflets. However, its usefulness is limited. The quality argument is much more powerful. For example, clients choose an organization based on what they hear about that institution. A good name or a good atmosphere is more important than colorful posters. This finding leads to a more client-oriented approach. The organizations must ensure that their own clients are satisfied and, therefore, become their own best ambassadors.

Of course, clients are not the only criterion that the organization should keep in mind. That could lead to a policy in which the organization only wants to please customers to avoid any form of dissatisfaction or criticism. Such an attitude could have a lowering effect on quality. The starting point must remain the vision and the project of the organization itself. Of course, an educational organization, for example, can consider the fields in which graduates will work and other schools where they will continue their studies. The success figures in that educational niche and the satisfaction of the professional field with the quality of its graduates make it clear that an organization must also take the satisfaction of external customers into account in addition to the satisfaction of internal customers. Negative feedback from the field or poor success figures can make an organization think and function as an external lever for quality initiatives. In any case, external incentives are often necessary to make employees aware of the need for an integrated quality approach.

However, awareness alone is not enough. Employees also need to adjust their behavior and attitudes. The trick is to get and keep them motivated in the long term. Experiences in the profit sector, for example, show that the quality candle quickly goes out if the flame is not consciously kept awake. That is why employees must also receive incentives from within that convince them of the need for quality development.

4.6.2. Internal factors

It would be one-sided to present an organization merely as a responsive system. Even before the government's involvement, several organizations (in education and the health and welfare sector) were actively involved in systems of integrated quality development. This is clear, among other things, from the development of specific methods for quality control and from the organization of refresher courses on quality. There are two ways to enable change from within.

On one hand, the confrontation with internal problems may stimulate the need for a different approach (for example, clients dropping out, constant grumbling or protest, burnout among employees). On the other hand, employees or managers can have an infectious effect on colleagues through their enthusiasm. Innovative ideas do not necessarily have to come from senior employees. However, it is necessary for managerial staff to support creative ideas from colleagues. If the group that is ignited is large enough, motivating people can stimulate change.

Nevertheless, we must warn against naivete here. If organizations can be characterized as professional bureaucracies, the individual freedom of the employee can often put a damper on initiatives that require more joint work on integrated quality development. We must hope that training will lead the recently hired employee to a new job concept in which cooperation in support of the vision of the organization is central. That is, of course, no guarantee of change because a new employee often has little authority in the new work situation.

At the same time, it is important that other stimuli also break through the unilateral autonomy in favor of cooperation (such as certain government requirements). We are reminded that change often starts with new behaviors, whether imposed due to internal or external factors. Only when the other behavior is also successful can beliefs change along with it.

4.7. Quality development as a form of continuing learning

The term "development" refers to dynamism. The process of quality development never ends. An organization never reaches a point at which there is nothing further to improve or where there is a certainty that the future is firmly set up. Therefore, learning from new experiences repeatedly is a fundamental characteristic of quality development.

4.7.1. Individual learning and organizational learning

The success of quality development depends on the extent to which the organization and employees are willing to learn continuously. Quality improvement means nothing more than learning from experience. The focus on learning in organizations is not new. Argyris and Schon (1978) had already developed a comprehensive theory of organizational learning in the 1970s. Yet the investigation of this learning was undoubtedly accelerated by the book *The Fifth Discipline* by Peter Senge (1990). Moreover, it is no coincidence that the learning organization has become a buzzword in management thinking at a time when most organizations are confronted with rapid change. According to Van Den Broeck (1996), the concept is now also given a chance because the narrow, mechanistic way of thinking about organizations is gradually being abandoned.

Attention to organizational learning is important here (Than and Olaore, 2021). Excellent quality is more than the sum of the efforts of individual employees. If quality assurance only came down to individual employees having to work differently and perhaps harder, it would be a difficult project to digest. The new, fascinating, but also tricky thing about integral quality development is that it also entails a form of organizational change, and that is a collective process. In addition to individual learning, organizational learning is equally necessary.

When individuals learn, it does not mean that the organization also learns. Suppose a manager decides that one employee is performing less well than another. If he does not discuss this finding with those involved, he has learned something himself, but the organization has not. To speak of collective learning, the behavior change of an individual must influence the behavior of other individuals. For example, if a training worker finds that a group of students cooperates much better during his sessions if he takes time to address their questions, experiences, and disappointments, that is an individual learning process. He can discuss this finding with colleagues and clarify for them how he works. There is a chance that these colleagues will also learn from that experience, and the organization will be able to improve. An organization, therefore, only learns when someone not only performs his individual task better but also allows other members of the organization to function better as a result. Collective learning is organizational change. Senge (1990, p. 3) defines learning organizations as follows:

"Learning organizations are organizations in which people are constantly increasing their capacities to create outcomes they really want to achieve, in which new expansive patterns of behavior are nurtured, and in which people are constantly learning how to learn together. That is also the challenge for integral quality development."

In practice, however, the relationship between individual learning and organizational learning appears to be an important field of tension (Dillen & Romme, 1995; Stelmaszczyk, 2016). How and to what extent is organizational learning dependent on individual learning? That is the central question. To this, organizational experts have formulated quite different and often contradictory answers. Some see organizational learning because of individual learning (Antonacopoulou, 2006). Others reject that view as an anthropomorphism: organizations are viewed as if they were human beings. Organizational learning is, therefore, fundamentally different from individual learning. I hold the view that learning in organizations should be done by individuals but that learning should be embodied in knowledge, rules, and procedures that help the entire organization.

Individual learning must, therefore, be permanently anchored in the organization (Basten & Haarmann, 2018). Finding ways to ensure that this anchoring takes place smoothly is therefore important. To speak of an organization, there must be implicit and explicit rules that show what the desired behavior is in that organization. If those rules lead to behavior that produces the desired results, there is no reason to change them. The organization, therefore, does not have to learn. The only learning needed then is individual learning. This means, for example, learning to behave according to those rules through vocational training, skills training, introductory programs, refresher courses, and so on. Only when the rules no longer lead to the desired result does the organization feel the need to learn—that is, to change collective behavior and, with it, the rules.

4.7.2. Levels of learning

In Figure 4.6 I have schematically represented the different forms of learning. I briefly explain them.

Figure 4.6. Levels of learning

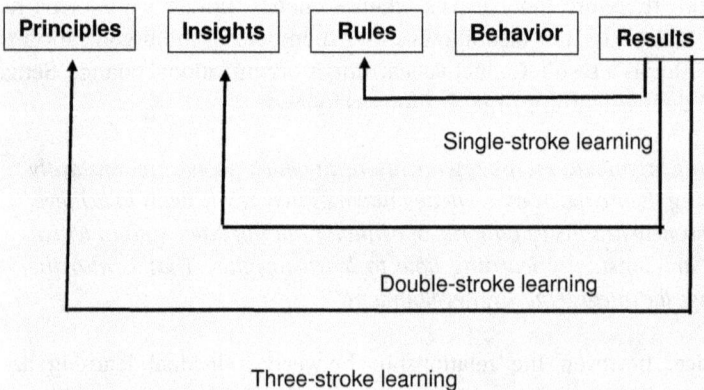

Single-stroke learning

If collective learning only leads to rule changes, then that is single-stroke learning. That learning only leads to an improvement without tracing the causes of the problem. It also implies that existing principles and insights are supported. In other words, no drastic changes are taking place. This learning is reflected in the following examples:

- The maintenance personnel in an organization complain about stressful working conditions. The management decides to hire someone extra.

- Patients are increasingly complaining about the qualities of a particular nurse. The management sends him to a refresher course.

Double-stroke learning

Both the rules and the underlying insights change. This learning leads to innovation. It goes much deeper than single-stroke learning because the causes are now being investigated. An organization is forced into double learning when conflicts arise between employees or between departments and groups. External signals can also make it clear that merely changing the rules no longer helps. A condition for this learning is that those involved are prepared to enter a dialogue about the fundamental causes. Simple solutions, such as single-stroke learning, are no longer sufficient. The innovation that must be the result of double learning still leaves the basic principles of the organizations intact. Double learning would occur in the examples mentioned above if the personnel director sat down with the maintenance personnel to find out the causes of the stress or commissioned an investigation into the stressful aspects of maintenance work in the organization. The director of the hospital should at least ask the other nurses for their opinions and evaluations of the offending colleague.

Three-stroke learning

If the essential principles on which the organization is based are under discussion, then there is three-way learning. In that case, the identity of the organization, its role in the environment, and its mission itself come up for discussion. The organization can reflect on the type of service it wants to provide. Management can develop a serious personnel policy plan to improve the quality of the employees over a period of five years. In Table 4.4, I have summarized the characteristics of the three learning forms.

Table 4.4. Characteristics of learning forms

Learning	Domain of learning	Result
Single-stroke	rules	improvement
Double-stroke	insights	innovation
Three-stroke	principles	development

Source: Adapted fromSwieringa & Wierdsma (1990).

4.7.3. In summary: Characteristics of a learning organization

Following Mensink (1994), we can characterize a learning (nonprofit) organization using several characteristics:

Strategy

- Management describes the organization's environment as a network of partnerships.

- There is a shared, powerful vision in the minds and hearts of the employees.

- Based on the shared vision, the members of the organization see the development of a strategy as a permanent learning process.

- Plans are drawn up and adjusted interactively with the employees in the organization.

Structure

- The organization consists of a network of teams grouped around an aspect of the core process.

- Teams are given responsibility and decision-making power.

- Coordination occurs through lateral relationships and is not imposed from above.

Culture

- Being outward-oriented is a central value.

- Asking critical questions is encouraged.

- Experiments are normal.

- Making mistakes is allowed.

- It is normal to exchange ideas with internal and external stakeholders.

Work processes

- Teams and departments treat each other as partners.

- Added value for the stakeholders partly decides the design of the turning processes.

- Integral quality development is seen as a learning process.

Finally: What is really important?

- Involvement and exemplary behavior of the managers is crucial.

- Leaders create support for quality development.

- Everyone in the organization takes part in quality development.

- Trust is a basic value in relations between stakeholders.

- Individual learning and learning must take place in teams so that the organization can learn.

- Teams need to take ownership of their processes.

But also, pitfalls

- Wanting to go too fast without the majority following.

- Paying no attention to employees' uncertainties.

- Taking too complicated an approach.

- Wanting too much; too little focus on what is important.

- Paying too little attention to external partnerships.

- Being too slavishly busy with numbers; doing too little with the stories.

Part 2.
Integral quality
development: Practice

No problem can be solved with the same thinking that created it.
We must learn to look at the world in a new way.

— Albert Einstein

Chapter 5

Basic methodologies

It should be borne in mind that nothing is more difficult in preparation, more doubtful in success, and more dangerous in effect than presenting oneself as someone who wants to implement innovation.

— Niccolo Machiavelli

In this chapter, I describe several basic methods. These are general methodologies that can be applied in any organization that takes quality development seriously. First, I discuss how the appreciative approach can have a specific place in quality development. I then discuss the PDCA method. Next, the practice of self-evaluation is discussed. Finally, I discuss how an organization can become and remain a learning organization.

5.1. Getting started with the appreciative approach

Cooperrider (2000) described four phases, the so-called 4D cycle, to achieve effective organizational development through the appreciative approach. The 4D stands for Discovery – Dream – Design – Destiny. This cycle is applicable to the process of quality development. The starting point is the choice of a positively defined theme. Examples could include the following: How do we reach satisfied employees or customers? How do we become a leading organization in policymaking? How do we achieve the best teamwork?

The starting point of an appreciative approach is a certain theme on which the organization wants to work. The reason for the theme can be an evaluation, a complaint, a new development in the outside world, or an event in the organization that makes people think. The characteristics of this approach are that it does not allow the organization to be paralyzed by negative feelings or by a narrow point of view that focuses only on the problem. I often find that a negative experience leads to the organization being approached exclusively or predominantly from a negative angle. From the outset, the trick is to articulate the theme in a positive way. This requires a constant awareness of one's own strengths and, at the same time, the conviction of being able to develop the organization in a positive direction in the future. I first present the cycle visually (see Figure 5.1) and then discuss its different steps.

Figure 5.1. Phases in the appreciative approach

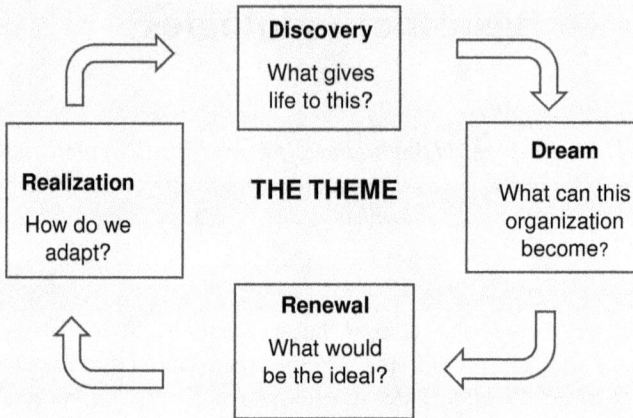

Source: Adapted from Cooperrider (2000).

The beginning of any appreciative approach is choosing the right theme for change. The theme must be chosen carefully because it decides the scope of the research and because it is central to the four phases that I discuss in Sections 1.1 to 1.4. At the same time, the choice of theme decides the direction in which the thinking will take place. Organizations develop in the direction of what they study about themselves. For example, when relational conflicts in the organization are chosen as a theme, the result will be that the number and severity of complex and problematic themes will increase. However, if teamwork or excellent quality is the theme, these phenomena will flourish and develop. Organizations help create their worlds. The choice of themes is, therefore, crucial. In any case, the appreciative approach starts from aspects that give strength to an organization.

The key question here is: What gives life to this organization? Contrary to the traditional evaluation, which must bring several shortcomings to the surface, I start with what the organization was good at in the past. What factors inspired the organization at the time when it was most successful? From there, forces and possibilities can be detected that can make the quality of the organization and its processes even more effective. Let us recall that the seeds of change and development are already implicit in the first questions that are asked. The trick is, therefore, to encourage employees to think about those subjects that offer the most opportunities for further quality development. If employees experience that their organization is developing in the direction of the themes they are questioning, this motivates them to select those topics that they would like to see developed in the organization.

The trick in this phase is to identify the strengths of the organization. This can be done by focusing on those moments when the organization performed very well or when people felt particularly good within the organization. The point here is to understand the factors that made such positive experiences possible. Examples could be good leadership, good peer relationships, the presence of modern technology, clear structures, strong shared values, and good working practices. In this way, employees are prevented from concentrating unilaterally on the analysis of shortage experiences, and at the same time, they learn from (even small) positive experiences.

In this phase, employees share their stories of extraordinary experiences with each other and, in effect, discuss the core of what inspires and drives their organization. They also look for those factors that can best stimulate the organization in its future development. This creates a sense of collective meaningfulness. In this way, the history of the organization becomes a dynamic stimulus for the future rather than a frozen set of bad, romantic, or forgotten events. History then becomes an opportunity. When such an appreciative approach really lives in an organization, and when all stakeholders of the organization or community are connected in the search for those strong experiences, hope grows, and the qualities of an organization are strengthened. Examples of themes that organizations have chosen are diversity, quality, employee empowerment, organizational learning, shared vision, client satisfaction, innovation, partners, and consensus decision-making.

> *The exhilarating quest for discovery, the search to find what magic lies beyond the stars and inside the atom, is at once wonderfully insatiable and wonderfully satisfying. We cannot find happiness in contemplating ourselves, but we can find it in contemplating infinity. Reaching out, with our imaginations, toward its majesty, it will in turn embrace us and inspire us.* (Jacques Cousteau, cited by Nystrom, 2002)

It is important in this preparatory phase that people brainstorm in a creative way. To stimulate that process, the following four questions can serve as guidelines:

1. What was a top experience or highlight in your organization?

2. What do you value most about:

   - yourself?

   - your job?

- your organization?

3. Which factor makes your organization most vital?

4. Name three wishes to strengthen the vitality and health of your organization.

In this phase, it is important that influential employees take part in designing the future of the organization. It is, therefore, useful to form a steering group in which all levels of the organization are involved, if possible. It is also essential that the chosen themes be formulated in an appreciative, positive manner.

5.1.1. Discovery phase

Looking for factors that inspire and energize an organization is a kind of discovery process. The data gathered in appreciative interviews should point the way to the forces that energize the organization when it functions at its best. In this phase, data and stories about the theme are collected. This is a core process, as it serves for the dialogue that follows and for the organizational changes that must result. In a traditional research approach, objective data are looked for with the assumption that those facts exist outside the person who is investigating. It is, therefore, a kind of objective reality outside of man. In an appreciative approach, we do not look for objective data. Rather, it comes down to empathizing with the stories that employees tell about their organizations. That is why it is good that people are enthusiastic when they tell their stories about values and experiences, the history of their organization, and their wishes for the future. It comes down to stimulating thinking and speaking about those positive forces because they are often forgotten in problem-setting and deficient thinking about organizations.

The appreciative interview is the core of this phase. This is a mutual learning process: both the interviewer and the interviewee learn as they explore values, top experiences, and desires together. To ensure that this process runs smoothly, it is important to clearly define in advance which stakeholders will be interviewed. Particularly important are those employees who are highly interested, who have sufficient impact on the development of the organization, and who also have sufficient insight and information about the selected theme. In smaller organizations, it may be possible to consider involving everyone. Of course, an interview protocol must also be developed. What we ask determines what we will find. What we find decides how we will speak. How we speak decides how we can imagine together. How we imagine together decides what we will achieve. Ideally, an interview protocol should include at least the following three parts:

1. *Preliminary questions*

    What do you value most about:

    - yourself?

    - your job?

    - your organization?

2. *Questions about the core theme*

It is good to briefly introduce the theme in a positive way. For example, when it comes to quality, the following introduction could be used: "Quality development is the priority for everyone in the organization. Everyone who experiences quality appreciates it and recognizes its importance. People also feel proud when they have been able to take part in a high-quality project, when they feel that their contribution really mattered, or when they notice that the client really appreciates the quality."

    - Think about a time or period when there was a strong or extraordinary expression of quality development in teams, groups, or across the organization. What made that quality development possible? (Explore working methods, communication, leadership, etc.)

    - Give an example of an extraordinarily strong moment of quality development that you experienced yourself. What factors made that moment possible?

3. *Closure*

    - Which key factors ensure vitality in your organization?

    - If you look to the future, what should we become as an organization?

    - If you could develop your organization in the direction you would like, what three things would you do to strengthen the vitality and health of the organization?

Good questions encourage the interviewee to tell his story and put people on the trail of valuable experiences. They also bring out people's essential values and aspirations.

5.1.2. Dream phase

In this phase, stability, the status quo, and inertia are challenged by imagining a richer and more positive future. This is in line with the basic aim of any quality development, namely, permanent quality improvement. We base this on the strong moments in the history of the organization, and at the same time, we want to further develop the possibilities of the organization. The quality of this phase is strongly influenced by the extent to which examples from the past are fascinating. In this phase, the stakeholders commit themselves to the future of the organization. Often, for most stakeholders, this is the first time they have been invited to consider the exciting potential of their organization. It is also important that they dare to think beyond what they previously thought possible. People must, therefore, dare to imagine an exciting future for their organization that far exceeds the limitations of the current situation.

This phase can go ahead as follows:

- Small groups consider the data and stories from the interviews and use that material to form a picture of what their organization could look like in the future.

- The small groups discuss the ideal organization together.

- The groups consider what could happen in the organization in a period of five years, for example.

- Each group makes a creative representation of the future organization (a drawing, a model, a commercial, etc.).

- Each group presents that creative presentation to the other groups.

5.1.3. Renewal phase

This phase follows the creation of the social architecture that is necessary to support the future organization. The key element here is the formulation of provocative propositions that make the dream of the organization concrete. Here, the essential elements of the infrastructure of the organization are mapped out: leadership, strategy, structure, HRM, culture, client relationships, values, communication, results, and so on. The focus is on the functioning of the organization in all its facets. The question is, which organizational changes are necessary to be able to realize the new goals? The process also involves more people, especially those who have a stake in the future design of the organization. All important aspects of the organization should be carefully considered here.

The next step is to formulate provocative statements in which the desired qualities of the organization are clarified. Such statements bridge the gaps between the best of what is and ideas about what should be. The statements are provocative in the sense that they provoke and challenge traditional beliefs and practices while at the same time suggesting real possibilities for the organization. The aim is to develop a series of provocative statements about the ideal theme. What would the organization look like in all areas if it developed as told in the statement?

The following is an example of a provocative statement: "The process of quality development in our organization empowers the employees in such a way that they feel like valued co-owners of this organization. They constantly take the initiatives to improve quality. The organization is a learning organization in which there is a mutual fertilization of ideas. The organization is a leader in the sector." A provocative statement must:

- Be challenging and stimulating.

- Be well founded: Are there examples that make it clear that the ideal is realistic?

- Be wanted: Do all the employees in the group support it?

- Be expressed in positive terms.

5.1.4. Realization phase

In this phase, images of the new future are realized. This is the period of learning and adapting, improvising and trying out. The potential for new developments is high in this phase. With a view to the shared positive view of the future, everyone is invited to take part in creating the new development together.

People and teams talk together about how they can contribute to realizing the organization's dream, as expressed in the provocative statements. Engagement incorporated into relationships should become the basis of new development. It is important here to develop an appreciative eye for all elements of the organization, in systems, procedures, structures, and working methods (for example, a department of "evaluative studies" was renamed "appreciative studies").

Actions, goals, resources, and people necessary to make the provocative statement come true are described. To also build in a time dimension, it makes sense to ask yourself what should be ready in four years, four months, four weeks, and four days. It comes down to selecting several goals and activities and accurately indicating what means, by whom, and within what period the organization will achieve them. Classical working methods are suitable for this, such as project management, working groups, and so on.

With the appreciative approach, I want to add an extra dimension to quality development based on the observation that many good intentions in the field of quality care do not lead to lasting improvement. The change in thinking consists of dynamizing quality development based primarily on the qualities, possibilities, and positive experiences of an organization and much less on shortages. I believe that the impulse to achieve quality development and improvement that emanates from the strengths of an organization is stronger and has a longer effect.

5.2. The PDCA circle as a learning tool

If an organization wants to become a learning organization and work permanently on quality improvement, it must also have access to instruments that support it in that endeavor. The classic final inspection is not enough. Yet, I see many examples in which quality is only checked in the final phase. Consider, for example, exams at the end of the year that test whether students meet the requirements. Employees are not evaluated enough about the quality of their actions. Hardly any moments are planned in which the employee can adjust his process through interim evaluations.

Figure 5.2. The PDCA circle

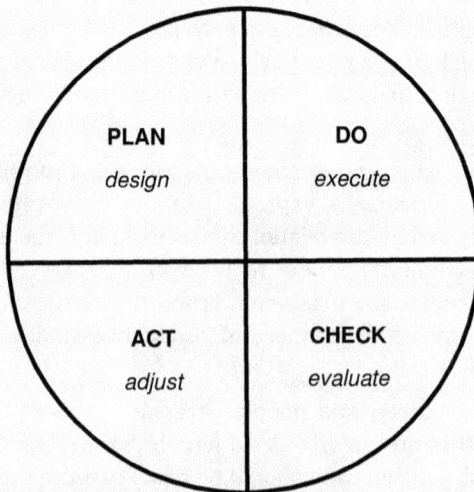

5.2.1. The method

A permanent concern for quality improvement must be based on a systematic way of working. Isolated, non-targeted initiatives are not enough, even though they can be quite valuable in themselves. Such a system can be found in the four-step plan of the PDCA circle in figure 5.2. The fascinating thing about this model is that it can be applied at various levels: both the individual employee can use it (in the preparation, implementation, evaluation, and adjustment of his assignment) and the organization.

Plan

Quality should not be the result of chance but should be the result of a conscious quality policy. The starting point for any quality improvement lies in the goals that we must describe as concretely as possible. Knowing exactly what we are working toward is important. I no longer need to repeat here that goals should be formulated in workable and observable behavioral terms as much as possible. They must stand for the result of a process. As management and employees describe the result in concrete behavioral terms, the evaluation will then be able to continue more efficiently. Without quality awareness among management and employees, the employees easily experience this concretization of the goals as a tight straitjacket. This entails the danger that employees will become demotivated and that their creativity will stiffen. At the same time, such a tight description easily leads to a minimal commitment to the finish line and not a step further. Employees are often used to working with goals for their own activities. They are much less involved in the formulation of goals for the entire organization through organizational policy. That is why I advocate involving employees at the level of the organization in formulating the goals. Quality planning is, therefore, especially important in integral quality development. It consists of the organizational-level planning of short-term actions. Ideally, an organization makes such a quality plan every year. Priorities are decided each year and elaborated in action plans. Based on his experience with the PDCA, Bruggeman (2014) argued that many organizations start planning too quickly. Planning without first thoroughly exploring the problem and the situation is short-sighted. He, therefore, proposed to extend PDCA (Plan, Do, Check, Act) to APDCA (Analyze, Plan, Do, Check, Act), where the first A stands for a thorough analysis of the problem.

Not only employees but clients can have a say in the matter. It is important to know what clients' needs are. This is particularly important when it comes to individualized service, care, or help, such as in-home care.

- Collecting information

  o We collect information on the client; in addition, we also involve others, including relatives and other professionals.

- Figuring out wishes, needs, and problems

  o We enter into dialogue with the client and periodically identify which values are important to him and what his wishes and needs are.

  o We discuss dilemmas (conflicting values) and make well-considered choices in consultation with the client.

  o We investigate whether (as a result) there are or could arise potential risks.

  o Setting goals.

  o Together with the client, we determine which situation is desirable and/or which behavior is proper, as well as which goals must be achieved in an agreed time schedule.

- Deciding on and planning activities

  o Based on the goals set, we decide in consultation with the client which activities are needed.

  o We determine which activities the client can conduct himself and what the employee needs to do.

  o We draw up the schedule and record the agreements made in the care plan.

Execute (Do)

After the planning phase, of course, follows the goal implementation phase. Management needs data to find out whether and to what extent employees have achieved their goals after a set period has elapsed. An efficient internal registration system can prove useful here. However, many employees in the nonprofit sector have negative experiences with registration. The clients almost never verify its usefulness. Without accountability, the government or management imposes a schedule. Employees rarely see the results of processing. As a result, they are hardly motivated to register adequately. For them, registration is often synonymous with useless bureaucracy. If management wants to collect good data, it must be prepared to develop a practical registration scheme together with the employees. The employees experience daily what is or is not workable. They must also be given access to the results of the processing. These data are the basis for new operationalizations of the goals. Only if policymakers involve their employees in registration in this way can the insight grow from the practice itself that registration is a necessary working tool. In Chapter 6, I discuss the problem of measurement and figures.

It can also be worthwhile for an organization to gradually develop its own quality system. Such a system is a description of the way in which the quality of the basic processes of the organization must be realized, evaluated, and assured. It holds a description of, among other things, the following elements:

- the most important quality requirements (e.g., the basic competencies that students must have developed at the end of their education to meet the professional profile).

- the basic processes and associated procedures (e.g., the examination regulations).

- the way in which basic processes are regularly assessed.

- persons responsible.

- the paths to be followed if the stated quality is not achieved (i.e., the description of the way in which quality improvement will be improved).

The quality system is, therefore, a set of standards, procedures, and tools. A quality system should not become an end because then it is experienced as a burdensome formality that does not supply added value. Such a system should give clarity to everyone in the organization so they can all work together in the same direction. A quality system enables new employees to find out what the organization expects of them, ensures that ad hoc solutions do not have to be sought each time problems arise, and gives the organization orientation. The development of a quality system is a long-term task. Naturally, that quality system must be written down in one way or another. The concrete form that this can take is the quality manual.

In addition to the mission statement and the vision, the quality manual also describes the quality policy and the quality system. It describes how the organization wishes to achieve its goals in a high-quality manner. Such a handbook, if developed in an expert manner, can become a necessary working tool for an organization. Here lies the challenge—on the one hand, to prevent employees from considering the handbook as a piece of bureaucracy and, on the other hand, encouraging them to find correct solutions to their questions and problems in the handbook. Ideally, the handbook is put on the computer so that everyone can consult it. In practice, a quality manual is only really used often if employees have no other resources to solve their problems.

PREZO (2017) concretizes it as follows:

- Execute the activities according to the plan.

- Supply the care or support following what has been agreed upon and laid down in the care plan.

- Observe whether the agreements need to be adjusted during the implementation of the care provision.

Evaluate (check)

After a certain period, employees must examine the extent to which they have achieved their goals. The evaluation of their functioning takes place based on the collected facts. I distinguish two types of data in quality management, each of which is important: (1) The data are based on people's subjective experience, the so-called perception data. For example, an employee survey gauges satisfaction, which is a subjective perception. Evaluations of employees by students or clients are also part of the perception data. (2) The objective data are the results of measurements (e.g., the number of graduates according to intake characteristics). On one hand, an evaluation is the determination of the differences between the actual and the desired results. On the other hand, evaluations examine the shortcomings and their probable causes. Simple tools are available for this that every employee can learn to use, such as the Pareto analysis, brainstorming, and the fishbone diagram, which I discuss in Chapter 8. For the evaluation to be meaningful, it must take place in an atmosphere of trust. If the employees only experience the evaluation as a control measure, they will have little motivation to cooperate. The strength of well-organized quality management lies precisely in the fact that employees check themselves and derive part of their work motivation from this.

It should be noted that Deming, who adopted this method from Stewart, proposes changing the C for Check to S for Study because Check is easily associated with Control. This would make it more difficult for people to be involved in quality development. PDCA then became PDSA (Plan, Do, Study, Act) for Deming.

PREZO (2017) applies the check as follows:

Evaluate care and support

- We discuss whether the client experiences the agreements being fulfilled by the parties involved.

- We discuss whether the client's experiences with the care supplied meet his values, wishes, and needs.

- We discuss whether the client feels that the set goals have been achieved.

- We also involve the client's relatives and other professionals in this process.

- We do this structurally and systematically through consultation moments (e.g., care life plan discussion, multidisciplinary consultation, evaluation interview).

Act

The evaluation has a double function. On one hand, it is the basis for a new operationalization of the goals. On the other hand, it serves to adjust activities and employees. The adjustment of the activities may mean that the organization includes new activities in its program. It may turn out that other activities are not possible. Adjustment also means responding to new developments in society and in the professional field.

The employees will recognize their strengths and weaknesses in the evaluation. It is very motivating if they can retrain their professional skills. That is why good management will ensure the ability of the employees to adapt to new circumstances and develop further. Management must, therefore, make space, organizational, and financial resources available for permanent training. The wide range of courses and further training offers many opportunities here. However, consultations between your own employees or with employees of different organizations also supply opportunities. Larger organizations can introduce work consultations and, at a later stage, quality circles to allow employees to work autonomously on quality improvement.

'Act' can also mean that the organization is on the right track according to the evaluation and wants to keep that course. In practice, I see that both individual employees and organizations invest energy in planning and implementation. I often miss evaluations that are the source of adjustments. I also see that people are willing to adjust but that there is no solid basis for doing so. For example, employees are concerned with how they can do their work even better. The legitimate desire to do better next time often leads to a guess-and-miss approach.

PREZO (2017) suggested:

Adjust care and support if necessary.

- We adjust care and services where necessary and as often as necessary.

5.2.2. Checklist

In the questionnaire below, management and employees will find tools to work purposefully with the quality plan according to the (slightly changed) PDCA method.

Analysis

- What is the problem, and for whom is it a problem?

- What is the situation of the organization? In what environment does it work (economically, politically, socially, and culturally)?

- What is the culture of the organization: Which values are important?

- What kind of leadership? How are the relationships with the employees?

- What are the possible causes of the problem? > What are the needs of the clients?

Objectives

- What goals have been formulated for the organization as a whole?

- Can employees and clients take part in the formulation of goals?

- To what extent do management and employees regularly operationalize official goals?

- To what extent is the operationalization of the goals based on a needs analysis of the target group?

- Are the goals unambiguously understandable for clients and employees?

- To what extent and by what means does the organization communicate its goals to the public?

Execution

- What quality level must employees achieve?

- What standards exist for this, and are they known to the employees?

- What room for maneuvers are employees given in the performance of their duties? > To what extent can employees adjust the goals themselves? > What happens when an employee can achieve the set goal in the relationship with the client?

- What resources do employees receive to achieve their goals?

- What help do employees receive if they experience difficulties in achieving goals?

- Are there standard registration forms?

Evaluation

- Does management regularly discuss the extent to which employees are achieving the goals?

- On which facts do both management and employees base their assessment of effectiveness?

- How do management or employees decide whether clients are satisfied with their experience with the organization?

- Do employees know under what conditions management is satisfied with their performance?

- How does management check the quality of the employees?

- Are there performance reviews? Who performs them?

- What are the consequences for employees? Do they know these consequences?

- How does management calculate error costs?

Adjustment

- Do employees develop their own abilities at the expense of the organization?

- Which further training initiatives can they take part in? Under what conditions?

- To what extent are employees given incentives to learn from their mistakes?

- Through which channels does the organization stay abreast of developments in society and in the professional field?

Anchoring

- How will the organization ensure that the solution is permanent? Does the wheel have to be reinvented every time?

- How does the organization try to prevent the same mistakes in the future?

- How does the organization ensure that new employees know the proven approach to problems?

- What agreements does the organization make to re-evaluate the solution after a certain period?

5.2.3. Systematic reflection

As a further concretization of the PDCA method, I now discuss systematic reflection. Systematic reflection is often lacking, making PDCA a technique that no longer contributes fundamentally to quality development. Such a system is offered in Korthagen's reflection cycle in Figure 5.3. I briefly describe each step (Kelchtermans, 2000).

According to Korthagen (1998), a good reflection process has five phases that must be repeated continuously:

- Phase 1: Gaining experience—acting.

- Phase 2: Reviewing the action.

- Phase 3: Becoming aware of and making explicit the essential aspects of the experience.

- Phase 4: Develop alternatives for the approach and make a choice.

- Phase 5: Trying out the chosen alternative in a new situation (new experience).

Figure 5.3. Process of reflection

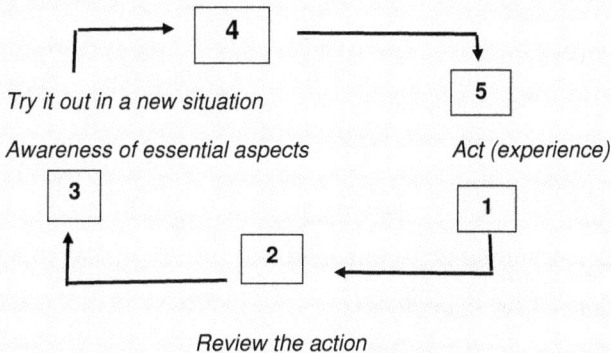

Developing alternatives for the approach and making choices

4

Try it out in a new situation

5

Awareness of essential aspects   *Act (experience)*

3

1

2

Review the action

Source: Adapted from Benders (2003).

Every instance of learning to reflect starts with gaining experiences (phase 1), which must then be reflected on step by step.

Phase 2 examines what happened. This is an important phase because people often tend to quickly look for alternatives for action without first considering what happened. The person seeks answers to the following questions about the experience:

1. What did I want?   5. What did the client want?

2. What did I feel?   6. What did the client feel?

3. What was I thinking?   7. What did the client think?

4. What did I do?   8. What did the client do?

The employee must have an eye for the questions from the client's point of view. He does not know enough about what he thought and felt. Therefore, he should not only examine his own experiences but also put himself in the client's position. Thus, the service relationship is understood as a situation of meaningful interactions. The different participants in the situation interpret it in their own way as a function of many factors, such as earlier experience, knowledge, needs, expectations, and so on. It is necessary that the reflection here be limited to the experience itself. It is not yet a diagnosis.

Only in phase 3 does the person come to a responsible diagnosis. It is important that our own interpretation framework be discussed here. In phase 4, the person looks for action alternatives. How can he manage it differently in the future? In phase 5, which is also phase 1 of a new reflection process, the person tries out the alternatives and gains new experiences on which he can then reflect. In this way, it becomes clear that reflection is a cyclical process that is never finished.

Questions that can give direction to the reflection process:

Phase 1 (acting = phase 5 of the earlier cycle)

- What did I want to achieve?
- What did I want to pay attention to?
- What did I want to try?

Phase 2 (looking back, what happened concretely?)

Employee perspective	Client perspective
1. What did I want?	5. What did the client want?
2. What did I feel?	6. What did the client feel?
3. What was I thinking?	7. What did the client think?
4. What did I do?	8. What did the client do?

Phase 3 (awareness of essential aspects)

- How do the answers to the earlier questions relate to each other?
- What is the influence of the context?
- What does this mean for me now?
- So, what is the problem?

Phase 4 (alternatives)

- What alternatives do I see?

- What advantages and disadvantages do they have?

- What will I resolve next time?

5.2.4. Some Critical Remarks on the PDCA

The PDCA circle as a method has meanwhile become firmly proven in the practice of quality development. Based on their experiences, several authors formulated some justified concerns and adjustments (Van Kemenade, 2013; Bruggeman, 2014; De Saeger, 2014).

A first consideration is that the rigid use of the PDCA circle leads to a form of control thinking. As if standard use would automatically lead to the right solution so that critical thinking would not be given enough attention. In addition, if the check is given too much emphasis, the method becomes a form of control. According to Van Kemenade, there is also a vision of reality behind which predictability and repetition are characteristics. If predictability becomes too dominant, innovative and critical thinking are endangered. People then approach reality with a blindfold and, therefore, have too little eye for the continuous changes in people, contexts, and organizations. The belief that reality can also be effectively changed with good planning is misleading because reality itself is constantly changing. As a result, a tight schedule is often unproductive. Strategies often do not develop the way they were conceived. It is better to adjust the goals and strategy when the circumstances make it necessary rather than sticking tightly to predetermined plans. Tight planning and using the check too strongly as a control lead to people dropping out. There can then be no question of a real quality culture.

De Saeger (2014) argued that the PDCA is often misused. People jump to planning far too quickly without first thoroughly analyzing the situation, of which Deming was aware. In addition, too many organizations would put a lot of effort into planning without being consistent in their actions. Thinking and doing are not compatible with each other. He also warned that only PDCA circles go around to solve recent problems, often with the effect that the solutions are not secured. That is, they are not permanently anchored.

Van Kemenade (2014) also argued that PDCA is a Western concept that is not automatically valid for other cultures. Therefore, he proposes to let go of the need for control thinking. The world is less malleable than planners assume because of the rapid change in context and people. As an alternative, he advocates ACCRA. That acronym then stands for Attention (giving attention and building relationships), Context (knowing and considering the environment in which one finds oneself), Commitment (creating the involvement of people), and Reflection in Action (reflecting on what one is doing).

5.3. Self-assessment

The first step in the procedure for permanent quality development is self-assessment. I limit myself here to self-evaluation with a view to an improvement perspective. Self-evaluation can also take place with a view to accountability, for example, in preparation for an external evaluation. With the self-assessment, the organization shows a situation about the quality of the input, the processes, and the results. This form of self-assessment should supply data that the organization can use to plan and implement quality improvement.

5.3.1. Definition of terms

Self-evaluation is not a new phenomenon. What is new is the fact that it now receives systematic attention and is also managed professionally. In the context of the OECD's International Organization Improvement Project, Hopkins, Ainscow and West (1994) distinguished four stages in thinking about self-evaluation:

Organizational development

Ideas from organizational science about organizational development form the basis. Organizations apply methodologies from organizational development to bring about change. The core lies in the survey: data in the organization are collected and then discussed with those involved.

Organization-based review

In this phase, instruments for mandatory self-evaluation were developed (self-evaluation was regarded as the preeminent tool for bringing about change). Self-evaluation is used here both as a source of accountability to third parties and for implementing innovations. A well-known tool developed by the University of Bristol is the GRIDS (Guidelines for Review and Internal Development). The entire organization takes part in this process, which is aimed at improving the internal nonprofit organization. Responsibility for that process lies jointly with management and the employee group.

Organization-based development

In this phase, the emphasis shifts to development. Organizations are given more autonomy and responsibility so that they themselves become responsible for design and development. Self-evaluation is a development tool here.

Holistic organization improvement

The central question here is the relationship between self-evaluation, innovation, and performance. Before that, many innovations had led to changes in components, for example, working methods. The comprehensive approach focuses on the organization.

A crucial point of discussion is still the extent to which self-evaluation can be used simultaneously as an instrument for accountability to third parties and as an instrument for improvement. Many authors state that the two goals are difficult to reconcile. It is a conflict between control and the means of stimulating professionalism, between responsibility toward society and responsibility toward oneself.

Van Petegem (1998, p. 104) defines self-evaluation as follows: "Self-evaluation is the process, mainly initiated by the organization itself, whereby well-chosen participants systematically describe and assess the functioning of the organization with a view to taking decisions or initiatives in the context of (aspects of) general organizational policy development."

I will explain this description point by point:

- Self-evaluation is a permanent and cyclical process that fits in with quality management. The emphasis is on the process, not on the product. Even if the result of the self-assessment can be a report, the report is not the primary intention.

- Self-evaluation takes place at the initiative of the organization itself. Employees are responsible for making the data available and for what happens to the results afterward. This is a different starting point than the external evaluation, where third parties request data to arrive at an opinion.

- Well-chosen participants. To arrive at valid information, it is necessary to involve the data of people who are actively involved in what happens in the nonprofit organization: employees, clients, and management. In addition, partners can also be surveyed (for example, suppliers and partner organizations).

- Self-evaluation takes place systematically. Ideally, self-assessment meets the standards that a scientific study must meet: reliability, validity, and objectivity. Reliability means that the results are not dependent on chance, and therefore, the choice of the participants is important. Validity refers to the content of the research. Is the information relevant to obtaining a picture of the organization indeed being collected? Objectivity in this context means that the results may not be influenced by the person who organizes the self-evaluation. In any case, a self-evaluation should be more than a collection of loose impressions.

- The self-evaluation must relate to the functioning of the organization. In contrast to the classic inspection of employees' actions, a self-evaluation must cover the organization. This means that, in addition to the service provision process, the conditions (such as leadership, vision, personnel policy, and resource policy) must also be examined. It is also important to try to gain insight into the results. This can be done, for example, by measuring the satisfaction of employees, clients, and partners and by mapping the results of the process (number of dropouts, recidivism, etc.).

- Self-evaluation is both describing and judging. In addition to providing a correct description of the situation, the self-assessment must also allow for an assessment. If the self-evaluation is to have a function in the pursuit of permanent quality development, the organization must, of course, be able to compare in order to determine to what extent the quality is indeed improving. This can be a comparison over time so that a quality development plan can be put in place. However, it can also be a comparison of standards. In a self-evaluation, the assessment takes place based on the standards that the organization itself chooses. These standards may also make it possible to decide how the organization is performing in comparison with other organizations. Of course, it is not possible for standards to be imposed from outside during such a self-evaluation, as can be the case with an external evaluation such as an accreditation.

- Self-evaluation takes place with a view to making decisions. The results of a self-assessment are not intended to be used without obligation. They must form the basis for concrete initiatives that lead to quality improvements. In section 5.3.2, I will discuss how we can arrive at initiatives and decisions based on a self-evaluation. However, it is necessary to work with the results afterward. If this does not happen, there is a substantial risk that the participants will drop out at the next evaluation. It must eventually become clear to everyone in the organization that the effort of self-evaluation leads to actual changes.

5.3.2. Self-evaluation in practice

In this section, I describe how self-evaluation can take place in an organization. To this end, I present a simple four-step plan in Figure 5.4: (1) preparation; (2) performance; (3) progress actions; and (4) follow up.

Figure 5.4. Self-evaluation roadmap

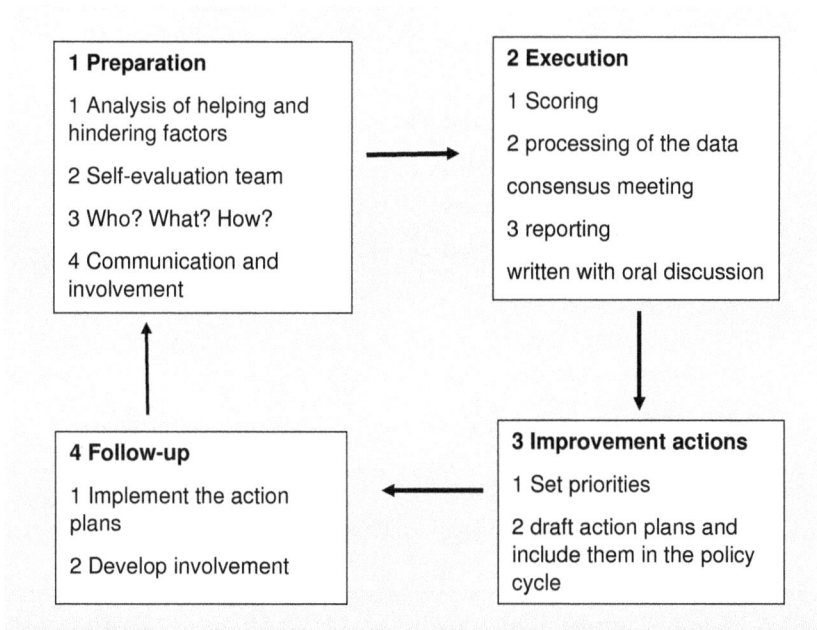

5.3.2.1. Preparation

Good preparation determines the success of a self-assessment process. Preparing is more than just rational planning. Good planning is a necessary, but not sufficient, condition for success. Preparing certainly also means considering and predicting psychological situations.

Analysis of helping and hindering factors

The first element of good preparation is the research into hindering and helping factors (Devos et al., 1999a). When discussing the pillars of quality management, I have already outlined how factors such as leadership, vision, and personnel policy determine the chances of success. Naturally, these factors now also play a role in the concrete organization of a self-evaluation. I briefly review these and other factors (from Devos, Verhoeven & Van den Broeck, 1999a).

Facilitating factors are:

- an open organizational culture characterized by open communication, mutual trust, and peer support.

- stimulating organizational leadership with a democratic leadership style. The management must ensure that quality management, including self-evaluation, is supported by the entire organization.

- active involvement of the various levels of the organization in the policy.

- collaborative working: stability in the team and cooperation.

- availability of resources.

- strong conviction of the usefulness and necessity of self-evaluation among as large a part of management and employees as possible.

- willingness to take a critical look at one's own performance.

- willingness to change at all levels of the organization.

- sufficient skills to solve problems.

In addition, I can distinguish several factors that jeopardize the success of a self-evaluation. The organization should be aware of these factors in advance and consider how and to what extent something can be done about them before starting the self-assessment procedure.

Hindering factors are:

- no clarity about the purpose of the self-evaluation, hidden agendas, or concealed goals.

- incorrect insight into the meaning and procedure of the self-assessment and, therefore, poor communication and information flow.

- certain characteristics of the organization, for example:

- ○ an unclear organizational structure,

- ○ lack of willingness to change,

- ○ an oversupply of innovations,

- ○ open or hidden conflicts.

- • absence of helping factors.

Self-assessment team

It has already been said, but I repeat it here: to the extent that quality management and therefore, self-evaluation is the concern of only one person, it must fail. A large group, if possible, the entire organization, must form the support base. The self-assessment must, therefore, be prepared and conducted by a team. This can be an existing quality working group or an ad hoc self-assessment team. It is desirable that the working group be composed on a voluntary and expert basis. It is also useful to have the various sections involved in the self-evaluation also represented in the team.

For the success of the self-assessment team, it is necessary to clearly define the tasks, responsibilities, resources, and authorities in advance and to communicate these to all members of the organization.

The extent to which an external expert should also be included in the self-assessment team depends on the experience the organization already has with quality management and self-assessment. If the organization is still inexperienced, it may be useful to hire an outside expert. She or he can recommend the organization, check the step-by-step plan, supervise the procedure, teach skills, and supervise the interpretation of the results. She/he must ensure that the organization can autonomously organize future self-evaluations as quickly as possible.

Even though the team plays a significant role in self-assessment, the role of leadership is crucial. It is leadership that must, on the one hand, put the organization on track to self-evaluation and, on the other hand, inspire and encourage the process. Of course, leadership is also in charge of providing the self-assessment process and the team with the necessary resources.

Who, what, how?

The self-evaluation process requires considerable effort from the organization. Deciding the goals of self-assessment is a process that ideally occurs in consultation between management and the self-assessment team. It must be made clear in advance what the purpose of the self-evaluation is and what will be done with the results. I myself advocate that self-evaluation be used in the first instance in the context of a permanent pursuit of quality improvement and that learning from the organization comes first. Naturally, the self-assessment will also have to be conducted by external parties, such as inspectorates and accreditation bodies. In the context of internal quality management, the results of self-evaluation must lead to concrete progress actions.

If employees get the impression that self-evaluation is an end in itself (i.e., a measurement for the sake of measurement), it will undermine their motivation. It must be a means that contributes to better quality. Does management only want to figure out its own position for one of the standards? Does management intend to have a learning effect among employees? It is important to mention here that the goals of self-evaluation must, of course, fit in with the vision and the general goals of the organization.

Subsequently, it must be clearly agreed upon in advance what will be evaluated: the entire organization or a part of it. It should also be made clear what is meant by "leadership" in concrete terms. Is it about the director, the head of the department, or the board? It is essential that everyone has the same people in mind when evaluating. Usually, these are those who have direct authority over those who complete the self-assessment.

It must also be clear in advance who will take part in the self-assessment. Sometimes, that can be everyone in the organization. However, that is difficult due to limited resources, and one must limit oneself to a sample. Moreover, it must also be made clear which categories will take part: only employees, or also clients, partners, support staff? One criterion is, of course, that participants must have sufficient experience with the evaluated organization.

Self-evaluation can be done using many instruments. Nonprofit organizations have many options in that area and do not have to rethink everything themselves. Whichever instrument is used, it is often necessary for participants to become familiar with the instrument, especially when using it for the first time.

Finally, clear planning must also be drawn up in advance. This plan includes the timetable, as well as the necessary infrastructure and the selection of the participants. Since self-evaluation can become a labor-intensive activity, it is necessary to plan it well in advance. In addition to the preparation of the employees, attention must also be paid to the concrete implementation, the processing of the data, the feedback of the results, the determination of progress actions, and the follow-up. If self-evaluation is to become an element of integral quality management, regular evaluation should be a possibility—if possible, annually, but at least every two years. The entire organization does not need to be evaluated annually, but various aspects of quality can be evaluated each time, and a global evaluation can be conducted every three to five years in which the entirety is examined. There may be no one-size-fits-all method; everything depends on the intended purpose. What is certain, however, is that integral care for quality aimed at continuous improvement requires regular evaluation.

Communication and involvement

The realization of a self-evaluation requires considerable effort from those involved. It is therefore necessary to obtain the strongest possible involvement of as many employees as possible. Communication is an important link in this regard. Particularly for nonprofit organizations that have no experience with self-evaluation, the realization of that involvement requires special attention.

The first condition for involvement is that everyone is properly and promptly informed. Management must prevent rumors from arising by supplying the necessary information to those involved in a timely manner. Too often, management waits too long to inform employees, leading to rumors and misinterpretations. As a result, the organization must invest a lot of energy in correcting the information. In any case, the who-what-how questions must receive a clear answer. Information alone is not enough for effective communication. As I discussed in section 2.3, there must be room for dialogue in which resistance can be discussed, among other things.

To motivate people to cooperate, it is necessary to create a solution in which everyone benefits. It must be clear to the employees what the added value of self-evaluation can be for themselves and for the organization. If the organization does not yet have experience with self-evaluation, it is necessary to train employees in the use of the method. Refreshing the method is sufficient for later self-evaluations. Naturally, new employees will always have to be trained.

5.3.2.2. Execution

After the preparation period, the self-evaluation takes place. First, the instrument must be used, then the data must be processed, and finally, the results must be recorded in a report for all parties involved.

Scoring

To begin with, all those involved—a sample or the entire group—must conduct the self-assessment. Depending on the instrument used, they score items or answer questions. It must be decided in advance whether everyone will participate in the entire self-evaluation or whether diverse groups will be examined on a different part of the method each time. In any case, the results must be representative so that a reliable picture of the organization is obtained. If a sample is used, the composition must be fully correct. It is about getting the best and broadest picture of the organization. If the organization has not yet gained experience with this, guidance from an external expert is needed. Most instruments are initially scored individually. In some methods, the staff must discuss the individual results in a consensus meeting. It is necessary to have someone from the self-evaluation team available to answer questions from employees.

Data Processing

Once the evaluation forms have been completed, processing can begin. This is quite a job, especially if many employees have taken part in the self-evaluation. Here again lies an important task for the self-assessment team. If they do not conduct the processing themselves, they must organize it. In any case, an image of the organization must be distilled from the raw data that accurately reflects the nuances of the various levels. This picture can be based on statistical or qualitative descriptive material. In any case, the result must be that those involved recognize themselves in the result. Some instruments also have an electronic version that can be scored via computers and the Internet. In that case, the processing can also be automated so that the results become available without much effort.

For some instruments, it may be useful to present the results to those involved and to have them commented on. Soon after the scoring, preferably not much longer than a week, the group meets for a consensus meeting supervised by a trained quality management officer, preferably someone from the self-assessment team.

When scoring, differences always arise between sections and employees. For example, management as a group usually scores higher than the other employees. The aim of the meeting is to seek consensus based on arguments. It is about finding and discussing differences to arrive at a common result. In the normal procedure (a sample), the staff examines an overview of the scores, in which score differences are clearly visible. Prior to the consensus meeting, a score overview is made of the individual scores per focus area and per sub-aspect. This can be done by showing the frequency of the score for each phase on a special score sheet. A list with all areas of attention and criteria can be used for this purpose. A bar or line chart with a separate bar or line for the various levels (management, clients, employees, support services) is also insightful.

It is essential to let employees express their motives for scoring in a certain category. For example, start with the people who scored in the modal category. In the discussion that follows, employees who scored in the other categories put forward their arguments. Pay attention to possible systematic differences between scores of subgroups (full-time and part-time employees, lower and upper management, etc.).

Of course, holding a consensus meeting is optional. Nevertheless, I recommend it, because it stimulates involvement and indeed makes quality care integral to everyone's business.

Reporting

It is essential that the results of the self-assessment be communicated to all those involved if they are to remain motivated to cooperate in the future. It is usually not sufficient to communicate the results in writing. Precisely because a next step must be taken later, in which the group takes progress actions, it is also necessary that the written report also be explained orally. The report is, therefore, a working tool and not a final text.

The interpretation of the data is a delicate process. What does a certain result mean? It is useful to have reference points, both internal and external. I give some examples (Devos et al., 1999a).

Internal reference points:

- results of earlier investigations, earlier inspection reports, etc.
- results of other sections within the nonprofit organization.
- expectations agreed upon in advance.
- applicable standards in the organization.
- values and norms that live in the organization.

External reference points:

- standards set by the government.
- standards for accreditation.
- results of other nonprofit organizations.
- data from government reports.
- research reports.

The self-assessment team must, therefore, clearly decide in advance, in consultation with management, who will see the results. These are, of course, primarily the employees because they must continue to collaborate with the data. I often see that management wrongly keeps the results to themselves, especially when the role of management is not assessed positively. Existing relationships and organizational culture also decide how the information is used. If self-evaluation is to stimulate lasting quality improvement, a great deal of openness toward the internal stakeholders is necessary.

The extent to which external stakeholders receive information must also be determined. The question is also whether the actual report should be made available to everyone or whether the outside world will receive an abbreviated version.

The organization must also decide to what extent it restricts itself to a business-like representation of the results or whether a detailed self-assessment report is presented. A self-assessment report is needed for external quality management, such as inspections. In addition to this external goal, I find an extensive self-assessment report, albeit labor intensive, a powerful instrument that can promote quality development.

5.3.2.3. Progress Actions

If self-evaluation is to be given a place in an integrated quality approach, it must lead to progressive actions. The organization must realize this based on the results of the self-assessment report. First, the strengths and weaknesses must be found; then, priorities must be set. Finally, those priorities must be translated into actions for progress.

Strength-weakness analysis

Scoring is not enough. In addition to positioning in relation to certain standards, it is important for an organization to get a picture of its own strengths and weaknesses. But, of course, quantitative scores can be a starting point for making a strengths-weaknesses analysis. It is necessary that both strengths and weaknesses be shown for all relevant dimensions of self-assessment to arrive at a nuanced picture.

A strengths-weaknesses analysis is best linked to the discussion of the results or to the consensus meeting. Naturally, this requires a meeting for which sufficient time is set aside (even on a study day).

Finally, I must point out that it is especially important to define the strengths and weaknesses in such a concrete way that they can be interpreted clearly and unambiguously by everyone. This is followed by the phase in which the group must make choices based on the analysis.

Set priorities

The danger of an integral analysis of the entire organization is that many points of progress appear. This can create skepticism and pessimism or the tendency to start everything at the same time. However, it is impossible to work on all the points at once. It is, therefore, important that the group try to reach a consensus on several progress priorities based on the strengths-weaknesses analysis. This can be done empirically: each group member individually shows three progress points and assigns one, two, or three points to them. Then, all the points awarded are added up, and a ranking follows. For example, the three highest-ranked progress points could be chosen as priorities.

Experience shows that employees tend to choose progress points for which management is responsible. Nevertheless, permanent quality improvement is the responsibility of everyone in the organization. It is useful to distinguish between progress points for which employees (teachers, for example) are responsible (these usually have to do with processes) and progress points for which management is responsible. Priorities should then be set for both employees and management.

Action Plans

The last step is to develop action plans to work on the priorities. The organization must develop an action plan for each priority. An action plan includes a description that is as concrete as possible and includes the following:

- goal (SMARTI: Specific, Measurable, Achievable, Relevant, Time-Bound, and Inspiring).
- time planning.
- resources.
- criteria for judging success.
- reporting (when, what, to whom).

The composition of working groups is suitable for organizing the implementation of the action plans. A working group can be installed per priority, for example, led by a member of the self-assessment team or the quality working group. Even though the work is done in a smaller working group, it is essential that the rest of the organization be regularly informed of progress. Quality development must remain everyone's business. In the end, this method is only useful if it leads to results (i.e., to real improvements). Therefore, it is necessary to choose only a limited number of workable priorities.

5.3.2.4. Follow up

Working on quality improvement implies a long-term policy. In practice, quality management repeatedly runs the risk of being extinguished like a candle if the organization does not pay explicit attention to embedding. This is why I propose several measures to ensure that quality initiatives started with great enthusiasm also remain vital. It should be clear that the role of management is of decisive importance in this regard. The attitude of management is still too often minimalist; it tolerates quality development if it does not become too critical of the functioning of management itself. Tolerance is not enough; real commitment is necessary.

First, quality assurance, self-evaluation, and prioritization must be an essential part of the overall policy of the organization at any level. Again, if quality development is only a concern of a few, it lacks the power to lead to permanent quality improvement. This requires that the goals of quality development be included in the general goals of the organization.

Second, it is necessary that someone in the organization has the responsibility to coordinate quality development and, therefore, self-assessment and progress actions. Ideally, that person takes part in consultation with management, but he does not necessarily have to be a member of it. In many nonprofit organizations, the quality manager is a staff officer. Smooth and regular communication with management is essential.

In quite a few organizations, the authority of the quality manager is a problem. Often, he has a list of tasks and responsibilities but no powers to make decisions or to intervene.

The efforts of the working groups regarding the priorities should lead to concrete proposals. These can then be presented to management, preferably to the entire organization, and then possibly adjusted to details. A decision will have to be made on these proposals, preferably based on consensus. Ideally, the proposals will then be integrated into day-to-day business. The renewal is then no longer an innovation but a daily routine.

If people experience self-evaluation as merely an extra burden in the long run, it must yield several benefits (Devos, Verhoeven & Van den Broeck, 1999 b):

- more organizational unity.

- strengthening team spirit.

- more willingness to implement changes.

- more incentives to develop new problem-solving skills.

- better atmosphere and more open climate.

5.4. How to become a learning organization?

A psychosocial support organization has developed a mentoring system for new employees. Guidance talks are attended by the mentor and discussed with the person concerned. Sometimes, conversations are also tape-recorded. If a conversation holds interesting elements that can also be instructive for others, they will be discussed in the beginner group. These discussions often lead to conclusions and learning points that are important for all employees, including experienced colleagues. Guidance conversations on video are also sometimes viewed and discussed together with a view to learning how to critically analyze guidance practice. These discussions then form the basis for further collective training sessions in which both experienced and novice colleagues take part.

Another instrument used by new employees is systematic reflection after each coaching meeting. Points of attention appear from this personal reflection that receive special attention during the next meeting. These reflections are also discussed in the performance interviews between mentors and new employees. Another form of learning takes place through the InterVision sessions. In these sessions, colleagues bring in work questions that are explored in depth by the group. The sessions end with an inventory of learning points that each member of the group writes down for themselves. This can then lead to more training sessions that are useful for all members.

A final learning path consists of the use of a self-evaluation tool. All employees first score individually on the functioning of the organization and the quality of the core processes. Once a year, the processed results form the starting point for the collective determination of progress priorities, which are then worked on in working groups.

The example above illustrates that learning in the learning organization must meet specific requirements, which I briefly describe here:

Problem-oriented, cyclical learning by doing

Learning processes are driven by existing or expected problems or experiences. Learning, therefore, takes place when the current situation no longer corresponds to the desired situation. Problems are signals for necessary change. Learning is linked to work because that is where problems arise. Problem-oriented learning is cyclical learning: one first acts then reflects, then thinks about workable solutions, and finally decides what to do.

Collective learning

In the learning organization, team learning is given a lot of emphasis, in addition to individual learning, of course. Changes in a learning organization arise from the meeting of different perspectives, interests, and contributions.

Conscious learning

A learning organization stimulates conscious learning. That means working methodically by asking each other questions. Conscious learning requires the collective will, courage, and skill to ask what someone is doing, for what purpose, why, and how. Because learning is always linked to a task, work, or a concrete problem, discussions are prevented from flowing.

Versatile learning

This term refers to the various levels: rules, insights, and principles. The organization must have sufficient diversity to cope with the diversity in the environment. This diversity can manifest itself in:

- people: thinkers next to doers, individualists next to group workers.

- strategies: planned, rational as well as pragmatic strategies.

- structures: complex next to simple structures.

- systems: complex as well as simple systems.

A learning organization consciously allows contradictions and paradoxes. Conflicts are not threats to avoid but challenges to solve.

Learning to learn

To learn, the organization must develop its learning ability. This ability rests on self-knowledge and on knowledge of how and why a person learns. Naturally, a learning organization must also have a collective learning ability so that employees have the courage to look at themselves.

To speak of a learning organization, the focus on continuous learning must be the starting point. This is based on the conviction that quality can only continue to develop if everyone and the entire organization want to learn from mistakes. Continuous learning is vital for the survival of an organization in a dynamic and competitive environment. Whether that focus can be there depends on the leadership. It must create space in which errors can be discussed, it must itself serve as an example of that willingness to learn and openness, and it must create a safe climate in which employees and teams dare to speak about errors.

Learning in the learning organization requires that information be anchored in the entire organization in the form of knowledge, rules, and procedures.

Therefore, it is necessary that the starting point be dependable and correct. To obtain valuable information, employees must be prepared to expose themselves and discuss their mistakes. In addition, they must be open to feedback from others. Of course, such an attitude is only possible if the culture allows for mistakes to be made. If that were not the case, people would tend to hide their mistakes for fear of negative consequences. According to Senge (1990), employees must be aware of their mental models: entrenched beliefs and ideas that neither the person nor the organization uses consciously. These models decide the view of reality and the actions of individuals and groups. It is necessary that people become aware of their current mental models and, if necessary, formulate alternatives for them.

Learning also requires the organization to be problem-solving. Therefore, opinions and points of view should be judged based on their merits and not according to the person expressing the opinion. As a result, problem orientation contributes to the democratization of the organization and to the participation of every employee. It is not who says something that matters but what is said. Only when employees have the certainty that their superiors will not use their views against them will they be inclined to openly discuss the behavior and mistakes of their superiors as well. The importance of problem orientation also allows us to clarify the difference between control and learning in quality development. If control prevails, the quality of the results will be pursued by ensuring the reliability of the process from above and top-down, via inspection. A learning-oriented approach can pursue the same goal, namely the best quality of the products, but through a bottom-up approach, through the cooperation of everyone in the organization.

Finally, this learning is only possible if everyone takes responsibility for their own behavior and for the learning of the organization. Learning from your own mistakes alone is not enough. Individual learning must be anchored in the organization. Being focused on the entire organization is an important condition.

To enable continuous learning, the organization must also take structural measures. At least the four following measures are needed:

Developing a shared vision

The charisma of leadership is often the driving force of an organization. Yet, true inspiration means that individual visions can be translated into a shared vision. This vision supplies an intrinsic motivation that makes real learning possible.

Learning in teams

The learning unit of a learning organization is not the individual but the team. A good team is more than the sum of its parts. To realize this, it is necessary that a free flow of opinions and visions arise in the team. To achieve that real learning, the organization must create forums where that learning becomes possible. For example, there must be times when information about errors and experiences is systematically exchanged and when anchoring in the organization is sought.

Promote participation

One of the core conditions for becoming a learning organization is the intrinsic motivation of all employees to learn and to share that learning. A condition for realizing such involvement is that employees are given the freedom to evaluate the learning mechanisms that they consider most desirable. This means real participation in learning decisions.

Stimulate an open culture

If it is true that the learning organization is the opposite of a mechanistic organization, then it is necessary that the employees develop a sense of belonging to the entire organization. The saying that "the whole street is clean if everyone sweeps before his own door" does not apply. In the architecture of the organization, forms must be looked for in which this involvement in the entire organization can be realized. Usually, this will lead to the conversion of functional organizations into flatter organizational forms with a lot of horizontal communication. For nonprofit organizations, it is usually necessary to adapt the buildings so that they invite collaboration. The traditional architecture of nonprofit organizations often makes collaboration difficult, if not impossible.

Community of practice

If an organization wants to develop a quality system that has support, it must invest heavily in the training of employees, not only in quality management but also in those competencies that make the processes possible. Such training should not only be instructive but should also offer employees the opportunity to pass on their experiences so that the entire organization can learn from them. One way to achieve this is to set up a community of practice, a forum in which experiences are exchanged in such a way that everyone benefits, not only individually but also as an organization. Schön (1983) spoke of a "community of reflective practitioners" when employees interweave their task performance with learning and passing on learning experiences to each other. However, such learning forums can also become ineffective when learning becomes an artificial ritual or when information is obscured by a self-protective attitude.

Finally: What is really important?

- Looking before you leap. A good study of the problem and situation is essential for quality action.

- Learning from positive experiences and strengths gives more opportunities for the involvement of many than focusing on problems.

- Reflecting systematically on the actions of individuals as well as the team and the organization is a prerequisite for deep learning.

- Learning permanently is a condition for quality development in an organization.

- Completing a systematic self-evaluation requires a methodical approach.

Chapter 6

To measure is to know, or not?

Collecting numbers uncritically gives you a false sense of security; patient listening leads to a deeper understanding of what is really happening in an organization. Every quality development requires some form of evaluation. For too long, this has been interpreted unilaterally as measuring. This is one of the reasons why the term "quality management" in the nonprofit sector has long been viewed in a less positive light. Without wanting to deny the importance of meaningful measurements, in this chapter, I want to explain the limitations of a one-sided quantifying approach from the broader perspective of quality development. Evaluation can also take place with qualitative methods. In this chapter, I discuss several methods to realize the evaluation. I also place the theme of measurement in a broader context.

6.1. Measurement, a critical reflection

"To measure is to know" is a slogan that conquered the world from the first quality management approach and is still often used. The reasoning is that if you really want to gain insight into what is happening in an organization, you must measure it. That measurement is, therefore, at once reduced to collecting figures. This way of thinking ignores what really matters in quality development—namely, keeping the organization focused on its goals based on information, as well as checking whether and how the organization has achieved its goals and adjusting its policy and approach where necessary. It is about valuable information, not numbers, for their own sake. In addition to figures, qualitative data are also especially important. Employee stories express in their own way how the organization works toward its goals. Moreover, those stories help to discover the meaning of pure numbers. I must, therefore, take a nuanced, critical approach to the slogan "to measure is to know." Figures without the underlying stories leave much unclear.

Especially in the nonprofit sector, there appears to be much unfamiliarity with the requirement to prove one's own quality with figures. Control bodies impose indicators that the organization must also substantiate empirically. For a long time, there was hesitation and resistance to measuring (Goubin, 2005). However, gradually, everyone has evolved, often out of necessity, sometimes silently, into counting and measuring culture. What cannot be measured does not really count as proof of quality work. A modern application by some governments and inspectors is to require that everything be evidence-based. Of course, we must be critical of such trends and developments and not just accept everything that is pre-chewed. When numerical measurement becomes too important, there is usually no longer an ear for the story behind it. Measuring threatens to make us forget the immeasurable essence. Looking, listening, and thinking critically about things remains necessary. After all, measurements are based on assumptions that do not apply to all processes within the nonprofit sector. Therefore, it is necessary to consider several questions deliberately at the beginning of an evaluation process. I call them VIP questions:

1. Where are we going to collect or measure facts, or where are we going to listen to stories?

   • Does it involve manufacturing, services, care, and so on?

2. What is the nature of the processes being evaluated?

3. What is the goal of the evaluation?

   • Describe what is happening?

   • Improve the quality?

   • Measure results?

   • Improve processes?

   • Compare processes with those of other organizations?

4. What tools are available for this purpose?

5. Is there evidence that this tool is suitable for achieving this goal?

Bullen (1999) argued for the use of the right evaluation tools by pointing out the quite different processes that can be the subject of evaluation. He distinguishes manufacturing processes (creating new products), administrative processes (standardized processes that should produce a standardized output), service processes (clients change during the process), and social change processes (long-term processes whose outcome is unknown).

Bullen characterizes these processes according to two dimensions: X-characteristics and Y-characteristics. Table 6.1 provides a schematic overview. Each type of process shows a unique mix of X and Y characteristics. X-characteristics are associated with uncertainty and can be described more accurately with qualitative tools, such as storytelling (the telling of stories and experiences); Y-characteristics are associated with more certainty and are easier to describe with figures and indicators.

Table 6.1. X and Y characteristics of processes

X Characteristics	Y Characteristics
People change along the way	People don't change
The intended result is not known in advance	The intended result is known in advance
The results are not precisely defined	The results are precisely described
The processes are not well defined	The processes are well defined
The processes are individualized	The processes are standardized
The results are individualized	The results are standardized
Multiple causes and multiple effects – it's hard to prove the causal relationships	Processes proceed according to proved causal relationships
The process goes from person to person	The process proceeds from person to object
Meaningfully described as an open system	Meaningfully described as a closed system
Often looking for long-term results	Often looking for short-term results

Source: Adapted from Bullen (1999).

An example. A social service organization aims to change people (X); the result is not fully known in advance (XY) and is often not well defined (XY). The processes that will take place cannot be written out properly and completely in advance (XY). Since these are human realities, there are usually many factors involved, and not everything can be attributed to a specific cause (X). The process is usually person-to-person (X). The relationship with the client can be meaningfully described as an open system (X). Results can usually only be expected in the longer term (X).

According to Bullen, many measuring instruments are designed for processes with many Y characteristics. If we also attack processes with many X characteristics using the same instruments, we will get into trouble.

A one-sided emphasis on figures also arouses resistance because these practices are quickly linked to control and, therefore, to order. Without control, there is no order, no balance, no manageability. However, such a conception of measurement carries the risk of becoming particularly destructive to quality development. The reasoning is that only if organizations behave like machines would control make sense. Organizations, however, are organisms that dynamically interact with their environment and are constantly developing internally. Processes are more important than fixed structures. Wanting to realize a rigid structure through measurement and control is disastrous for an organization's development opportunities. However, I am not advocating a laissez-faire attitude.

Naturally, an organization must be able and willing to account for itself internally and externally, among other things, about the realization of its goals, its use of resources, and its deployment of people. However, accountability must take place in interactions with employees, stakeholders, and the environment. Quantitative measurement has limited value in this context if it is framed in the stories of the organization. Accountability also means investigating how and to what extent the organization dynamically deals with what presents itself from within the organization itself and from the environment. Numerical measurement is meaningful only if it supports and stimulates the development of the quality of the organization.

6.2. Measurement as a process

In addition to accountability, measurement is also a dimension of management. This is the process of monitoring activities to ensure they are performed as planned and correcting significant deviations. This can also be an element of quality development. I briefly discuss here those processes in an organization that lend themselves to quantitative goals (such as the number of absences due to illness, percentage of graduates, number of work accidents, and amount of waste).

For that type of process, control consists of four steps (see also Figure 6.1):

1. set standards.

2. measure performance.

3. compare performance against standards.

4. take action.

Before the actual follow-up can begin, the organization must set clear standards and performance requirements. These standards are the criteria against which actual performance is compared afterward. It is necessary that these standards be defined as concretely as possible. This means that both the concrete activities and the required quantity must be shown (for example, reducing the amount of waste from 15 percent to 3 percent). It is obvious that these standards should be known to everyone involved in the process. These standards should also contribute to improving the quality of service. Standards, then, are the guarantee that must prevent quality from deteriorating again.

Figure 6.1. Process of control

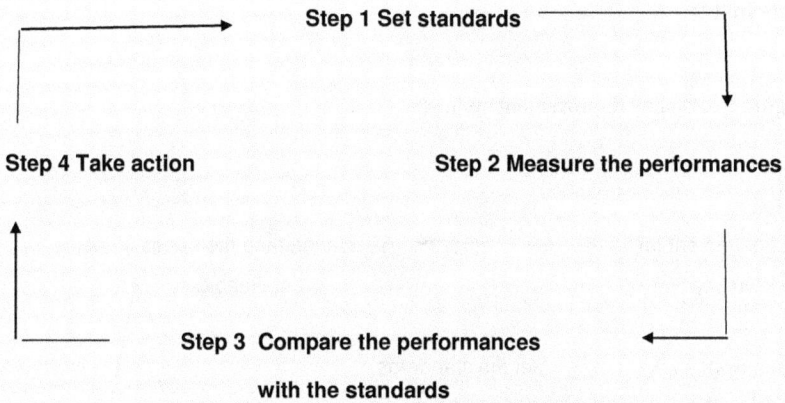

It is useful to distinguish between hard and soft standards. Hard standards are quantitative and, therefore, measurable in nature. They are also referred to as performance indicators. Examples are the number of clients, dropout rate, and recidivism rate. Soft norms are qualitative in nature and based on subjective judgments or perceptions. They are the so-called perception indicators (for example, satisfaction and courtesy toward clients).

Figure 6.2. The role of standards

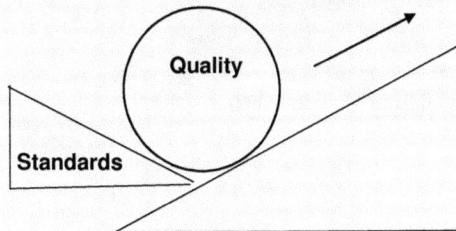

After the description of the standards, it is necessary to check the extent to which the set standards are also being achieved during the provision of services to be able to adjust quickly if necessary. Finally, it appears that the needs of the stakeholders are evolving, so the standards must also evolve. This is why it is necessary to go through the cycle repeatedly. In Figure 6.3, I schematize the process of quality improvement and the role that standards play in it.

Figure 6.3. Quality improvement cycle

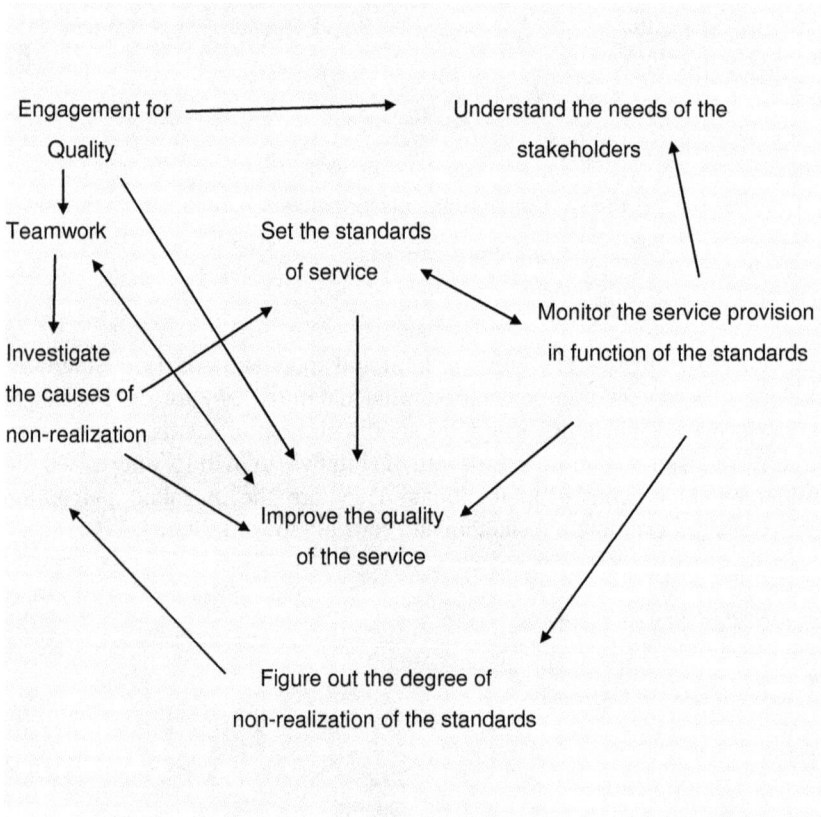

Source: Adapted from Moullin (2002).

In the measurement process, the organization collects information about its performance. It can base this on four sources: (1) personal observations of quality managers and managers; (2) statistical reports; (3) oral reports; (4) drafted reports. Each of these sources has advantages and disadvantages. Naturally, a combination of various sources increases the chance of reliable information. Even more important than how to measure, however, is the question of what to measure. Wrong criteria lead to dysfunctional results.

The information obtained is the basis for the comparison between the determined performance and the standards set. To what extent does the result deviate from the norm? In order not to have to respond to every deviation, margins are set within which deviations are acceptable. Deviations that fall outside the set limits are significant and require adjustment. Figure 6.4 shows schematically how to work with boundaries.

Figure 6.4. Determination of an acceptable variation range

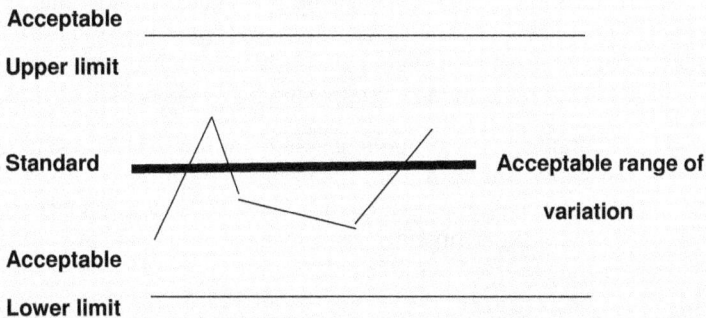

The last step of the verification process involves several options. If the performance meets the standards, nothing needs to be done. If the performance is below average, a change is needed. Various interventions are then possible. If the deviation is due to inferior performance, the organization must take corrective action. This may consist of changing the structure or strategy, redefining the work, supplying further training, and so on. However, it must first be decided whether immediate corrective action or a basic correction is to be taken. In the latter case, the organization looks for the causes of the variation and removes those causes. The organization, therefore, wonders how and why a performance deviated strongly. Based on the answer, it tries to come to grips with the cause of the problem. Immediate correction tries to address the problem at once so that performance varies within limits again. Organizations often take too little time for fundamental corrections and miss opportunities to really learn. They are too easily satisfied with an immediate action that quickly brings performance back within acceptable limits. In fact, that "firefighting" leaves the causes untouched. An effective approach is to analyze errors and deviations to learn from them and thus avoid the same problems in the future.

It is, of course, also possible that the variation is due to unrealistic standards and that the target was set too high. In that case, the standards should be reviewed, not the performance itself. So, let's talk about those standards.

6.3. Characteristics of effective measurement

If measurements are required, it is better to take them properly. Robbins, Decenzo, and Coulter (2013) outline the following characteristics that an effective measurement process must meet:

- Accuracy: A measurement system that produces inaccurate information misleads management, which in turn can lead to wrong decisions and errors.

- Timeliness: Measurements should highlight variations over time to avoid a serious impact on one's performance. Even the best information becomes worthless when it becomes obsolete. Effective measurements supply the right information on time.

- Economical: A measurement system must also be economically workable. The gain from a measurement must outweigh the effort needed to obtain the information. Hence, management should ideally organize as few measurements as possible, yielding the best possible results.

- Flexible: Effective measurement systems must be flexible enough to adapt to changing circumstances and take advantage of new opportunities.

- Intelligibility: A measurement that is not understood is worthless. Therefore, it is sometimes necessary to use simple measurement systems. What is too complicated can cause errors, frustration, and resistance.

- Reasonable criteria: The standards used in the measurement process must be reasonable and, therefore, achievable. If the standards are too strict and employees find it difficult to achieve them, they will not be motivated. Because employees do not want to risk being labeled incompetent by their supervisors, they prefer to resort to dishonest practices rather than admit that they cannot meet the standards. Standards should present employees with a challenge that motivates them to perform well.

- Strategically placed: Quality managers cannot control everything that happens within an organization. Even if that were theoretically possible, the benefits might not outweigh the costs. Therefore, the measurement should mainly relate to factors that are of strategic importance to the organization. This may mean, for example, that they must take place where deviations from the standards are the most common.

- Multiple criteria: Managers and employees mainly want to look good on the criteria they know are being measured and will put less effort into points that are not covered. This is why it is important to organize a broad measurement. Multiple criteria have a double-positive effect. First, several criteria are more difficult to manipulate at the same time than a single criterion. Second, an evaluation based on different criteria will give a more correct picture of performance.

- Corrective action: A good measurement system not only shows deficiencies but also gives advice on the measures to be taken to improve performance. The system must both detect the problem and suggest a solution.

6.4. Types of measurement

6.4.1. Time of measurement

Management can take measurements before, during, and after an activity.

Figure 6.5 shows several types of measurements.

Figure 6.5. Types of measurements

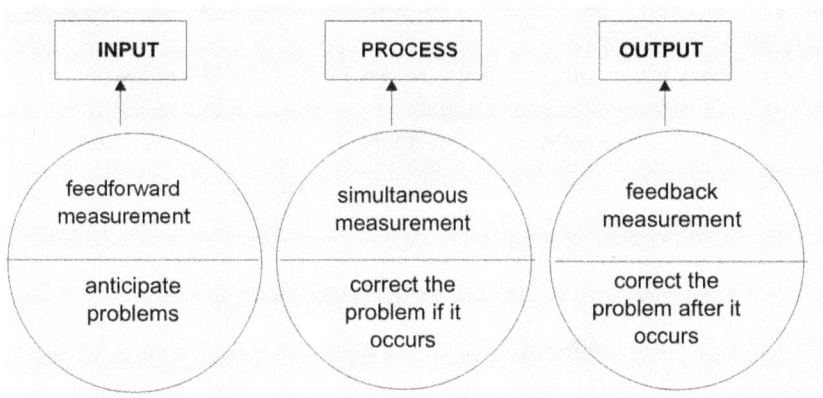

6.4.1.1. Pre-measurement (feedforward measurement)

This form of measurement is the most desirable: after all, it tries to prevent problems so that the organization does not have to invest energy in solutions later. The condition is that correct information is available in advance, and that is often difficult. Therefore, executives usually need to use one of the other two forms of measurement. Preliminary measurements mainly focus on the human, material, and financial resources entering the organization. This measurement is necessary, for example, when selecting or hiring new employees. In this way, the organization wants to be sure that it has recruited the right person so that no problems arise afterward.

Quality assurance

Quality assurance, or quality management, is a form of quality assessment that precedes the process. Although the system has so far mainly been used in industry, it also offers many opportunities for the nonprofit sector. With quality assurance, organizations want to ensure that they themselves do not have to perform access control on the incoming elements. Instead, the quality specialists at the supplier analyze and check the quality assessment system. If that investigation is positive, the organization receives a certificate that guarantees quality. As a result, it can enter networks without the partners having to conduct quality assessments on-site each time.

Accreditation is an example of this. Accreditation guarantees partner institutions that the system of quality development and the quality itself meet strict standards. In European higher education, for example, accreditation has become a standard procedure. This should guarantee that students who go to an institution abroad end up in a place that meets the necessary quality requirements. The institution sending the students no longer must check the quality on site. Accreditation already fulfills an important function in other sectors as well. In the healthcare sector, for example, clinics collaborate only with suppliers who have a quality certificate.

In concrete terms, quality assurance means that the client proceeds to a system audit by partners or suppliers to arrive at an assessment of the effectiveness of the quality assurance there. This review covers, among other things:

- evaluation planning.
- procedures for detecting and correcting errors.
- control of processes.

Several factors contributed to the introduction of quality assurance. Of course, there is an exemplary role of industry. After all, high-risk industries have long been obliged to apply quality assurance (the nuclear industry; the military, space, and aviation industries). In addition to government requirements, the market also plays a role.

6.4.1.2. Simultaneous measurement

This form of measurement takes place at the moment people perform the activity. As a result, problems can be addressed before they cause too much damage. Permanent process control is an example of integral quality development. Another example is direct supervision. The manager observes the actions of his employees and can intervene at once when he detects errors. Of course, there is time between the error and the manager's intervention, but compared to the feedback check, that time is minimal. For example, computers can be programmed to react at once after an error. Process control aims to rectify major deviations from the standards during the process as quickly as possible.

For example, a teacher in the first grade can regularly evaluate whether all children achieve the required minimum level of reading or math. If that is not the case, he/she can quickly adjust. After all, if a child is held back a grade, he or she can suffer adverse consequences.

Of course, the process in nonprofit organizations is not about the production of measurable products. Accurate measurement with precision measuring instruments is, therefore, not possible. Process control is, therefore, likelier to take place by assessing performance and attributing traits to people.

For example, in healthcare, patient satisfaction measurements can provide an indication of the quality of the reception and support process in the hospital. In education, students can evaluate their teachers with a view to adjusting their teaching behavior if necessary. Therefore, it usually involves subjective evaluations or perception measurements. The count of objective indicators, such as the number of attendees, the number of dropouts, etc., also provides an indication, of course, but has yet to be interpreted. Sudden high absenteeism during a course can be due to student dissatisfaction with the quality of the course but can also be the result of a flu epidemic.

The function of the final inspection has been expanded in integral quality development. In the past, the final check was often the only measurement aimed at determination. For example, the practical driving test is the decisive moment for the aspiring driver, passed or failed driver's license or no driver's license.

Now, the function of the final check is double. In the first place, it has an external function; it has a responsibility toward the client and must give the client the guarantee that he will receive excellent quality. For example, the field that recruits graduates of a certain school must be able to rely on the fact that students have the necessary competencies. If it later turns out that this is not the case, the organization will no longer employ graduates of that school.

Second, the final inspection also has an internal function: it is a check on the earlier quality inspections. In this position, it can supply information about the weak aspects of the quality assurance process.

6.4.1.3. Feedback measurement

The most-used form of measurement takes place after the fact. The problem here is that the moment the manager receives information about the problem, the disaster has already happened. However, this measurement also has advantages over the other two forms. Primarily, this measurement supplies meaningful information about the efficiency of the planning process. When the feedback check showed a minor variation between actual performance and standards, planning was very efficient. However, if the deviation is large, that information can be used to develop new plans. Feedback control can also boost employee motivation. After all, people want to know how well or how badly they have performed. A performance appraisal system can have a valuable motivational dimension. Feedback control mainly focuses on the results of the process, the output.

One form of feedback measurement is customer satisfaction research. The technique of mystery shopping apparently proves useful here. Mystery shopping is a way to assess a distribution or sales network. Researchers knock on the door of the company and pose as customers, with different customer profiles, contact scenarios, and types of questions. Depending on the organization, such an investigation can range from one hundred to several thousand contacts. The customer himself is not involved. Mystery shopping only probes one aspect, albeit an important one, of the purchasing process, namely contact. It is important that it be done incognito so that the addressee does not suspect that it is a test.

Robbins et al. (2013) supply the following guidelines for formulating adequate feedback:

1. Focus on specific rather than general behaviors. Be as concrete as possible and avoid vague feedback that usually supplies little useful information to improve a problem.

2. At least support negative feedback with hard factual material. If you must inform an employee why a performance is unsatisfactory, you must prove to him with as clear as possible factual evidence why you judge the performance to be unsatisfactory. Concrete evidence also clarifies which behaviors should be avoided in the future.

3. Comment on the task, not the person. Negative feedback should be descriptive rather than judgmental in nature. Therefore, the feedback should only relate to the task and should not concern the personality of the employee. Person-oriented feedback is usually perceived as threatening and puts employees on the defensive. In that situation, the person is no longer open to the content of the feedback and is hardly able to learn lessons for future performance.

4. Make sure the employee has correctly understood the feedback. The feedback must be communicated so clearly that the employee can unambiguously understand the message. The least you can do, therefore, is have your employees paraphrase the feedback so that you can check whether the content has been correctly understood.

5. Focus the negative feedback on behavior that the employee can control. Only behavior that the employee can do something about is eligible for feedback. It is, therefore, important that the assessor give concrete suggestions with which the employee can improve his performance.

6.4.2. Scope of measurement

By analogy with the planning process, I must distinguish here between strategic and operational measurement.

Strategic measurement

I speak of strategic measurement when management follows a strategic plan and makes changes when circumstances require it. Control of the entire organization is usually strategic in nature. If the control only concerns activities within the organization, that control does not help to realize the strategic plans. In strategic control, the link with the environment is essential because a strategy has to do with changes in problems and opportunities in the environment of the organization.

Operational control

Operational control refers to daily, weekly, or monthly measurements, while strategic control encompasses a much broader time perspective. Moreover, operational control is not conducted by the top but by middle management. After all, it is their responsibility to ensure that the daily or weekly deviations from the plans are corrected.

6.4.3. Contingency of measurement

There is no one good measurement system that functions optimally in all circumstances. What constitutes a good system largely depends on the situation. In Table 6.2, I list important contingency factors (Robbins et al. 2013).

Table 6.2. Contingency factors in measurement

CONTINGENCY FACTOR		INSTRUCTIONS FOR MEASUREMENTS
Size of the organization	small	informal, personal, management by walking around
	big	formal, impersonal express rules and procedures
Position and level	high	many criteria
	low	few criteria that are easy to measure
Degree of decentralization	high	more and wide measurements
	low	limited number of measurements
Organizational culture	open	informal, self-control
	closed	formal, imposed measurements
Importance of the activity	high	intensive and extensive measurements
	low	limited, informal measurements

Source: Adapted from Robbins, Decenzo & Coulter (2013).

- Measurement systems should vary according to the size of the organization. Small organizations can use personal and informal systems; direct supervision is perhaps the most appropriate there. As organizations grow, immediate supervision is less possible, and a more formal system must be developed.

- As employees move up the hierarchy, they need a system with multiple criteria. Lower-ranking positions usually have more clearly defined tasks and achievements that are easier to define in terms of criteria. Higher functions are more difficult to define and, therefore, less easy to measure with precision.

- As departments become more decentralized, managers need more feedback on the performance of subordinate decision-makers. Of course, since they are still responsible for the performance of those to whom they delegate tasks and responsibilities, they must be sure that their subordinates' decisions will be efficient and effective.

- The organizational culture largely determines which type of measurement is useful. In an organization where trust and openness reign, self-monitoring and informal investigation are possible. In an authoritarian organization, measurement will be done more formally and from the outside to ensure that the performance meets the set criteria. The measurement system must, therefore, be consistent with the organizational culture.

- The importance of the activity is the final factor that decides the type of measurement. If the measurement is expensive and the consequences of errors are not serious, a measurement system should not be very extensive. However, if an error can cause severe damage to the organization, a thorough measurement is necessary.

A measurement system that becomes rigid or uses unreasonable criteria becomes dysfunctional. Measurements should also encourage employees to continue taking responsibility for themselves. If the system becomes very rigid, employees will ensure that they meet the set standards but will show little responsibility in other areas, leading to inferior performance. For example, if the measurement system focuses only on quantity, employees will neglect quality. When a system assesses the activities themselves rather than the results, the employees mainly want to score well on those activities. If employees experience a measurement system as unreasonable, they will try to influence the results in such a way that they make a good impression. Research shows that the manipulation of measurement data is an important phenomenon. The general conclusion is that a measurement system alone does not guarantee motivation and quality. As employees can reconcile with the measurement system, it can play a role in employee motivation and the quality of the results, thus gaining a meaningful place in the organization's strategy.

6.5. Adverse reactions to measurement

Let us again point out the risks of equating measurement with control. If quality development is to be applied only through control, it is likely to fail. It is impossible for management to control all aspects of the service process and of its organization. Measurements and control often have a disastrous effect without the active and motivated cooperation of employees. This is why management must consciously look for ways to give employees responsibility in the measurement process. Self-monitoring by everyone in the organization is likely to be much more effective than external monitoring. Moreover, control by the client is also essential. Effective control, therefore, also requires the involvement of the client.

Although measurements supply the necessary information for management, employees often find it difficult. If the measurements are only used for management purposes, they carry the risk of demotivating employees. However, even if measurements are to be a stimulus in the development of the organization, many psychological factors still lead to resistance. Naturally, the organizational context itself is also often a source of resistance.

- Inappropriate measurement: If the measurement has nothing to do with the organization's goals, it is irrelevant. If the wrong thing is measured, it has the counterproductive effect that employees may also be less motivated to do important things well.

- Unattainable standards: If employees are aware that the expectations of the organization are not realistic, there is a danger that they will become demotivated and, therefore, work below their capabilities.

- Unpredictable standards: If the measurement system is unpredictable and constantly changing, employees become frustrated and resistant to the system. After all, the situation is uncertain for them because no matter what they do, they never know if they will do it well enough.

- No control over the situation: It is very frustrating for everyone to be blamed for things that the organization cannot control itself.

- Conflicting standards: Standards may exist in organizations that contradict each other. For example, the requirement to achieve high quality can conflict with the requirement to realize enormous quantities.

6.6. Road map

At the end of this chapter, I formulate a step-by-step plan for a meaningful measurement and evaluation culture.

Use a balanced set of tools

Evaluating is more than collecting figures. Qualitative methods are also valuable, such as storytelling, focus group discussions, and in-depth interviews. These qualitative methods are very suitable for gaining insight into a phenomenon (for example, to find causes or to explore new phenomena). Usually, a mix of quantitative and qualitative methods is suitable for obtaining both deeper insight and a numerical overview. Figures enable better comparisons over time and with other organizations. It is also important to measure both perception and performance indicators. After all, perception measurements map out subjective experiences, such as employee and customer satisfaction. The performance indicators are then purely objective data that can be derived from the registration data, such as absence, absenteeism, waiting times, etc.

Measure and evaluate only what the organization really needs

To make and keep evaluation valuable, it is necessary to decide in advance which measurements are necessary to achieve the goals of the policy plan. It makes little sense to measure as much as possible and then do nothing with the results afterward. It is, therefore, justifiable to properly check a limited and workable number of indicators so that not only data can be collected, but also comparisons can be made over time and with other organizations. It is then necessary to interpret that data as a function of the goals set. It is disastrous for employees to feel that they are endlessly measuring (too) much or must fill in (too) many questionnaires.

Involve stakeholders in setting the standards

Quality development as a relational practice is also useful when deciding the standards for involving as many stakeholders as possible—clients, employees, and interest groups—in the question of which standards are meaningful and feasible. In this way, employees avoid experiencing the measurements as a strange event in which they themselves are only the object. Of course, it is impossible to consider most individual wishes, and the goals of the policy plan remain the main guideline. However, if stakeholders perceive the standards as irrelevant, unrealistic, or unfair, they are counterproductive and demotivating. It is therefore necessary to decide together with stakeholders which standards are necessary and useful. If they are not involved, or if they interpret the standards differently than management, there is a significant risk that they will flout the standards, and the quality of service will deteriorate.

Map both results and processes

An integrated approach to evaluation must pay attention to both results and processes. Measurements should clarify the extent to which the organization achieved its set goals. That is the result measurement. After all, this knowledge is necessary to either continue working on the goals or set new goals. That is why it is so important that the measurements are also processed and related to the goals set. By measuring the results, we check the effectiveness. Ultimately, it is also necessary that the organization demonstrate that the results were not obtained by chance but are the result of a targeted approach. That is why it is also necessary to question the way in which the results are worked toward (efficiency). The analysis of the processes can reveal any problems or lack of efficiency in the pursuit of the results. Naturally, it is necessary that processes and results are in line with each other. After all, what good are the processes that run smoothly if they do not deliver the desired results?

Develop a system to effectively use the results of the evaluation

Too often, I see that the results of evaluations are not fed back into the policy plan and, therefore, have no consequences for the goals and the strategy. The results should at least be compared with the desired results, and if they deviate, causes and remedies should be looked for. It is also necessary that the organization have an approach to disseminate the results within the organization so that all involved can learn lessons. Effective communication is essential. Too often, employees complain that they must fill in many questionnaires or supply figures but that they rarely see the results.

Do not use results to blame, but to improve

Often, the analysis phase is followed by a phase in which the guilty are looked for. Someone may have to pay for less attractive results. Moreover, managers often point downward and dismiss their own responsibility. Such practices lead, on one hand, to fear of measurement and, on the other hand, to fraud: an attempt is made to hide the real facts. The art of good leadership consists of giving people the space to learn from their shortcomings without sanctions being linked to this. Moreover, the results can be used in a negative sense (the glass is half empty) or in a positive sense (the glass is half full).

Confronting the negative carries the risk that energy will seep out and that people will not be stimulated at all.

Finally: What is really important?

- Measurement is only one dimension of evaluation. In addition to numerical measurements, sufficient attention must be paid to the stories.

- Figures in themselves mean nothing; they still must be interpreted.

- Numbers without meaning do violence to reality.

- Measurement must be a function of the goals that an organization pursues.

- When evaluating, one must always determine which approach(es) are useful.

- Other processes require a different evaluation method.

- When measuring, it is necessary that the method be applied judiciously.

What is really important

Chapter 7

Quality models

A quality model is merely the vehicle through which organizations work systematically on the development of their quality.

In this chapter, I describe some concrete methodologies and instruments that nonprofit organizations can use. First, a system for self-assessment is discussed: the EFQM model. Because the EFQM method is quite complex, I developed a questionnaire that is more useful for small organizations, associations, working groups, and teams, the OAWT. I then discuss CAF, a derivative of EFQM intended for government services. I then discuss Investors in People, a model with a more specific focus on personnel in organizations. Then, I explain ISO 9001, a model that has many applications in the profit sector. I then focus on higher education and finally on the healthcare sector.

7.1. EFQM (european foundation for quality management)

7.1.1. Introduction

Since 2021, EFQM has reorganized its model after thorough consultation with stakeholders. The new EFQM model has shifted from being a simple assessment tool to one that offers a vital framework and method to help with the changes, transformation, and disruption that individuals and organizations face every day.

While the specific content and visual identity of the EFQM model may have changed over time, what has not changed are the underlying principles on which it is based. Regardless of the size of the organization or whether it is a public, private, or third sector, these principles are as important today as they have ever been, and this latest edition of the EFQM model is no different in continuing to stress the importance of:

- The primacy of the customer

- The need to take a long-term, stakeholder-centric view

- The importance of understanding the cause-and-effect linkages between why an organization does something, how it does it, and what it achieves because of its actions.

The EFQM model, like its predecessors, acknowledges the existence of a set of European values best expressed in the EU Charter of Fundamental Rights, the European Convention on Human Rights, the European Union Directive 2000/78/EC, and the European Social Charter. The model also integrates the United Nations 17 Sustainable Development Goals and the United Nations Global Compact (2000), ten principles for sustainable and socially responsible businesses. The foundation bases its operation on the assumption and expectation that any organization using the EFQM model will respect and act upon the essence of the messages contained in the above documents, regardless of whether it is legally obligated to do so.

Figure 7.1. Structure of the EFQM model

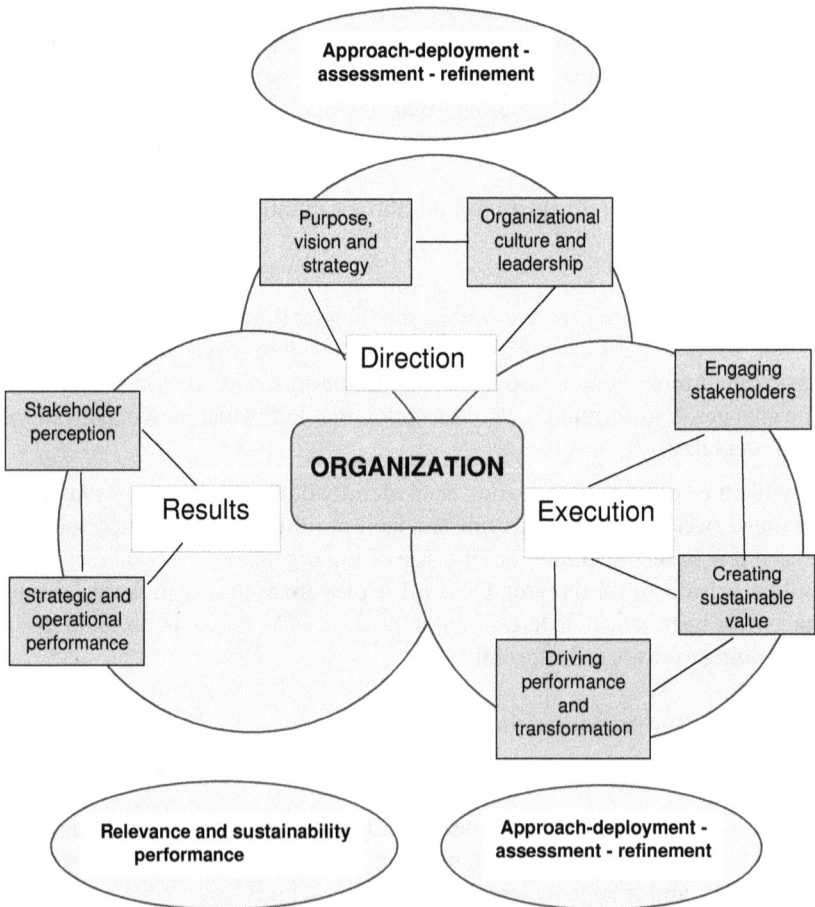

Source: Adapted from EFQM (2021).

7.1.2. Concept and structure

The EFQM model structure is based on the simple but powerful logic of asking three questions:

- "Why" does this organization exist? What purpose does it fulfill? Why this particular strategy? (Direction)

- "How" does it intend to deliver on its purpose and its strategy? (Execution)

- "What" has it achieved to date? "What" does it intend to achieve tomorrow? (Results)

Central to the rationale of the EFQM model, the "red thread" is the connection between the purpose and strategy of an organization and how that is used to help it create sustainable value for its most important *stakeholders and the delivery of outstanding results.

I clarify the basic elements: direction, execution, and results.

Direction

For an organization to achieve and sustain outstanding results that meet or exceed the expectations of its stakeholders, it:

- Defines an inspiring purpose.

- Creates a vision that is aspirational.

- Develops a strategy that is centered on creating sustainable value.

- Builds a winning culture.

This direction setting prepares the way forward for the organization to be seen as a leader in its ecosystem and well-positioned to execute its plans.

Criterion 1 Purpose, vision & strategy

An outstanding organization is defined by a purpose that inspires, a vision that is aspirational, and a strategy that delivers.

The purpose of the organization:

- Explains why its work is important
- Sets the scene for creating and delivering sustained value to its stakeholders
- Provides a framework in which it takes responsibility for its contribution to, and impact on, the ecosystem in which it operates.

The vision of the organization:

- Describes what the organization is trying to achieve in the long term.
- Serves as a clear guide for choosing current and future courses of action.
- Provides, along with the organization's purpose, the basis for setting the strategy.

The strategy of the organization:

- Describes how it intends to fulfill its purpose.
- Details its plans to achieve the strategic priorities and move closer to its vision.

Criterion 2 Organizational culture & leadership

Organizational culture is the specific collection of values and norms that are shared by people and groups within an organization that influences, over time, the way they behave with each other and with key stakeholders outside the organization.

Organizational leadership relates to the organization as a whole rather than any individual or team that provides direction from the top. It is about the organization acting as a leader within its ecosystem, recognized by others as a role model, rather than from the traditional perspective of a top team managing the organization.

An organization that aspires to be recognized as outstanding, a leader within its ecosystem, achieves success through a focus on the following activities:

- Steer the organization's culture and nurture values
- Create the conditions for realizing change

- Enable creativity & innovation

- Unite behind & engage in purpose, vision & strategy

Execution

For an organization to achieve and sustain outstanding results that meet or exceed the expectations of its stakeholders, it is necessary, but not sufficient, for it to:

- Define an inspiring purpose.

- Create a vision that is aspirational.

- Develop a strategy centered on creating sustainable value,

- Build a winning culture.

The Direction setting, as outlined above, prepares the way forward for the organization, but it then needs to execute its strategy effectively and efficiently, ensuring that it:

- Knows who the stakeholders are in its ecosystem and engage fully with those that are key to its success.

- Creates sustainable value

- Drives the levels of performance necessary for success today and, at the same time, drives the necessary improvement and transformation if it is to be successful in the future.

Criterion 3 Engaging stakeholders

Positioning statement in Criterion 1, the purpose, vision & strategy of an organization is linked with identifying and understanding stakeholder needs within the context of its unique ecosystem.

There is also a clear linkage between how an organization executes its engaging stakeholders strategy (Criterion 3) and the perceptions of its performance by those stakeholder groups (Criterion 6) that it serves.

Independent of the specific groups identified, it is highly likely that there is a degree of similarity in applying the following principles when engaging with key stakeholders.

An outstanding organization:

- Identifies the specific types and categories within each of its key stakeholder groups.

- Uses its understanding of key stakeholders' needs and expectations to achieve continued engagement.

- Involves key stakeholders in deploying its strategy and creating sustainable value and recognizes the contributions it makes.

- Builds, supports, and further develops relationships with key stakeholders based on transparency, accountability, ethical behavior, and trust.

- Collaborates with its key stakeholders to develop a collective understanding and focus on how, through co-development, it can contribute to and draw inspiration from the United Nations Sustainable Development Goals and Global Compact ambitions.

- Actively gathers the perceptions of its key stakeholders rather than waiting for them to make contact.

- Evaluate its performance in relation to key stakeholders' needs and decide on the right actions to be taken to help secure its future, as perceived by these key stakeholders.

In practice, I find that an outstanding organization will include the following groups in the classification of its key stakeholders:

- Customers: Build sustainable relationships

- People: Attract, engage, develop & retain 3.3 business & governing

    Stakeholders – secure & sustain ongoing support

- Society: Contribute to development, well-being & prosperity

- Partners & suppliers: Build relationships & ensure support for creating sustainable value

Criterion 4 Creating sustainable value

An outstanding organization recognizes that creating sustainable value is vital for its long-term success and financial strength. The organization's clearly defined purpose, enriched by its strategy, defines for whom the organization should be creating sustainable value. In most cases, customers, segmented appropriately, are the target group for creating sustainable value, although some organizations might also focus on selected Key Stakeholders within their society or business & governing stakeholder segments.

An outstanding organization acknowledges that key stakeholder needs may change over time and that it is important to collect and analyze feedback to improve or change their products, services, or solutions.

The different elements of creating sustainable value are shown below in a step-by-step sequence. It is recognized that the organization's plans for today and the future may well run in parallel or overlap at times, depending on the nature of the organization's business.

- Design the value & how it is created
- Communicate & sell the value
- Deliver the value
- Define & implement the overall experience

Criterion 5 Driving performance & transformation

Now and in the future, an organization needs to be able to meet the following two important requirements at the same time to become and remain successful.

On one hand, it needs to continue successfully managing the delivery of its current business operations ("Driving Performance.") On the other hand, there are constant changes inside and outside the organization that need to be managed in parallel if it is to remain successful. ("Driving Transformation.")

The combination of driving performance & transformation confirms the necessity for the organization to deliver for today while preparing for the future.

Major elements in enabling performance & transformation are innovation and technology, the ever-increasing importance of data, information & knowledge, and the focused use of critical assets and resources.

- Drive performance & manage risk
- Transforming the organization for the future
- Drive innovation & use technology
- Leverage data, information & knowledge
- Manage assets & resources

Results

What the organization has achieved in relation to what has been described in the direction & execution sections, including the forecast for the future. In practice, I find that an outstanding organization provides results data for:

- Stakeholder perceptions

- Creating sustainable value

- Driving performance & transformation

Criterion 6 Stakeholder perceptions

This criterion concentrates on results based on feedback from key stakeholders about their subjective experiences of dealing with the organization—their perceptions. These perceptions could relate to past as well as current key stakeholders and could be obtained from several sources, including surveys, focus groups, ratings, the press or social media, external recognition, advocacy, structured review meetings, investor reports, and compliments/complaints, including feedback compiled by customer relationship management teams.

In addition to the perceptions that a key stakeholder may have of an organization based on individual experiences, perceptions may also be shaped by the environmental and social impact reputation of the organization. For instance, the degree to which the organization is perceived by its key stakeholders as contributing successfully to one or more of the United Nations Sustainable Development Goals and Global Compact ambitions.

As fully described in Criterion 3, there is a clear linkage between how an organization executes its engaging stakeholders strategy and the perceptions of the stakeholder groups that it serves (Criterion 6). The weighting factor decided by the organization and applied for each of the five different stakeholder groups is set in Criterion 3 and mirrored in Criterion 6.

In practice, I find that an outstanding organization:

- Knows how successful it is at executing its strategy to meet the needs and expectations of its key stakeholders.

- Uses its analysis of past and current performance to predict future performance.

- Uses key stakeholder perception results to stay informed and influence its current direction and the execution of its strategy.

Examples of key stakeholder perception results and topics to be covered could include but are not listed in any priority order or limited to:

- Customer perception results

- People perception results

- Business & governing stakeholders perception results

- Society perception results

- Partners & suppliers perception results

Criterion 7 Strategic & operational performance

This criterion concentrates on results linked to the organization's performance in terms of:

- The ability to fulfill its purpose, deliver the strategy, and create sustainable value

- Its fitness for the future. These results are used by the organization to check, understand, and improve its overall performance and to forecast the impact this performance will have on both the perceptions of its key stakeholders as well as its future strategic ambitions.

In practice, I find that an outstanding organization:

- Uses both financial and non-financial indicators to help it measure its strategic and operational performance.

- Understands the linkages between key stakeholder perceptions and actual performance and can predict, with a high degree of certainty, how future performance will evolve.

- Considers the current and future needs and expectations of its key stakeholders when deciding on the most proper performance indicators to match its strategic & operational goals.

- Understands the cause-and-effect relationships that impact performance and uses the results achieved to stay informed and influence its current direction & execution.

- Uses the results currently being achieved to forecast its future performance with an expected degree of certainty.

Strategic and operational performance indicators could include the reported results and forecasts used to show how well the organization is achieving its strategic goals and the reported indicators and forecasts used to show how well the organization is achieving its operational targets. The indicators could include, but are not limited to, the following examples:

- Achievements in delivering purpose, strategy & creating sustainable value

- Fulfilment of key stakeholder expectations

- Economic & financial performance

- Achievement in driving performance & transformation

- Predictive measures for the future

7.1.3. EFQM Diagnostic tool: RADAR

The RADAR logic states that an organization needs to:

- Decide the **R**esults it is aiming to achieve as part of its strategy.

- Have in place an **A**pproach that will deliver the required result, both now and in the future.

- **D**eploy this approach appropriately.

- **A**ssess and **R**efine the deployed approach to learn and improve.

Figure 7.2. Elements of Radar

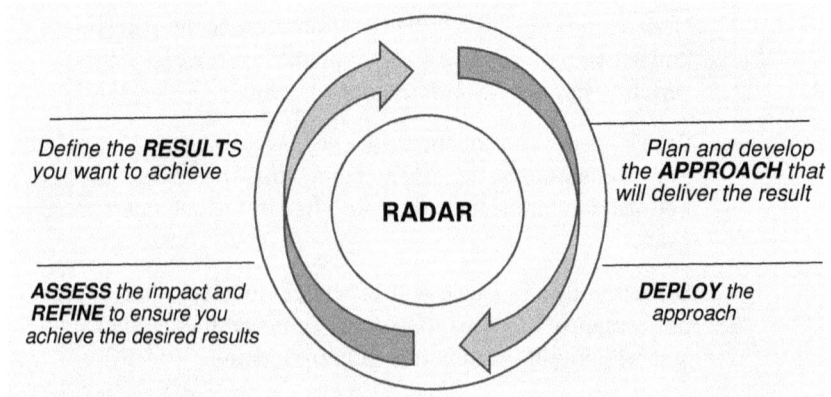

Define the RESULTS you want to achieve

Plan and develop the APPROACH that will deliver the result

RADAR

ASSESS the impact and REFINE to ensure you achieve the desired results

DEPLOY the approach

Source: Modified from EFQM (2021).

7.2. OAWT – Application for (small) organizations, associations, workgroups, and teams

7.2.1. Introduction

The EFQM method is far too heavy for small organizations, associations, working groups, and teams (OAWT). Because I believe in the usefulness of the integrated approach, I have developed a tool that should be easier for these particular entities and help them get an idea of their own strengths and areas for improvement (Cuyvers, 2007).

The questionnaire consists of statements that all have equal importance. Naturally, this does not allow a detailed picture of the entire organization to be developed. The questionnaire does, however, offer a workable starting point for concretely starting with quality improvement and development. The fact that the statements are of equal value helps these groups to decide on which aspects of action should be taken first. After all, they will have an equal share in the improvement of quality.

Advantages

Using this questionnaire has the following advantages:

- It helps your OAWT to decide its current position and to set priorities for the future on that basis.

- It allows possible comparisons with the performance of other OAWTs.

- It encourages your OAWT to take control of its own processes.

- It makes it possible to find out to what extent the members of an OAWT share the same views on the strengths and weaknesses of a working group, team, or council.

- It ensures that the working group, team, or council does not become overstressed by wanting to undertake too many improvement actions at the same time.

- By thinking together about the interpretation of concepts such as manager, processes, and stakeholder, you automatically get more coordination and more involvement within the group. It makes some things much clearer. It is sometimes difficult to define these concepts, but it does create clarity.

Positive approach

I want to emphasize that, when choosing actions, it is also important to consider strengths. A group can rightly choose to take its own strengths as a starting point, which reduces the impact and importance of the weaknesses because the strengths "flatten out" the negative impact of the weaknesses. Of course, this does not mean that weaknesses are swept under the carpet by means of a kind of ostrich policy. Peter Drucker said, "We learn from our mistakes, but we grow through our successes."

Opportunity for dialogue

This scoring is also an excellent opportunity for dialogue among the members of the OAWT. That is why it is necessary that everyone have input and be given the space to speak freely. Finally, it is important that enough time be spent clarifying meanings: How should we interpret a score? What does this statement mean for our group? How should we interpret the result?

7.2.2. Method

It is necessary that the group decide several things clearly in advance. Who is the leadership that will be assessed? What are the core processes that the group will focus on? Who are the stakeholders that the working group, team, or council will mainly deal with? In short, everyone who takes part in the exercise must judge the same things. The group should also agree on how to assess the result areas.

The questionnaire can be used each time you take a closer look at an area of interest. Go through the four successive steps each time before discussing the next area of interest.

Step 1 Evaluation

First, the members of the group individually decide their personal scores for each sub-criterion of the focus area. If, in their opinion, the sub-criterion does not apply to their OAWT, they can also indicate this. During the preparations, the group agrees that, in other words, it will critically examine whether there are matters that are not applicable. In this way, those involved know during the scoring that all the other points apply.

Step 2 Discussion

Subsequently, each member expresses the individual results, which are then noted on a summary sheet (or board). It is especially important in this phase that different members of the group articulate why they gave their scores. If the group has little time, it may suffice to discuss the highest and lowest scores.

Step 3 Introducing action points

After the discussion of the scores, each group member has an idea of the highest and lowest scores per sub-criterion. Each member then individually devises an action point for that area of interest. I emphasize that both strengths and points for improvement are the starting points for new ones.

7.2.3. Scoring the questionnaire

Goal

Scoring a questionnaire is a challenge for every OAWT. It comes down to understanding the meaning of each statement and then deciding on a realistic and fair score. If you want to place your OAWT in a good light, it can be difficult to paint an objective picture. However, an objective description is necessary. After all, this allows you to identify the areas that are eligible for improvement actions. It can help if you keep asking yourself: Can I back up my judgment with facts?

The purpose of this questionnaire is to help you map out the current situation of your working group, team, or council based on the statements. Each of these statements has equal importance.

Each time, you must indicate to what extent the approach of the OAWT is effective and to what extent the working group, team, or council applies that approach. An effective approach is evidenced by the following features:

- systematic (a planned sequence of activities rather than ad hoc responses).

- routine (the extent to which the approach is part of the normal processes); subject to regular evaluation cycles for improvement; effectiveness is measured based on evidence.

- more proactive (focused on prevention) than reactive (focused on repairing errors).

- the fact that the approach applies to:
  - all relevant areas, including support activities, customers, and suppliers.
  - all forms of services and all employees.

The principles

- Successful OAWTs focus on understanding and meeting stakeholder needs.

- All approaches and methods are subject to regular review and improvement cycles, and the results are applied.

- Chairs or coordinators should lead by example in the constant pursuit of high performance.

- All processes must be measured regularly.

- The OAWT bases its policy on factual material; results and data are readily available.

- Two-way communication is clear in the OAWT.

In all processes, the aim is to reduce throughput time. Benchmarking processes and performance is a frequent practice. This means that you compare the approach of your working group, team, or council with that of a working group, team, or council that is known to be very good. You can draw lessons from this comparison for your own working group, team, or council.

- The concept of the internal customer is clear; every employee considers his colleagues as customers.

- Teamwork is a normal way to improve performance. Management acknowledges the effort to improve.

- Continuous improvement involving every employee is the custom.

Scoring in practice

For each statement, you must indicate in which phase your working group, team, or council is. It is necessary that the members of the OAWT first score the questionnaire individually. Then, they can try to reach a consensus. Below, I describe the meaning of the four stages. It is helpful to keep these descriptions handy while assessing the statements. I must emphasize that it is sometimes necessary to clarify what the positions mean before scoring. Each group member must interpret the statements in the same way.

Table 7.1. Meaning of the scores

SCORE		DESCRIPTION
D	Not started yet	Nothing much happens. Sometimes clever ideas come up, but they have not yet been developed.
C	Some progress	There is some indication that something is happening.
B	Clear progress	There is evidence that attention is being paid to this topic. It is regularly evaluated and adjusted. However, its application has not yet been universally or fully realized.
A	Fully realized	There is an extraordinary approach. It is hard to make any more progress.
N/A	Not applicable	You do not recognize this point in your working group, team, or council.

Since this questionnaire must be usable for diverse types of OAWTs, I cannot indicate, for example, which are the core processes of the service. The group members must first describe these together.

7.2.4. OAWT questionnaire

7.2.4.1. Leadership

This focus area explores the activities and behavior of the OAWT coordinator, chair, or leader. It examines its role in setting up clear goals and in supporting and realizing them in the OAWT. It mainly emphasizes the personal involvement and actual behavior of the coordinator, chairman, or leader rather than his/her words and texts. It also examines how the goals and operations are communicated and reinforced. For the sake of convenience, we will use only the term manager hereafter. Decide in advance who you consider to be your manager(s)!

Table 7.2. Leadership

	D	C	B	A
1.1 Vision The manager has a clear picture of the function and tasks of the working group, team, or council and ensures that these are known to the members.				
1.2 Personal Involvement The manager actively takes part in the operation of the OAWT.				

1.3 Recognition and Support The manager positively appreciates the efforts made by colleagues in the OAWT.				
1.4 External Action The manager personally meets internal and external stakeholders of the OAWT and is actively working to improve relations with them.				
1.5 Reflection on own actions The manager collaborates with colleagues to improve the functioning of the OAWT.				

7.2.4.2. Strategy

This focus area examines how the OAWT realizes its values and goals through the planning of activities. It examines to what extent goals and planning are based on reliable facts. In addition, this focus area has an eye on the extent to which the plans are expressed in realistic operational plans. Finally, it also examines the extent to which the possibilities for change are supported by the employees. Decide in advance who the group's stakeholders are!

Table 7.3. Strategy

2.1 Use of relevant information The OAWT uses factual material for long-term planning and day-to-day operations (factual material relating to core processes, performance, requirements, and satisfaction of internal and external stakeholders). The OAWT has therefore defined key indicators that are important for its own operations.				
2.2 Developing policy The values and strategic goals are sufficiently concretized in concrete goals, action plans, and tools for both the short (one or two years) and the long term (more than three years).				
2.3 Communication about policy Most employees can name the important goals of their OAWT, and they know the plans to achieve them.				
2.4 Member engagement Members take part in the formulation of concrete annual policy goals.				

2.5 Testing and improvement The OAWT evaluates its own action plans at least once a year and adjusts them if necessary.				

7.2.4.3. Members/employees

This focus area investigates how the OAWT develops and involves its members in the operation and improvement of the OAWT. It's about attracting the right people, developing the skills needed to help achieve the OAWT's objectives and to change as a group. That is why it examines to what extent personal goals are in line with the goals of the working group, team, or council. Moreover, this also concerns the extent to which employees are given responsibility for improving the working group, team, or council.

Table 7.4. Members/employees

	D	C	B	A	N/A
3.1 Development The OAWT provides new members with training and guidance in support of its strategic plans, goals, and needs (and not ad hoc).					
3.2 Competencies The OAWT fully appeals to the individual competencies of its members.					
3.3 Participation The members of the OAWT are sufficiently represented in meetings, and their ideas are valued.					
3.4 Care for members The OAWT monitors the workload (work for the OAWT) of its members.					
3.5 Upskilling The members are given sufficient opportunities for further training and guidance.					
3.6 Testing and improvement The OAWT regularly evaluates the way in which the members of the OAWT interact with each other and makes adjustments where necessary.					

7.2.4.4. Partners & resources

This focus area relates to the most important resources of the OAWT, such as finance, information, material, infrastructure, and new technologies. It examines the extent to which resources are carefully planned and used.

Table 7.5. Partners & resources

	D	C	B	A	N/A
4.1 Partners The OAWT is looking for partners within and outside the organization who can support and strengthen its operations and with whom cooperation is possible.					
4.2 Finance If the working group, team, or council has financial resources, it must use them in an efficient and careful manner, and it must account for their use at least annually.					
4.3 Information The working group, team, or council can ensure that the information used (on the core processes, stakeholders, etc.) is reliable, up-to-date, and user-friendly for those who need it.					
4.4 Infrastructure The OAWT treats materials and buildings with respect and has an eye for sustainability. Members may discuss their infrastructural needs with the organization.					
4.5 Testing and improvement The OAWT regularly evaluates the way in which it deals with partners and resources and adjusts where necessary.					

7.2.4.5. Management of processes, products, and services

This area of interest investigates how the OAWT plans and realizes its core processes. This also concerns the requirements that control of the core processes must meet. Examples are innovation and sustainability.

In this area of interest, it is necessary that you first agree with the group on what the processes, products, and services of the working group, team, or council are. You can then select the three (up to five) most important of them and score each of them for the sub-criteria.

Table 7.6. Management of processes, products, and services

	D	C	B	A	N/A
5.1 Identification of Processes The OAWT has mapped out its primary processes, products, and services.					
5.2 Stakeholders The processes, products, and services meet the expectations of the stakeholders.					
5.3 Evaluation The OAWT regularly evaluates whether all activities used for the processes, products, and services are efficient and suitable for achieving the set goals.					
5.4 Stimulating creativity and innovation The OAWT continuously innovates its processes, products, and services based on the innovative ideas of the members.					

7.2.4.6. Stakeholder appreciation

This focus area examines the way in which the OAWT identifies and segments its external target groups. It assesses the measures and results that indicate the level of satisfaction. It pays attention to both the current perceptions of the stakeholders, which can be retrieved through surveys, among other things, and to measures and results that predict trends and influence the satisfaction of the stakeholders. Examples are the number of complaints, late submission of information, and so on.

Decide who are the most important stakeholders of your working group, team, or council! In addition, discuss your way of working and the indicators you will use.

You have two options for this focus area. Either you only score globally for the three sub-criteria, or you decide for yourself which indicators, per sub-criterion, are useful and then score per indicator. We have always given a few indicators by way of example. It may well be that they are irrelevant to your working group, team, or council. You can then agree on your own indicators and score.

Table 7.7. Appreciation by stakeholders

	D	C	B	A	N/A
6.1 Evaluating relationships The OAWT evaluates its relationship management of the stakeholders with relevant criteria such as: the number of stakeholders (check accurately who you are dealing with as an OAWT), etc.					
6.2 Opinion of stakeholders The OAWT has a realistic view of the opinion of the stakeholders regarding: the efficiency of the OAWT's operation, the satisfaction with the results of the operation, etc.					
6.3 Complaints The OAWT has an exact and realistic overview of the number and content of complaints.					

7.2.4.7. Appreciation by the members/employees

This area of interest examines the trends and the extent to which OAWT members are satisfied. It asks for members' subjective perceptions as well as objective standards. In addition, it examines the extent to which results are made public. Essentially, the point here is to find out to what extent the working group, team, or council can motivate its members.

You also have two options for this area of interest. You can either score globally (you only score globally for the sub-criteria given here). Or you can decide in advance in the group itself which indicators are useful and then score per indicator.

Table 7.8. Appreciation by members/employees

7.1 Working Conditions	D	C	B	A	N/A
The OAWT regularly measures those aspects that influence or predict member satisfaction, such as: • appreciation of leadership • appreciation of policy and strategy • appreciation of personnel policy • appreciation of resources policy • appreciation of the management of processes					
7.2 Own indicators					

7.2.4.8. Influence on the wider organization (if relevant)

This focus area examines the activities of the OAWT that have an impact on the wider organization of which it is a part, as well as the extent to which it considers the organization in which it operates.

First, check how and to what extent your OAWT maintains relationships with the larger organization of which it is part.

Table 7.9. Influence on the broad organization

	D	C	B	A	N/A
8.1 Data availability The OAWT has an idea of the appreciation due to the larger organization of which it is a part.					
8.2 Contribution to the organization The OAWT can prove that its activities contribute to the realization of the goals of the organization of which it forms part.					

7.2.4.9. Key results

This focus area examines the general results of the OAWT. It assesses the extent to which the goals have been achieved and the efficiency with which this was done. Subsequently, the OAWT can also show the level at which it performs for several key indicators, which it figures out itself.

Table 7.10. Key results

	D	C	B	A	N/A
9.1 Objectives The OAWT can prove with factual material the extent to which it has achieved its operational goals.					
9.2 Efficiency The OAWT regularly assesses the efficiency of its operation.					

9.3 Indicators					
The OAWT has several indicators for which it: • collected facts • can indicate trends over several years • can link the realization to several objectives • demonstrably leads					

7.3. CAF (Common Assessment Framework)

7.3.1. Introduction

The Common Assessment Framework (CAF), or Common Self-Assessment Framework for Public Administrations, was developed at the initiative of the 25 European Ministers of Civil Service by the Innovative Public Service Group (IPSG), a group of European experts in the field of public administration. The first version was presented in May 2000 at the first European quality conference for public services in Lisbon. An updated version was introduced during the Second Quality Conference in Copenhagen in 2002. Finally, the CAF 2013 version is currently being used. An updated version was published in 2020 with a special focus on sustainability (linked to the Sustainable Development Goals (SDGs)), innovation, diversity, digitization (artificial intelligence), collaboration with citizens and civil society, and agility.

The goal of the CAF is to promote good policy in the public sector. CAF does this by facilitating self-evaluation of a service or organization with a view to arriving at a diagnosis and points for improvement; therefore, it is not an instrument for evaluation by external parties. CAF pursues four main goals:

1. help the civil service on its way to a culture of excellence and integral quality assurance.

2. coach her to develop a mature PDCA approach.

3. function as a bridge between the different quality management models and between the public and private sectors.

4. enable benchmarking between public administrations.

Principle 1: Results orientation

The organization focuses on results. Results are achieved that please all the organization's stakeholders (authorities, citizens/customers, partners, and people working in the organization) with respect to the targets that have been set.

Figure 7.3. Principles of excellence in the CAF model

Source: Adapted from EUPAN (2020).

Principle 2: Citizen/customer focus

The organization focuses on the needs of present as well as potential citizens/customers. It involves them in the development of products and services and the improvement of its performance.

Principle 3: Leadership and constancy of purpose

This principle couples visionary and inspirational leadership with the constancy of purpose in a changing environment. Leaders set up a clear mission statement as well as a vision and values; they also create and support the internal environment in which people can become fully involved in achieving the organization's goals.

Principle 4: Management of processes and facts

This principle guides the organization from the perspective that a desired result is achieved more efficiently when related resources and activities are managed as a process, and effective decisions are based on the analysis of data and information.

Principle 5: People development and involvement

People at all levels are the essence of an organization, and their full involvement enables their abilities to be used for the organization's benefit. The contribution of employees should be maximized through their development and involvement and the creation of a working environment of shared values and a culture of trust, openness, empowerment, and recognition.

Principle 6: Continuous learning, innovation, and improvement

Excellence is challenging the status quo and effecting change by continuous learning to create innovation and improvement opportunities. Continuous improvement should, therefore, be a permanent goal of the organization.

Principle 7: Partnership development

Public sector organizations need others to achieve their targets and should, therefore, develop and support value-adding partnerships. An organization and its suppliers are interdependent, and a mutually beneficial relationship enhances the ability of both to create value.

Principle 8: Social responsibility

Public sector organizations must assume social responsibility, respect ecological sustainability, and try to meet the major expectations and requirements of the local and global community.

These Principles of Excellence are integrated into the structure of the CAF, and in time, the continuous improvement of the nine criteria will bring the organization to a prominent level of maturity. For each principle, four levels of maturity have been worked out so that an organization can have an idea of its way forward toward excellence.

Even more, than private companies, which are subject to the rules of the market economy, public organizations must actively defend values such as good governance, democracy, the rule of law, civic orientation, diversity, equality between men and women, a suitable working environment, integrated prevention of corruption, social responsibility within the ecological limits of the earth, and the fight against discrimination. With this model, the CAF creates a common language for all civil servants.

The CAF attaches significant importance to the social responsibility of a government organization. The mission of a government organization is always dominated by several needs and expectations of society. In addition to its mission, a government organization must adopt a responsible attitude to contribute to sustainable development, being an ideal balance between economic, social, and environmental interests within the local, national, and international community. Examples include the organization's attitude and contribution to the quality of life, environmental protection, conservation of the world's natural resources, ensuring equal employment opportunities, ethically responsible behavior, community involvement, and contribution to local development at the national and international level.

Social responsibility mainly consists of the organization's will to include social and environmental considerations in its decision-making (criterion 2) on the one hand and to be able to respond to the impact of its decisions and activities on society and the environment on the other hand.

Social responsibility should be an integral part of an organization's strategy. Strategic goals must be checked for social responsibility to avoid undesirable consequences. An organization's performance compared to the community in which it operates (locally, nationally, or internationally) and its impact on the environment has become a critical element in measuring its overall performance. An organization working on its social responsibility will:

- improve its reputation and global image vis-à-vis citizens.

- will improve its ability to attract and keep new staff and to support staff motivation and commitment.

- will improve its relationships with businesses, with other government organizations, with the media, with suppliers, with citizens/customers, and with the community in which it works.

7.3.2. Structure

The structure of the CAF is based on the EFQM model. It is a light model that is especially suitable for getting a first idea of how an organization is performing. Moreover, it is mainly focused on self-evaluation. The method is a scoring of the nine areas for attention (referred to here as criteria) based on several points for attention, using a scoring form (see table 7.11). The condition areas (factors) and the result areas have their own scoring form.

The nine-box structure shows the main aspects requiring consideration in any organizational analysis. Criteria 1–5 (the enablers) deal with the managerial practices of an organization. These decide what the organization does and how it approaches its tasks to achieve the desired results.

Figure 7.4. Structure of the CAF model

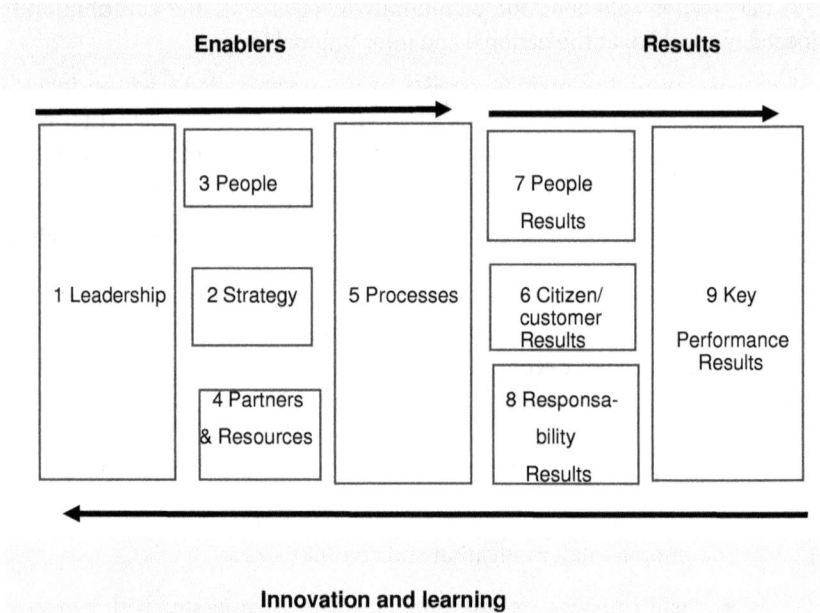

Enablers   **Results**

1 Leadership	3 People	5 Processes	7 People Results	9 Key Performance Results
	2 Strategy		6 Citizen/ customer Results	
	4 Partners & Resources		8 Responsa- bility Results	

Innovation and learning

Source: Adapted from EUPAN (2020).

7.3.2.1. Enablers

The five enablers boost the organization to perform at its best.

- Above all is leadership (1), which sets the strategic direction of the organization and creates the organizational foundations.

- Good leadership uses instruments of strategy and planning (2) as well as human resources management (3), cooperates with partners, and manages resources (4) such as budget, knowledge, and IT.

- On these bases, the organization defines and documents the internal processes (5) and develops these permanently.

- If the organization is well placed to boost the enablers, it will also deliver excellent results for its customers, stakeholders, employees, citizens, and society. The CAF defines four criteria that measure the results of the organization's work.

For the focus areas, there is always a definition and a summary of the main points for attention. Several examples are given for each sub-criterion that clarify what the sub-criterion means exactly, and that makes it possible to assign a score. I clarify this with the leadership criterion as an example.

Criterion 1: Leadership

A distinction should be made between the role of political leadership and the role of leaders/managers of public sector organizations. Self-assessment and improvement of the organization should focus on the role of management and its relationship with the political sphere. The Common Assessment Framework does not aim to evaluate the quality of public policy, but rather the management of an organization and the way in which policy is translated, and policy advice is given in terms of analysis, examination of the environment, and strategic planning.

It is typical for leaders/managers in a government organization to have to achieve customer-oriented goals in their work while ensuring balance with political or stakeholder goals.

Importantly, in leadership evaluation, leaders must demonstrate a good understanding of who their customers are, their expectations, and how they can be reconciled with political requirements, demonstrating a clear commitment to citizens/customers and other stakeholders.

Sub-criteria

1. Leaders give direction to the organization by developing a mission, vision, and values.

2. Leaders manage the organization's performance and ensure continuous improvement.

3. Leaders motivate and support the people in the organization and function as role models.

4. Leaders maintain good relations with political authorities and other stakeholders.

In Criteria 6–9, the results achieved in the fields of citizens/customers, people, social responsibility, and key performance are measured by perception and performance measurements.

7.3.2.2. Results

From criterion 6, the assessment shifts from the factors (the characteristics of an organization that determines how it operates) to the results (the results or outputs that the organization achieves). The assessment of the results requires a distinct set of answers, so from now on they are based on the scoring form for the assessment of the results (see Table 7.12).

- Customer/citizens results – e.g., how satisfied are the citizens with the work of the organization (the ministry, the municipality, the school, etc.)? How is telephone accessibility seen? What are the opening hours of the citizen service center?

- People's results – e.g., how satisfied are the employees with their work in the organization? How is the performance of people's work? Which training courses are attended?

- Social responsibility results – e.g., how much recycled paper is used? How many transparency/open data initiatives are supported?

- Key performance results – e.g., what output and outcome impacts does the organization achieve with its work (for public transport, police security, environmental protection, social services, quality of the laws, etc.)?

I clarify this with the results using the citizen/customer criterion as an example.

Criterion 6: Results with the citizen/customer

Criterion 6 describes the results of the organization book in terms of the satisfaction of citizens/customers with the organization and with the products/services they offer. The CAF distinguishes between observation and performance results. It is important that all types of government organizations measure the satisfaction of their citizens/customers directly (perception results). Performance results must also be measured. More information on citizen and customer satisfaction is obtained by measuring internal indicators. Working on better results on the internal indicators should lead to higher satisfaction among citizens/customers.

Examples of observations

Results related to the overall image of the organization:

- general level of satisfaction with the organization's performance.

- friendliness and correctness of the treatment.

- demonstrated and proactive behavior.

- flexibility and capacity to manage individual situations.

- openness to change.

- searching for proposals; gathering ideas for improvement.

- impact of the organization on the quality of life of citizens/customers.

Examples of performance measures

- number of citizen/customer proposals received and put into practice.

- indicators of conformity with gender aspects and cultural and social diversity about citizens/customers.

- opening hours of the diverse services (departments).

- to wait.

- handling/processing time at the service.

- cost of the services.

- number of information channels and their beliefs.

- number of interventions by the ombudsman.

- number of complaints and processing time of the complaints.

- number of files returned that have errors and/or situations in which the comparison of a new study is necessary.

7.3.3. Scoring

Why scoring?

Allocating a score to each subcriterion and criterion of the CAF model has four main aims:

1. To supply information and give an indication of the direction and priorities to follow for improvement activities.

2. To measure your own progress, if you conduct CAF assessments regularly; every two years is good practice according to most quality approaches.

3. To identify good practices, as indicated by high scoring for enablers and results.

4. To help find valid partners to learn from bench learning (what we learn from each other). The main aim of bench learning is to compare the diverse ways of managing the enablers and achieving results. Regarding bench learning, however, it should be noted that comparing CAF scores carries a risk, particularly if it is done without validating the scores in a homogeneous way in different public organizations.

How to score?

The CAF provides two ways of scoring: classical scoring and fine-tuned scoring. Regarding the enablers, the PDCA cycle is the f of both. The 'classical' CAF scoring gives a global appreciation of each subcriterion by indicating the PCDA phase of the subcriterion. The 'fine-tuned' CAF scoring reflects the analysis of the subcriteria in more detail. It allows you to score—for each subcriterion—all phases of the PDCA (PLAN, DO, CHECK, ACT) cycle simultaneously and independently. Comparing the performance with others by benchmarking and bench learning is at the highest level of both assessment panels.

CAF classical scoring

This cumulative way of scoring helps the organization become more acquainted with the PDCA cycle and directs it more positively toward a quality approach.

- In the enablers assessment panel, the organization is effectively improving its performance when the PDCA cycle is completely in place, based on learning from its reviews and from external comparison.

- In the results assessment panel, the trend of the results and the achievement of the targets are both taken into consideration. The organization is in a continuous improvement cycle when excellent and sustainable results are achieved, all relevant targets are met, and positive comparisons with relevant organizations for the key results are made.

Table 7.11. Score Form for Assessing Factors (CAF)

		We are not active in this field, we have no information or very anecdotal	**0-10**
PLAN		We have a plan to do this	11-30
DO		We are implementing/doing this	31-50
CHECK		We check/review if we do the right things in the right way	51-70
ACT		On the basis of checking/reviewing we adjust if necessary	71-90
PDCA		Everything we do, we plan, implement, check and adjust regularly and we learn from others. We are in a continuous improvement cycle on this issue.	91-100

Source: Adapted from EUPAN (2020).

Table 7.12. Refined scoring table of the results

	ENABLERS PANEL – FINE-TUNED SCORING				
	Scale	**0-10**	**11-30**	**....**	**Total**
Phase	**Evidence**	No evidence or just some ideas	Some weak evidence related to some areas	**....**	
PLAN	Planning is based on stakeholder's needs and expectations. Planning is deployed throughout the relevant parts of the organization or on an regular basis.				
	Score				
DO	Execution is managed through defined processes and responsibilities and diffused throughout the relevant parts of the organization on a regular basis				
	Score				

Check	Defined processes are monitored with relevant indicators and reviewed throughout the relevant parts of the organization or on a regular basis.				
	Score				
Act	Correction and improvement actions are taken following the check results throughout the relevant parts of the organization or on a regular basis				
	Score				

Source: Adapted from EUPAN (2020).

7.3.4. Development plan

Finally, CAF also developed a step-by-step plan for quality development, which I briefly outline here.

- Phase 1 The start
  - Step 1 Deciding how to approach the self-assessment and planning
  - Step 2 Communication about the self-assessment project
- Phase 2 The self-evaluation process
  - Step 3 Composition of the self-assessment group(s)
  - Step 4 Organization of the training
  - Step 5 Conducting the self-assessment
  - Step 6 Drawing up a report with the results of the self-assessment
- Phase 3 Improvement plan with the prioritization of actions
  - Step 7 Proposal of an improvement plan
  - Step 8 Communication about the improvement plan

    o   Step 9 Implementation of the improvement plan

    o   Step 10 Planning of a new self-assessment

7.4. Investors in people

7.4.1. Introduction

The importance of investing in employees is increasing. Human capital becomes especially important. Knowledge, skills, and motivation are the raw materials of the future. However, investing in employee development is not an optional exercise. A return is expected in the sense that the investments contribute to the achievement of the goals of the organization. A model for this was developed in Great Britain in 1991. The quality mark is recognized in 75 countries. Investors in People UK is now part of the UK Commission for Employment and Skills (Investors in People, 2005).

Investors in People developed a standard based on input from global best practices. The standard reflects what an organization needs to be successful and provides the development steps for achieving an excellent level of performance. The model has four levels and nine indicators.

Meeting the Investors in People Standard means that the organization is among the best in people management. Naturally, an organization can continue to evolve in the way it treats its employees. That is why performance levels have also been defined, which I will explain further.

IIP researched what is typical of the best-performing organizations. They found these six characteristics:

- powerful and inspiring leaders

- presence of strong core values

- recognizing and appreciating performance

- structure of the work

- continuous improvement and innovation

- sustainable practices adopted

Based on these findings, IIP developed a framework. This approach also uses the PDCA cycle as a methodology. IIP also offers organizations a benchmark tool with which they can compare themselves with other organizations in their sector.

7.4.2. The framework

The framework is based on three basic principles that are essential for an organization that wants to achieve top quality: leadership, support of employees, and continuous improvement (Investors in People, 2016). Based on these basic principles, the model describes nine indicators that are characteristic of organizations that always outperform comparable organizations.

Figure 7.5. Roadmap to quality in the IIP model

		ORGANISATION'S AMBITION
PHASE		
LEADING	1	Leading and inspiring people
	2	Living the organization's values and behaviors
	3	Empowering and involving people
SUPPORTING	4	Managing performance
	5	Recognizing and rewarding high performance
	6	Structuring work
IMPROVING	7	Building capability
	8	Delivering continuous improvement
	9	Creating sustainable success

Source: Adapted from Investors In People.

Leadership

Leaders play a vital role in quality development. They must inspire and motivate their employees to take part in quality development by propagating the values and culture of the organization and by involving and empowering people. The indicators for leadership are as follows:

- Leading and inspiring people. Leaders provide clear goals. They inspire and motivate people to achieve these goals and are trusted by people in the organization.

- Promoting the organizational values and culture. The behavior of people and leaders is always in line with the core values of the organization. They dare to act against deviant behavior and feel supported in this.

- Empowering and involving people. There is a culture of trust and ownership in the organization, such that people experience that they can make and implement decisions.

Support

Support is provided through performance management, by recognizing and rewarding superior performance, and by structuring the work. The indicators are as follows:

- Performance management. The goals of the organization are harmonized. Performance is measured, and feedback is used.

- Recognize and reward high performance. Recognition and rewards are clear and right and they create a culture that values people and encourages them to give their best.

- Structuring the work. The ambition of the organization is to lead the structure of the organization. Roles are designed to achieve the goals of the organization and provide engaging work for people in which they are encouraged to collaborate in diverse ways.

Improvement

The best organizations embrace change, flexibility, and continuous improvement. The philosophy of continuous improvement and innovation is the basis of the Investors in People Standard. Being a sustainable organization means paying attention to the development of competencies, resources, and plans for tomorrow. This means feeding innovation to constantly find new ways to realize the ambitions of the organization. The indicators are as follows:

- Develop competencies. People's competencies are actively managed and developed. This ensures that people are empowered to use their talents and that organizations have the right people at the right time and for the right roles.

- Continuous improvement and innovation. There is a focus on continuous improvement. People use internal and external resources to generate innovative ideas and approaches supported by a culture that encourages innovation.

- Pursuing sustainable success. The organization has a focus on the future and is open to change. Leaders have a good understanding of what is happening in society and how this affects the organization.

7.4.3. Development

The IIP performance model uses four levels that provide insight into the important phases an organization goes through on its way to becoming a mature organization.

Performance Level 1 – Developed

Employees and managers know what is expected of them. The organizational ambitions and working agreements are present and communicated.

Performance Level 2 – Established

Employees and managers are committed to the organizational ambitions and working agreements.

Performance Level 3 – Advanced

Employees and managers are active in achieving positive results and show ownership of ambitions and working agreements.

Performance Level 4 – High Performing

Employees and managers take responsibility for achieving sustainable positive results and have an eye for improvement. The organizational ambitions and working agreements are fully and sustainably integrated into the actions and thinking.

I give "Inspiring and leading people" as an example of how an organization can evolve on a criterion.

Table 7.13. Development table "Leading and inspiring people"

Themes	Developed	Established *Challenging and activating*	Advanced *Leading to positive results*	High Performing *Embedded and continuously improving*
Openness and trust	Leaders provide clarity about mission, vision, and goals	There is clear and interactive communication between leaders and people at all levels	Leading to positive results	Leaders are active role models who lead by example and are trusted by the people in the organization
People	People understand the goals of the organization	Line managers support people to achieve the goals	Leaders provide a consistent level of trust in the organization	Leaders motivate and inspire people achieve results that go beyond what is expected of them
Developing leader	Line managers know what is expected of them around people to effectively lead, manage, and develop	People know what to expect from their line managers and provide feedback on how they are managed and developed	Leaders are enthusiastic about achieving goals and motivating people to achieve them	Future leadership competencies are established in line with the core values of the organization, and leaders have these competencies

- To achieve IIP accreditation, an organization must score all nine indicators at the "developed" level.

- Investors in People Silver means that all nine indicators score at the "developed" level and seven of the nine at the "established" level.

- Investors in People Gold stands for all nine indicators, scoring "developed" and "established" and seven scoring "advanced."

- Investors in People Platinum means that they score "developed," "established," and "advanced" on all nine indicators and "high performing" on seven indicators.

7.5. ISO 9001

Implementing an ISO Quality Management System is a chance to rethink the true purpose of a nonprofit organization: Why should it exist? What are its priorities? For whom does it work? How does it comply with its environment? And what ought to be measured? All these topics are taken into consideration when a nonprofit organization applies for ISO 9001 certification. With the implementation of the ISO QMS standard, a nonprofit organization is obliged to focus its attention on what is extremely relevant for the future and, at the same time, to assess its everyday activities and to enhance its potency through the identification and standardization of its internal processes.

SO 9001 is defined as the international standard that specifies the requirements for a quality management system (QMS). Organizations use the standard to prove their ability to consistently supply products and services that meet customer and regulatory requirements. It is the most popular standard in the ISO 9000 series and the only standard in the series for which organizations can certify.

ISO 9001 was first published in 1987 by the International Organization for Standardization (ISO), an international agency composed of the national standards bodies of more than 160 countries. The current version of ISO 9001 was released in September 2015.

ISO 9001 is based on the plan-do-check-act methodology and provides a process-oriented approach to documenting and reviewing the structure, responsibilities, and procedures required to achieve effective quality management in an organization. Specific sections of the standard contain information on many topics, such as:

- Requirements for a QMS, including documented information, planning, and determining process interactions.

- Responsibilities of management.

- Management of resources, including human resources and an organization's work environment.

- Product realization, including the steps from design to delivery.

- Measurement, analysis, and improvement of the QMS through activities like internal audits and corrective and preventive action.

This ISO standard is based on 7 quality management principles:

- customer focus.

- leadership.

- engagement of people.

- process approach.

- improvement.

- evidence-based decision making.

- relationship management.

Figure 7.6. Management principles of ISO 9001

Source: Adapted from International Organization for Standardization (2015).

An ISO 9001 certification means that an external, independent party decides whether the quality management system of the organization meets all standard requirements. To decide this, a certification body (CI) conducts an audit.

7.6. ESG (standards and guidelines for quality assurance in the European higher education area)

7.6.1. Introduction

The first version of standards and guidelines for quality assurance in the European Higher Education Area was approved in 2005 by the European

Ministers of Education. It was the result of the cooperation of the E4 group: ENQA (European Association for Quality in Higher Education), EURASHE (European Association of Institutions in Higher Education), EUA (European University Association), and ESU (European Students' Union). After a revision in 2012, the 2015 version is currently in effect. The standards are intended for internal and external quality assurance. However, they do not want to be quality standards nor to prescribe how educational institutions should organize their quality assurance. Rather, they want to be a guide in those areas that are vital to a quality learning environment in higher education. Therefore, they relate exclusively to education and not to research and services. By quality care, they mean all activities related to the continuous improvement cycle.

ESG recognizes that the great diversity in political and educational systems, in socio-cultural and educational traditions, and in language and expectations makes it impossible and undesirable to pursue a monolithic approach to quality and quality assurance. Nevertheless, ESG wants accreditation bodies and other umbrella quality organizations to apply the same principles and to adapt processes and procedures to the requirements of their own context. The goals of ESG are as follows:

- propose a common frame of reference for quality assurance systems related to learning and education at the European, national, and institutional levels.

- promote efforts to watch and improve the quality of higher education in Europe.

- promote mutual trust so that recognition and mobility within and beyond national borders are encouraged.

- supply information about quality assurance in the European Higher Education Area.

7.6.2. The standards

The standards are based on four principles:

- higher education institutions are themselves responsible for the quality of their education and for monitoring it.

- quality assurance must accommodate the diversity of higher education systems, institutions, programs, and students.

- quality assurance should support the development of a quality culture.

- quality assurance considers the needs and expectations of the students, of all stakeholders, and of society.

The standards are divided into three groups: standards for internal quality assurance, for external quality assurance, and for quality assurance organizations.

7.6.2.1. Part 1: Standards for internal quality assurance

Policy for quality assurance

Institutions should have a policy for quality assurance that is made public and forms part of their strategic management. Internal stakeholders should develop and implement this policy through the right structures and processes while involving external stakeholders.

Design and approval of programs

Institutions should have processes for the design and approval of their programs. The programs should be designed so that they meet the goals set for them, including the intended learning outcomes. The qualification resulting from a program should be clearly specified and communicated and should refer to the correct level of the national qualifications framework for higher education and, consequently, to the Framework for Qualifications of the European Higher Education Area.

Student-centered learning, teaching, and assessment

Institutions should ensure that the programs are delivered in a way that encourages students to take an active role in creating the learning process and that the assessment of students reflects this approach.

Student admission, progression, recognition, and certification

Institutions should consistently apply pre-defined and published regulations covering all phases of the student "life cycle," e.g., student admission, progression, recognition, and certification.

Teaching staff

Institutions should assure themselves of the competence of their teachers. They should apply fair and transparent processes for the recruitment and development of the staff.

Learning resources and student support

Institutions should have the right funding for learning and teaching activities and ensure that adequate and readily accessible learning resources and student support are provided.

Information management

Institutions should ensure that they collect, analyze, and use relevant information for the effective management of their programs and other activities.

Public information

Institutions should publish information about their activities, including programs, which is clear, correct, goal-oriented, up-to-date, and readily accessible.

Ongoing monitoring and periodic review of programs

Institutions should monitor and periodically review their programs to ensure that they achieve the goals set for them and respond to the needs of students and society. These reviews should lead to continuous improvement of the program. Any action planned or taken as a result should be communicated to all those concerned.

Cyclical external quality assurance

Institutions should undergo external quality assurance in line with the ESG on a cyclical basis.

7.6.2.2. Part 2: Standards for external quality assurance

Consideration of internal quality assurance

External quality assurance should address the effectiveness of the internal quality assurance described in Part 1 of the ESG.

Designing methodologies fit for the purpose

External quality assurance should be defined and designed specifically to ensure its fitness to achieve the aims and goals set for it while considering relevant regulations.

Implementing processes

External quality assurance processes should be reliable, useful, pre-defined, implemented consistently, and published. They include a self-assessment or equivalent, an external assessment normally including a site visit, a report resulting from the external assessment, and a consistent follow-up.

Peer-review experts

External quality assurance should be conducted by groups of external experts that include (a) student member(s).

Criteria for outcomes

Any outcomes or judgments made as the result of external quality assurance should be based on explicit and published criteria that are applied consistently, irrespective of whether the process leads to a formal decision.

Reporting

Full reports by the experts should be published, clear, and accessible to the academic community, external partners, and other interested individuals. If the agency makes any formal decision based on the reports, the decision should be published together with the report.

Complaints and appeals

Complaints and appeals processes should be clearly defined as part of the design of external quality assurance processes and communicated to the institutions.

7.6.2.3. Part 3: Standards for quality assurance agencies

Activities, policy, and processes for quality assurance

Agencies should undertake external quality assurance activities as defined in Part 2 of the ESG on a regular basis. They should have clear and explicit goals and aims that are part of their publicly available mission statement. These should translate into the daily work of the agency. Agencies should ensure the involvement of stakeholders in their governance and work.

Official status

Agencies should have an established legal basis and be formally recognized as quality assurance agencies by competent public authorities.

Independence

Agencies should be independent and act autonomously. They should have full responsibility for their operations and the outcomes of those operations without third-party influence.

Thematic analysis

Agencies should regularly publish reports that describe and analyze the general findings of their external quality assurance activities.

Resources

Agencies should have adequate and proper resources, both human and financial, to conduct their work.

Internal quality assurance and professional conduct

Agencies should have in place processes for internal quality assurance related to defining, assuring, and enhancing the quality and integrity of their activities.

Cyclical external review of agencies

Agencies should undergo an external review at least once every five years to demonstrate their compliance with the ESG.

7.7. Quality in public health

In Great Britain, the Public Health System Group and some key national partners collaborated to develop a framework that protects and improves health outcomes and reduces health inequalities. The framework has been developed so that:

- People working in public health and related areas

- Providers of public health functions and services

- Commissioners and funders of public health functions and services

- Local authority councilors and directly elected mayors

National government, organizations, and policymakers are clear about what quality in public health means, the roles and responsibilities of key players in a public health system, and what steps can be taken to improve quality.

High-performing public health systems demonstrate the following strategic and enabling characteristics:

Strategic characteristics

- A shared goal of improving public health outcomes and reducing health inequalities with a strong ethos of accountability and collaboration among partners and communities.

- An assets-based approach, co-producing interventions with local communities and citizens.

- An approach that puts health outcomes at the heart of policy decisions to address the wider determinants of health.

- A proactive approach to enhancing and safeguarding health, keeping individuals and populations as healthy as possible, and reducing threats to health.

- Early intervention; adopting a life course approach across primary, secondary, and tertiary care settings and integrated services.

- A strong advocacy and influencing role for public mental health as well as physical health.

- An awareness and responsibility to future generations

Enabling characteristics

- Strong leadership (political and professional), which mobilizes and leverages action by multiple actors at all levels to achieve a common vision.

- Investment in the public health workforce and its continuous development.

- Continuous learning, improvement, and evidence generation.

- Measurement and evaluation with transparency about quality measures and outcomes.

- Decisions informed by evidence, needs, and insight and translated into deliverable commitments

- Use of innovative technology to stay ahead of the game.

Especially important in this framework is the focus on collaboration. A high-quality public health system is collaborative, maximizes investment in the public health system, ensures an assets-based approach, co-produces interventions with local communities, and has citizens at the heart of high-quality functions and services.

The framework describes seven steps that are useful in helping to set out how to improve the quality of public health in the key areas.

Figure 7.7. Stepstones to quality in healthcare

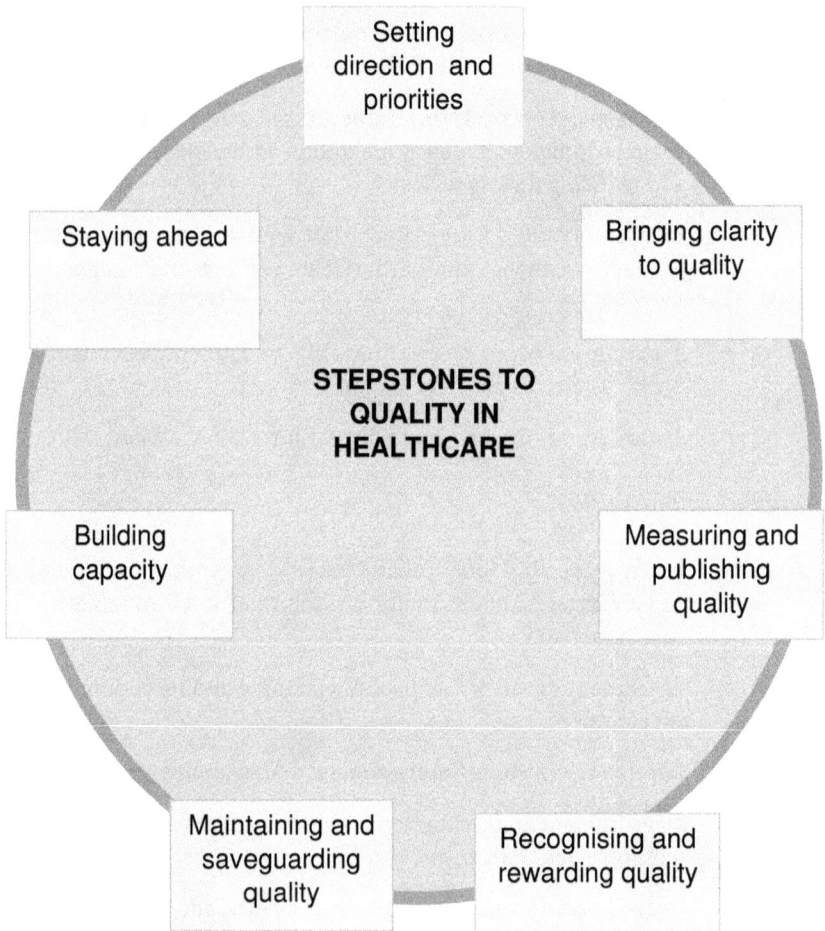

Set direction and priorities

- Work effectively as a system to set up and communicate clear, collective, and consistent priorities for quality.

- Identify any quality gaps and base future priorities on the evidence.

Bringing clarity to quality

- Supply support to the development of quality standards and align efforts to support their implementation.

Measuring & publishing quality

- Be transparent in driving improvement in quality, including the achievement of quality standards

- Find ways to measure and publish quality and support continuous learning.

Recognizing & rewarding quality

- Evaluate and encourage sector-led and peer-led improvement.

- Publish and disseminate examples of good practice.

- Develop reward mechanisms for high quality.

- *Maintaining and safeguarding quality*

- Support community-level capacity building.

- Continually strive to gain the views of the public, service users, and stakeholders, as we believe this is essential to safeguarding quality.

- Use evidence to set aims and measures for quality improvement.

Building capability

- Advocate the importance of education, training, and CPD for the workforce

- Support the leadership development for improving the quality of public health

- Create a learning public health system

Staying ahead

- Monitor developments in innovation and promote public health technologies

- Build a culture of continuous improvement that can accept change and innovation and share knowledge of what works.

7.8. Finally

I will just mention two prestigious prizes for quality management that are important outside Europe. I will not discuss them here.

The Malcolm Baldrige National Quality Award has become one of the most prestigious and important honors in the United States (Dooley et al. 2015). It is awarded to companies that consistently deliver high-quality products and services to their customers and have organizational structures, policies, and cultures to support such goals. The award guidelines form a definition of American-style Total Quality Control. The Baldrige Award follows the long-standing tradition of Japan's Deming Prize, which is given to organizations in Japan and now abroad that show excellence in Japanese-style Total Quality Control.

The Deming Prize is among the most significant awards for Total Quality Management. Established in 1951 by the Japanese Union of Scientists and Engineers, it has been positively influencing the Japanese economy since then and has become an international award. MBNQA is the highest award given in the United States to the most recognized companies for performance excellence ("Improve performance and get world-class results" (Panda, 2020).

Chapter 8

Quality tools

Not everything that can be counted is of value and what is
of real value usually cannot be counted.

— Albert Einstein

While quality models that I described in the previous chapter represent a coherent and theoretically based framework for arriving at quality, techniques are practical tools that describe a step-by-step approach to solving a problem. Models describe the why and the why; techniques are about the how. In this chapter, I describe a whole series of techniques that organizations can use in a meaningful way at many moments in their focused work on quality.

8.1. Techniques to develop ideas

In this section, I describe four techniques for creatively developing innovative ideas: brainstorming, relationship diagram, nominal group technique, and benchmarking.

8.1.1. Brainstorming

Description

Brainstorming is a simple technique that aims to collect many ideas about a certain topic in a brief time. The goals can be, for example, inventorying problems, collecting solutions, or developing an improvement proposal. In quality management, a brainstorming session is often followed by a Pareto analysis, which I describe in section 8.2.1.

Method

Initially, the employees or members of a quality circle or a team select a problem. Then, the group comments on the problem. The comments are noted on a flipchart or board. The employees do not yet use meeting or discussion techniques because these are often too structured and, therefore, put the brakes on the formation of creative ideas. Only after the session has run for some time can the group leader structure the conversation more. The group can then evaluate the ideas for their merits. The following rules will help make the process go smoothly:

- Phrase the problem in diverse ways to avoid one-way thinking.

- Assume that members are aware of the problem.

- Record all ideas.

- No one is allowed to criticize their own ideas or those of others during the brainstorming session. Early criticism inevitably puts a brake on the formation of creative ideas. The process will also quickly degenerate into a discussion about the first ideas, leaving too little room to put forward innovative ideas. Moreover, this method can spoil the atmosphere.

- Even seemingly silly or unusual ideas are positive. It is often precisely these ideas that associatively form a bridge to other creative ideas.

- Don't stop brainstorming too early. Only after the traditional ideas come the more creative ideas. Sometimes, several sessions are necessary to thoroughly explore ideas. To ensure the progress of a brainstorming process, the number of group members should not be too large. If too many people take part, some will no longer be sufficiently represented. Fifteen people are the maximum. You do not have to set a minimum since you can also brainstorm on your own. In addition, the atmosphere in the group should not be too tense or aggressive. In such a situation, the members are quick to express criticism, and criticism is disastrous for the course of the process.

Example

A group of students complain that they must spend too much time on their studies so that even their private lives suffer. As a result, the atmosphere in the group deteriorates. Under the guidance of a teacher, the students decided to investigate the problems. The question is what the causes of their problems are. The students may point to the amount of work and the study assignments as causes, but the core of the problems lies elsewhere. The brainstorming yields a range of probable causes for the tough situation. By assigning scores, the following causes appear as the most important:

- teachers give assignments without mutual consultation.

- students do not know how to plan substantial amounts of work.

- students do not know how to communicate effectively with teachers if they do not agree. In a later phase, they again brainstormed about remedies using the fishbone diagram (see section 8.2.2).

8.1.2. Relationship diagram

Description

The relationship diagram is a visual way to make relationships between ideas concrete. The technique was developed by the Japanese Kawakita Jiro. The diagram is a method of creatively collecting and organizing a large amount of information. It can be about ideas, experiences, opinions, and so on. It is creative because it can break through the classic ideas, and it is also a method that allows all team members to take part.

Method

Ideally, this chart is used in teams of six to eight people. It is important that the members have knowledge of or experience with the problem discussed. It is not necessary for members to already form a team. The technique can be used as a form of team development.

The starting point is a difficult theme, problem, or question. Individual brainstorming sessions are then held on that theme. The ideas are written down on post-its, which are then pasted on a board and arranged in certain clusters. Then, each cluster is summarized in a sentence. The following steps must be taken:

- First, take enough time to agree on the theme you are going to brainstorm.

- It is important to define the theme clearly so that everyone is talking about the same thing.

- Then everyone brainstorms silently and writes down ideas on post-its, only one idea per piece of paper.

- When the participants are ready, they silently stick their notes on the board in places of their choosing.

- Then everyone reads all the ideas.

- Next, the participants move their own notes to what they perceive as clusters or groups of similar ideas. In this phase, they can talk to each other and discuss the order. It is not a problem if not all notes can be placed in a group.

- In each phase, ideas that have arisen can be put on post-its.

- In the next step, members try to agree on a description of each group of ideas. In no more than one sentence, they write down what the group of ideas entails.

- In the next step, the group considers the ideas that have not yet found a place in one of the groups: either they will be placed in a group, there will be a separate group, or they will be removed if everyone agrees.

- If the number of clusters is too large – more than eight – the group will try to merge clusters to reduce the number.

- To further visualize the matter, connections between clusters can be shown with arrows.

When

This instrument is especially suitable when there is a wide variety of views or ideas in a team. It can also be used to bring order to complex, diffuse, or chaotic ideas. That way, the team can try to come to a consensus.

The relationship diagram is most useful when:

- the group is unsure about the facts and when it concerns a problem of which they do not yet fully understand all the consequences.

- it is necessary to organize all ideas before systematically analyzing them.

- there is little unity in the team, and the team must concentrate its energy to make progress.

Example

A group of employees decides to apply the diagram to the time problem. First, it is necessary to properly define the problem. Is it about real working time, about the time they still must work at home, about overtime, or about something else? Then, they collect all their experiences with time problems and write them down on Post-its. These are then glued to the board and clustered. For example, a cluster could be "Wasted Time."

8.1.3. Nominal group technique

Description

Nominal Group Technique (NGT) is a structured way of brainstorming that ensures everyone's contribution.

Usage

- When some group members are verbally stronger than others.

- When some group members think better in silence.

- When there is concern that some group members are not taking part.

- When the group does not spontaneously generate many ideas.

- When some or all group members are new.

- When the problem is too difficult or may cause conflict.

Method

Paper and pen for each group member, a flipchart/board, markers, and tape.

1. Clarify the topic until everyone understands it.

2. Each team member individually and silently writes down as many ideas as possible in a limited amount of time (for example, five or ten minutes).

3. Each team member takes turns presenting an idea. The discussion leader writes down the ideas on a board or flipchart.

4. There is no discussion, not even to clarify ideas.

5. As time goes on, members may also bring forward ideas they have not put down on paper. By hearing others busy, they can get innovative ideas themselves.

6. Group members may pass up their turns and add ideas later if they wish.

7. Continue until there are no more ideas or until a certain amount of time has passed.

8. Discuss each idea individually. Ideas can be crossed off the list if everyone agrees. Discussion means clarifying the meaning or logic behind an idea and asking and answering questions.

9. Prioritize the ideas by multivoting or narrowing down the list.

Additions

- The discussion should be divided equally among all ideas. The main purpose of the discussion is to clarify ideas, not to resolve differences of opinion.

- It is important that all ideas be continuously visualized. Hang up the flipchart sheets with the ideas so that they are visible to everyone.

8.1.4. Benchmarking

Description

Benchmarking is the process of comparing your own performance and the paths towards it with those of other organizations, with the aim of improving your own processes and performance. As a result of that process, you will:

- have better insight into your own processes.
- identify what can be changed and why.
- earn from the experiences of others.
- improve your own performance.
- learn to understand what the best organizations in your category can achieve.

Benchmarking can be used by any organization at any time to improve. The benchmarking process has five phases (Camp, 1989) (see also Figure 8.1).

Scheduling

Here, the classic questions must be answered concerning the what, the why, and the how:

- What should be benchmarked? Benchmarking is suitable for any service that an organization provides. Of course, you can also benchmark aspects of the organization, such as marketing, quality assurance, customer service, and so on.

- Who do you want to compare yourself to? Naturally, competitors are interesting candidates for benchmarking. Because this is often difficult to achieve from a competitive point of view, you can also compare certain functions of your own organization with comparable functions of organizations from other sectors. However, it is necessary to compare them with organizations that perform very well.

- How do you collect the data? There is no such thing as one right way to collect data about other organizations, but rather a multitude of methods. Quite a lot of data is publicly available. This is not just about facts and figures but about documenting good practices that can help you better achieve your own goals.

Analysis

The analysis phase should lead to a careful understanding of your own processes and practices and those of the benchmarked organizations. Internal performances with their strengths and weaknesses must be clarified. Therefore, the following questions are important:

- Is this organization better than ours?

- Why is it better?

- Is this organization much, much better?

- What good practices does this organization use that we can also apply?

- How can we apply these good practices in our own organization?

Benchmarking steps

By answering these questions, you gain insight into your own gaps, and you have a basis to fill those gaps.

Figure 8.1. Steps in benchmarking

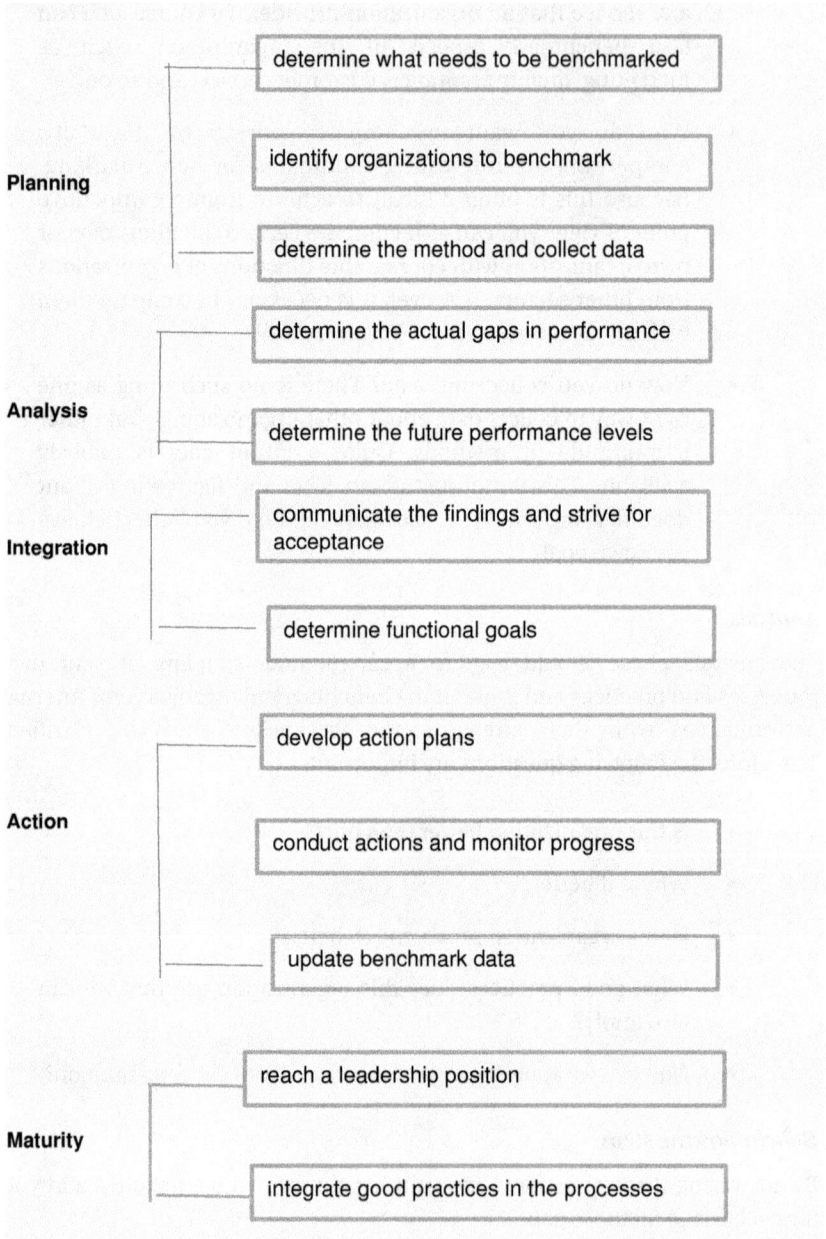

Planning
- determine what needs to be benchmarked
- identify organizations to benchmark
- determine the method and collect data

Analysis
- determine the actual gaps in performance
- determine the future performance levels

Integration
- communicate the findings and strive for acceptance
- determine functional goals

Action
- develop action plans
- conduct actions and monitor progress
- update benchmark data

Maturity
- reach a leadership position
- integrate good practices in the processes

Integration

Integration means that you process the findings from the benchmarking into operational goals for your own organization. This requires careful planning of the implementation of these new practices. In addition, you must ensure that the findings become a structural element of your own organization. For this, it is necessary to do the following:

- strive for the findings that both management and employees can accept.

- develop action plans.

- communicate the findings to all levels of the organization to gain support and involvement.

Action

The findings and the action plans must also be realized. Therefore, periodic measurement and evaluation of the actions are necessary. You also must set milestones at crucial times when you update the benchmarking findings and communicate the new findings to everyone again.

Maturity

The organization reaches a level of maturity when the entire enterprise is so permeated with best practices that other organizations come to benchmark their own processes. It also shows maturity when the organization and all levels within it use benchmarking as an ongoing process. Everybody takes part in benchmarking, not just the specialists.

8.2. Cause analysis techniques

In this section, I discuss four techniques that are particularly useful in analyzing causes and effects: Pareto analysis, fishbone (or Ishikawa diagram), WWWWH analysis, and force field analysis.

8.2.1. Pareto analysis

Description

With a Pareto analysis, the group members can select those problems whose solution yields the most significant quality improvement. The term originates from the Italian economist Vilfredo Pareto (1848-1923). Among other things, he studied property relations and concluded that 80 percent of the total assets were owned by only 20 percent of the population. His 80/20 rule later found application in his approach to diverse problems. In quality management, he stands for the proposition that 20 percent of all probable causes are responsible for 80 percent of all consequences. In the pursuit of quality improvement, therefore, it is not primarily a matter of tracing all causes of errors, but only the 20 percent most important causes because most problems can be solved through this. From that point of view, a systematic step-by-step approach to potential problems would be inefficient.

A Pareto analysis is useful if the organization has recurring problems and wants to know which of those problems to address first. This method is also useful if there are several problems and causes and if the organization wants to focus only on the most important of them.

Method

Step 1

After the members of a working group have come to an agreement on the subject they want to discuss, for example, through brainstorming, they must collect as much information as possible on that subject. The goal is to arrive at a selection of the problems to be treated on an objective basis during a specific period. The method can look like this:

- First, it is necessary to decide in which categories the information will be classified.

- Subsequently, it must be decided what kind of measurements are needed. Simple measures are frequency, quantity, cost, and time.

- Then, a period must also be agreed upon during which facts are gathered.

- The material must be effectively collected and organized into one of the categories.

Step 2

The group then draws up a frequency table that shows how often each error occurs. Then, the members rank the errors in order of frequency. The errors that occur most often make the largest contribution to the loss of quality and are the first to be treated. Therefore, for each error, the members calculate the percentage contribution to the total number of observed errors. In addition, they calculate the cumulative frequencies. They always add the percentage frequency to the frequency of the earlier error. These cumulative frequencies stand for how many errors account for the highest percentage.

Step 3

The results are displayed graphically. This makes it visually clear which errors are responsible for the highest percentage. A bar and a label must be created in the diagram for each category of facts. The smallest numbers are placed on the left, and the largest on the right. When there are many categories with small numbers, you need to see if you cannot group some of them into a more comprehensive category.

Step 4

The results obtained are now the starting point for selecting the problems to be treated. Measures to improve quality are only meaningful if they target the causes of the errors that account for most rejections.

If we can put a price on each error or problem, we calculate the most significant error based on the cost price and not on the cumulative frequency table. Sometimes, we also must consider the social importance of the problems. For example (in our example below), vandalism entails much higher economic costs than truancy. Truancy does not cost money, but it threatens the development of children and young people and, therefore, poses a greater social risk. We can offset this importance by, for example, assigning points to each problem according to its importance. The most important problem gets the most points. Then, we multiply the number of times it occurs by the points awarded per problem.

Example

In a provincial town, the police are receiving more complaints about cases involving school-aged youth. The director of one of the schools takes the initiative to consult with other school boards and the police commissioner. The Commissioner is already thinking aloud about a special youth brigade. The group agrees not to go ahead in a hurry and to collect sufficient information first. This is not available because agents do not draw up official reports about many activities (for example, when checking school absenteeism in cafes, when intervening in neighbor disputes, etc.). It is agreed that the agents register every performance for a month via a simple form. After a month, the working group will see the results as shown in Table 8.1.

Table 8.1. Complaints about young people received by the police

NR.	Definition	Number
1	vandalism	11
2	public intoxication	25
3	skipping class	35
4	bicycle theft	7
5	drug possession	9
6	indecent assault	1
7	violence	14
8	conflicts at home	6
9	traffic offenses	19
Total		127

The processing of this basic data in a cumulative frequency table is shown in table 8.2. It turns out that three problem behaviors are responsible for 62 percent of the complaints.

Table 8.2. Overview of problem behavior

	Definition	Number	% TOTAL	CUMULATIVE %
3	skipping class	35	27.5	27.5
2	drunkenness	25	19.7	47.5
9	traffic offenses	19	14.9	62.1
7	violence	14	11.1	73.2
1	vandalism	11	8.7	81.9
5	drugs	9	7.1	89.0
4	bicycle theft	7	5.5	94.5
8	conflicts at home	6	4.7	99.2
6	assault	1	0.8	100.0

8.2.2. Fishbone diagram

Description

The Ishikawa or fishbone diagram is a graphical diagram that the group uses in the problem analysis phase to gain insight into the probable causes of the problem selected, for example, through Pareto analysis. Around 1950, Japanese professor Ishikawa developed this diagram as a cause-effect diagram. Due to its simplicity and efficiency, the scheme has achieved remarkable success in dealing with quality problems. In its general form, the scheme looks as shown in Figure 8.2. Ideally, a fishbone diagram is linked to a brainstorming session. The brainstorming then produces a large amount of information, which is then systematically ordered in the fishbone diagram.

Figure 8.2. Fishbone diagram

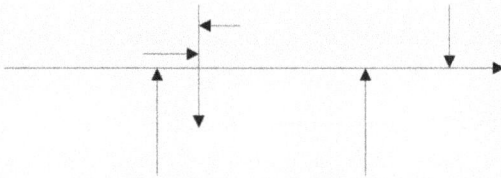

The vertical arrows are the main causes that give rise to the effect. The horizontal arrows against the vertical arrows are partial causes. I group the causes of the shortcomings into a few main categories, for example, student – teacher – subject matter – method – learning environment, and so on.

Method

I assume that the group members, after a Pareto analysis, have reached an agreement on the problem. They typify that problem with a keyword at the right end of the main horizontal arrow. The group then brainstorms plausible causes and sub-causes. They draw in the main causes as vertical arrows or bones and the sub-causes as cross arrows. When all putative causes and sub-causes have been listed, the group lets the diagram rest for a while. Later, group members check to see if they imagine any new causes. For this method to be effective, I must consider the following points:

- Involve everyone in drawing up the diagram to get as many ideas as possible.

- Distinguish between problems caused by people (e.g., students and teachers) by methods, contents, contexts, structures, and so on.

- For overly complex problems, first make an overview diagram for the main "bones" and then a detailed diagram for each main point on a separate sheet of paper.

After developing the fishbone diagram, you need to decide which causes you want to work on first. Here, too, the principle applies that you cannot be busy with everything at the same time. That is why you must make a choice again. This can be done quite empirically by having each member of the group link points to a few causes. For example, the worthiest cause gets five points, the second three points, and the third one point. Adding up the scores of all group members will show which cause has collected the most points. Of course, you can also try to come to a consensus on the worthiest cause based on mutual consultation. After the choice has been made, you can then forge plans to address the cause.

Example

In the example of the problems with young people, it turned out that truancy, together with drunkenness, were the most important complaints for which citizens called the police. After the working group had discussed the results of the observations, it considered the probable causes. The result is shown in Figure 8.3. The following were shown as possible main causes: the pupil, the home situation, the working methods used, and the school context. The working group was able to write down several elements for each of these causes:

Pupil

1. Feeling of loneliness
2. Not fascinated by study
3. No proper leisure activities

Home situation

4. Both parents work
5. Divorce issues
6. Inadequate arrangements concerning nightlife

7. No oversight of young people's expenses

School context

8. Too little focus on creating a school as a community
9. Teachers are little interested in the home situation of students

Work forms

10. Passive working methods
11. Subject matter is central
12. Little use of student-oriented working methods

   After the discussion, there was no longer any preference for a special youth brigade. The causes of truancy had to be tackled at the source by those involved. That is why a working group of the schools involved would develop a campaign to sensitize parents, students, and the catering sector of the city to the problem. In that context, this working group recommended that the city council appoint a professional. As a youth consultant, he would coordinate between the police, young people, schools, and youth associations. The consultant could also help problem youths and thus prevent repressive action.

Figure 8.3. Fishbone diagram of a practical example

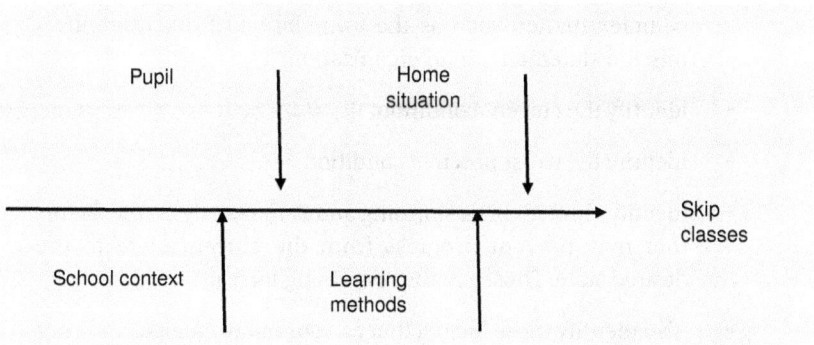

8.2.3. WWWWH technique

To define a process or problem as completely as possible, a work group or an individual employee can ask the following five questions:

1. What do people do? (What's the problem?)
2. When is it done? (When does the problem occur?)
3. Where is it done? (Where does the problem occur?)
4. Who does it? (Who takes part in the problem?)
5. How is it done? (How does the problem occur?)

The answers to these questions, or the lack of answers, may lead you to seek more information.

8.2.4. Force field analysis

Description

This technique helps to identify the factors that can inhibit or stimulate change processes and ensures that a balanced approach is used in the planning of change processes (by ensuring that existing strengths are not lost sight of). The technique can be used individually or in a team.

Method

- Name the desired condition. This can be a goal or a more complex matter, such as the formulation of, for example, a mission statement for an organization.

- Identify the current condition.

- Identify the worst possible condition.

- Identify, through brainstorming and Pareto analysis, the factors that may prevent progress from the current state to the desired state. Those are the restraining forces.

- Also identify those factors that can stimulate change.

- As the last and perhaps major step, formulate some basic actions that can minimize the restraining forces and enhance the stimulating forces.

When

A force field analysis is especially useful when the organization is facing significant changes. It can also be used as a planning tool for individual and group goals. This analysis leads to a balanced approach with sufficient attention to existing strengths.

8.3. Evaluation and decision-making techniques

Here, we discuss three techniques that are useful in evaluating a situation and making decisions: strengths-weaknesses analysis, decision matrix, and multivoting.

8.3.1. Strengths-Weaknesses Analysis

A strengths-weaknesses analysis is a useful tool to map out the current quality of an organization. Such an analysis starts from the collection of all assessment aspects that are relevant to an organization.

A strengths-weaknesses analysis consists of two phases. In the first phase, the members of the group brainstorm about what they consider to be the strengths of their organization as well as its weaknesses. Strengths and weaknesses therefore relate to the internal aspects of the organization and can be influenced by the organization.

They then discuss what they see as opportunities and threats to the environment. These elements are, of course, less easy to influence. I summarize the strengths-weaknesses analysis in Figure 84.

Figure 8.4. Strength-weakness analysis

STRENGTHS	WEAKNESSES
OPPORTUNITIES	THREATS

This analysis can still be refined. In quality assurance, it is important that the organization get a good insight into the criteria that stakeholders use when they look at the organization. That is not always easy. Still, this is valuable information that can help decide progress priorities. What assessment criteria do stakeholders use? How important do they consider each of those criteria? What conclusions do they draw from their assessment? Based on this information, the group can then fill in the diagram (see Figure 8.5).

Figure 8.5. Strengths and weaknesses

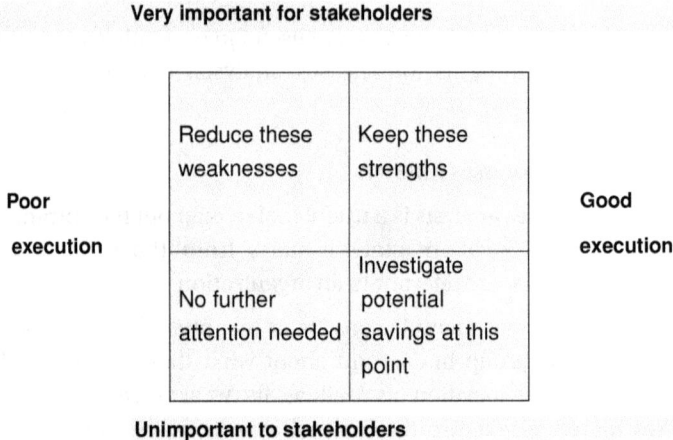

Very important for stakeholders

Reduce these weaknesses	Keep these strengths
No further attention needed	Investigate potential savings at this point

Poor

execution

Good

execution

Unimportant to stakeholders

Experiences, also in the socio-cultural sector, show that the SWOT easily leads to employees focusing too quickly on the negative points of their organization, the weaknesses, and threats. Socius (support center for socio-cultural adult work) thought that the SWOT should be given a more constructive and stimulating function. That is why Socius further developed the SWOT analysis into a SWOART analysis (Socius, Sd), which I briefly explain. The Socius website supplies more detailed information (https://beleidsplanning.socius.be/fase-4-van-uitdagingen-naar-Options-4-1-beleid schagen/). The acronym SWOART stands for Strengths, Weaknesses, Opportunities, Aspirations, Results, and Threats. What is innovative about SWOART is that the organization asks internal stakeholders what their aspirations are: what do they still want to achieve? What would they like to achieve within the vision and mission of the organization? The external stakeholders are asked what results they expect from the organization. The combination of the internal categories with each of the external categories produces a particular approach. As shown in Figure 8.6, these combinations lead to a total of nine action alternatives. Some examples. When an organization is good at something (internal strength), and society also offers (external) opportunities, then an organization has reasons to invest in this. The similarities between internal strengths and external opportunities lead to an advantage and a strengthening of the organization and its results. Those who are strong can dare to defend themselves against external threats; those who, on the other hand, evaluate themselves as weak have little choice but to try to repair the damage.

Figure 8.6. SWOART Analysis

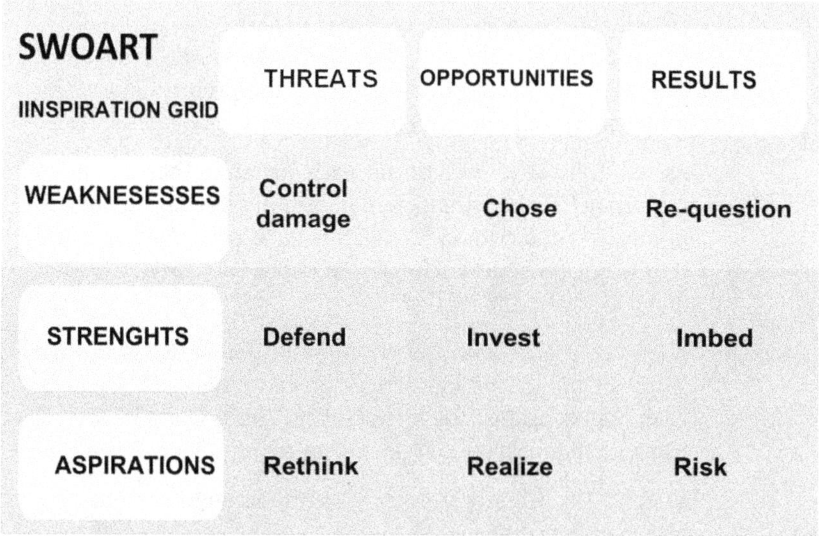

SWOART IINSPIRATION GRID	THREATS	OPPORTUNITIES	RESULTS
WEAKNESESSES	Control damage	Chose	Re-question
STRENGHTS	Defend	Invest	Imbed
ASPIRATIONS	Rethink	Realize	Risk

Source: Socius. https://beleidsplanning.socius.be/swo-art/

8.3.2. Decision-Making Matrix

Description

A decision matrix (other names are Pugh Matrix, problem matrix, opportunity analysis, and solution matrix) serves to evaluate and prioritize a list of workable options. The team first figures out several criteria against which it will assess the alternatives. Each alternative is then weighed against these criteria.

This method makes sense when you are forced to make a choice from many alternative options and when the decisions must be justified based on criteria. Examples are a problem to be selected to work on and when you can work on an alternative.

Method

1. Brainstorm about evaluation criteria that are appropriate for the specific situation. It sometimes makes sense to involve as many stakeholders as possible in this process if you have the opportunity.

2. Discuss and refine the list of criteria. Decide whether the criteria are necessary and relevant to assess the alternatives. When there are still many criteria left, you must narrow down the list and keep only the most important items. The multivoting technique can be used for this.

3. Assign a relative weight to each criterion based on its importance in that situation. For example, you can divide ten points over the criteria. Consensus is, of course, ideal, but if that is not possible, each team member can assign a weight and you add up the results.

4. Draw the matrix with the criteria and their weights on one side and the list of alternatives on the other side. Evaluate each choice against the criteria. That can happen in diverse ways. Rating scale options are the following:

   1, 2, 3: 1 = slightly present, 2 = moderately present, 3 = abundantly present.

   1, 2, 3: 1 = low, 2 = medium, 3 = high.

   1, 2, 3, 4, 5: 1 = little, 5 = much; 1, 4, 9: 1 = low, 4 = moderate, 9 = high.

It is important that the scales be composed consistently. A high value everywhere means that the alternative is chosen.

A second method consists of ranking the options from high to low for each criterion. One is then the option that least meets the criterion.

Example

Let us take the guests of an exclusive restaurant in Paris as an example. The intention is to first tackle the problem of long waiting times for guests. The problems they find are guests waiting for the host, the waiter, the food, and the bill. The criteria they find are:

- the burden on the guest (how does the waiting time negatively affect the guest).

- the ease of solving the problem.

- the effect on other systems.

- the speed of the solution.

(Originally, the 'easy to solve' criterion was defined as 'difficult to solve', so the rating scale had to be reversed. Now, all criteria can be scored the same way.) If a problem gets a high score on every criterion, it means that the problem will be selected more quickly: high burden for the guest, easy to solve, large effect on other factors, and quick to solve.

'Burden for the guest' has a weight of five points, which means that the team considers this to be by far the most important criterion compared to criteria that received 1 or 2 points. The team chose a three-point scale: high = 3, medium = 2, low = 1. As an example, the problem is 'guests waiting for food.' The burden for the guest is medium (2) because the atmosphere in the restaurant is pleasant. This problem is not easy to solve (the ease of solving the problem = 1) because it concerns both the people in the kitchen and the waiters. The effect on other factors is medium (2) because the waiters must walk to the kitchen several times.

It will take some time to solve the problem (speed of the solution = 1) because the kitchen is small and inflexible. To solve that, the kitchen would have to be renovated. Each score is then multiplied by the weight of the relevant criterion. For example, 'burden for the guest' (weight 5) multiplied by 'the guest waits for the host' (score 3) leads to a weighted score of 15. For each problem, the weighted scores for each criterion are added to get the total score. In this way, 'Guest waiting for the host' gets the highest total score of 28. That is why that problem must also be tackled first. Table 8.3 schematizes all aspects of this approach.

Table 8.3. Decision matrix

Criteria Problems	Burden for the client 5	Easy to solve 2	Effect on other systems 1	Speed of the solution 2	
Customers are waiting for the host	High - Nothing else for customer to do 3 × 5 = 15	Medium – Regarding host and waiters 2 x 2 = 4	High - Gives the customer a bad start 3 x 1 = 3	High - One can easily see if there are free tables 3 x 2 = 6	28

Customers are waiting for the waiter	Medium – Customers can already eat sandwiches 2 x 5 = 10	Medium – Regarding host and waiters 2 x 2 = 4	Medium – Customer still has the feeling of not getting attention 2X1+2	Low - Waiters are busy all sorts activities 1 x 2 = 2	18
Customers are waiting for food	Medium – Atmosphere is nice to meet you 2 x 5 = 10	Low - Regarding waiters and kitchen 1 x 2 = 2	Medium – Leads to extra trips to kitchen for waiters 2 x 1 = 2	Low - Design of kitchen is limited 1 x 2 = 2	16
Customers are waiting for payment	Low – Customers can wait at a drink 1 x 5 = 5	Medium – Regarding waiters and host 2 x 2 = 4	Medium – Customers standing at a table to wait, can see it 2 x 1 = 4	Low - Automated ticket system is needed 1 x 2 = 2	13

Additions

A lengthy list of alternatives can be shortened with a technique like multivoting. Commonly used criteria are effectiveness, costs, time commitment, support, enthusiasm of the team members, feasibility, and competence. Other criteria include:

Criteria for selecting a problem

- is the problem within the control of the team?
- required resources (e.g., money and people).
- inconvenience to the customer caused by the problem.
- urgency of the problem.
- importance of the team.
- effect on other systems in the organization.
- importance of management.
- degree of difficulty of the solution.
- time required.

Criteria for selecting a solution

- root causes addressed by the solution.
- comprehensiveness of the solution.
- cost to implement solution (e.g., time and money).
- availability of resources (e.g., people and resources).
- ease of implementation.
- time required to fully apply the solution.
- maintenance costs and ease of maintenance.
- support for or resistance to the solution.
- team members' enthusiasm for the solution.
- degree of control the team has over the solution.
- safety and health and environmental factors.
- necessary training.
- effect on other systems.
- effect on customers and suppliers.
- what is the value for the customer.
- possible negative consequences.

Other points of attention

- This matrix can be used to compare views, but it is more suitable for comparing data on different criteria.
- Sub-teams can be formed to collect data on the different criteria.
- Nevertheless, for several criteria, it is sometimes necessary to guess which solution would be best selected. For example: evaluating the necessary tools, the difficulty of a solution, or the time necessary to solve the problem. Therefore, the ranking of the options is only as good as the quality of the assumptions about the solution.

- It is necessary that the desired result in the scale is always indicated with the highest value (5 or 3). Criteria such as cost, resources, and difficulty can cause confusion. Low costs are always the most desirable. If the scale sometimes shows the desired result with a 5 and then again with a 1, you cannot achieve satisfactory results. So low costs should be scored with a 5. You can avoid confusion by scoring "low cost" instead of just "cost" or "ease" instead of "difficulty." Yet another possibility is to clearly indicate what a high and a low-value yield:

  importance: low = 1, high = 5; > cost: high = 1, low = 5; > difficulty: high = 1, low = 5.

If, in a team, the different members give different values to the same criterion, then it is necessary to get people to clarify their scores. This way, they can learn from each other and try to reach a consensus. It is not good to average the scores or to vote for the most popular score.

8.3.3 Multivoting

Description

Multivoting is a technique to narrow down a lengthy list of possibilities to a list of a few priorities or to make a final choice. This technique is preferred over regular voting because it is possible to prioritize items that everyone considers important but which are not given priority.

When

- After a brainstorming session or some other method that results in a lengthy list of possibilities.

- When a list needs to be shortened.

- When a decision must be made based on a group judgment.

Method

- Materials Needed: Flipchart or board, magnets or thumbtacks, five to ten strips of paper for each participant, and writing utensils.

- Show the list of possibilities and then remove the duplicates. You can shorten the list if necessary. You can use an affinity diagram to organize the data.

- Number each item.

- Decide how many items may remain on the final list. Also, decide how many choices each group member may make. Usually, five choices are allowed. For exceedingly long lists, there may be even more.

- All group members individually select the five items they consider most important. They then rank the five items by importance. The most important choice is at the top of the ranking. You can award five points to the most important choice, four points to the second choice, and so on, up to one point to the fifth choice. For example, each chosen item can be written on a separate note with the number of points.

- Counting the votes: collect the pieces of paper, read them one after the other, and put the points next to each item on the board. It is then easy to calculate the totals for each item.

- If a clear decision appears from that process, the process stops. If that is not the case, you can have any differences in points for the most important items substantiated (for example, by those who gave a 5 and a 1). The goal is not to force someone to change their score, but clarification can lead someone to the insight that they should change the number of points.

8.4. Process analysis techniques

Here, I discuss two techniques that are useful in the analysis of processes with a view to preventing errors: the simple Fault Tree Analysis and the Failure Modes & Effects Analysis.

8.4.1. Fault Tree Analysis

The fault tree analysis (Fault Tree Analysis, FTA) is a method to investigate in-depth, but not quantitatively, what can go wrong with the service, the process, or the product. For each form of failure, the question is asked: what is the cause? This creates downward root causes of the failure forms of the process or product. Fault tree analysis is convenient to conduct based on the job structure. The execution is as follows:

- Place a possible defect or failure of the product at the top.

- List all probable causes using logical structures.

- Explore this in-depth so that the problem becomes clear.

- The next step is the FMEA (see section 4.2). Here, the seriousness of the problem is assessed, and practical solutions are looked for.

8.4.2. Failure Modes & Effects Analysis (FMEA)

Description

This method (Failure Mode and Effects Analysis – FMEA) is a step-by-step approach to find all possible failures in a service or process. Failure modes are ways or ways in which something can go wrong. Failure means there are errors or defects, especially those that affect the customer. It concerns both actual and potential failures. Effects Analysis refers to the study of the consequences of those failures. Failures are prioritized according to the severity of their consequences, the frequency with which they occur, and the ease with which they can be detected. The goal of FMEA is to reduce or even avoid failures, starting with the most important ones.

This method can already be used in the planning phase but also later in the process or during aftercare. Ideally, of course, the method starts as early as possible during the planning process to prevent errors in advance. Such an analysis documents and increases knowledge about the risk of errors and is also a useful tool in the pursuit of continuous improvement.

When

The method originated with the US military and was later further developed by the aerospace industry and the automotive industry. The method can be used:

- when a process or service is still under development or when rethinking it.

- before the control process for a new or restructured process or service is developed.

- when improvement goals for an existing process or service are developed.

- to make an error analysis in existing processes.

Method

1. Assemble a cross-functional team with people with different abilities in the process or service, including planners, quality people, people who have contact with customers, and so on.

2. Decide the scope or scope of the analysis. Is it intended for a system, a process, or a service? What limits are there? How detailed? Put everything on a board or flipchart so that it is clear to everyone involved what it is about.

3. Identify the functions of the scope with these questions: what is the purpose of this system, process, or service? What does our customer expect? Use simple but clear sentences: a noun and a verb. The scope can often be subdivided into departments, sub-processes, and so on.

4. For each scope or sub-scope, identify the way things could go wrong. Those are the possible ways of failure. If necessary, you should go back and describe the function in more detail to make sure that the failure modes negatively affect that function.

5. For each failure mode, define the consequences for the system, related processes, the service, the customer, the product, and so on. For example, ask yourself what the customer will experience because of that failure.

6. Then, decide how severe each effect is (E – severity ratio). The severity is shown on a scale of 1 to 10 (1 = negligible, 10 = catastrophic). If a failure mode has more than one consequence, describe only the high severity ratio for that failure mode. Indicate the severity ratio per effect on the FMEA form (Table 8.4).

7. Then, decide all possible root causes for each failure mode. A cause-effect diagram can be used for this.

8. Decide the probability of occurrence for each cause (F – rate ratio). Use a scale of 1 to 10 (1 = almost non-existent chance, 10 = unavoidable). You indicate the ratio per cause on the FMEA form.

9. For each cause, identify the actual forms of control or detection being used. These are tests, procedures, and mechanisms that you already use to prevent the customer

from being confronted with failures. They are forms of control that should prevent the causes from occurring or reduce the likelihood of such happenings.

10. For each type of control, decide the detection ratio (D) or the extent to which that control can detect causes or failure modes after they have occurred, but before the customer must deal with them. Again, a scale of 1 to 10 is helpful (1 = control is confident to detect cause, 10 = control is confident not to detect cause). This can be shown on the FEA form.

11. Then calculate the most important risk (RPN, risk priority number) by multiplying E x F x D. Also, calculate the critical point by multiplying the severity by the probability of occurrence (E x F). Those numbers are a means of ranking potential failures and then acting accordingly.

12. Identify actions to reduce the severity or likelihood of failure. Also, determine who is responsible for the actions.

8.5. Form FMEA

Table 8.4. Form FMEA (Heron Technologies, 2005)

Number	Process Service Product	Possible Failure Mode	Possible Consequences	Severity Rate S	Possible Causes	Frequency Rate F	Current Method of Detection Detection Rate D	Possible Actions	Responsible and End Date
1									
2									
3									
4									

Source: Adapted from Heron Technologies (2005).

1. *Severity ratio*

   10 Dangerously high – failure can cause severe damage

9 Very high – failure leads to non-compliance with legal requirements

8 Very high – failure results in clients not getting what they expect

7 High – failure leads to client dissatisfaction

6 Medium – failure cannot be corrected in the short term

5 Low – failure leads to client complaints

4 Very low – failure can be corrected but will slow down the process

3 Minimal – failure will cause client annoyance but can be rectified without slowing down the process

2 Minor – failure is not noticed by the client and has only a minor effect on the process

1 None – failure is not noticed and has no effect on the process

2. *Frequency ratio (probability of failure)*

10 Extremely often – more than once a day

9 Very often – once every three days

8 Often – once a week

7 Very regularly – once a month

6 Regularly – once every three months

5 Intermittently – once every six months

4 Occasionally – once a year

3 Low – once every three years

2 Low – once every five years

1 Nil – once in more than five years

3. *Detection rate (probability of prompt detection)*

10 Virtually impossible – no inspection or defect not detectable

9 Very unlikely – random check

8 Unlikely – spot check

7 Very low – product or process is controlled entirely manually

6 Low – product or process is controlled entirely manually with a go/no-go or other forms of error prevention

5 Medium – some form of statistical process control is performed

4 Above average – some form of statistical process control is performed with immediate response to out-of-bounds

3 Likely – a qualified statistical process control is being performed with a critical tolerance limit

2 Very likely – all products are checked fully automatically

1 Almost certain – the defect is clearly visible, or fully automatic control takes place with regular calibration and preventive maintenance of the control equipment

8.6. Planning techniques

As planning techniques, I discuss here the Gantt Chart and the Process Decision Program Chart.

8.5.1. Gantt Chart

Description

A Gantt Chart (milestone chart, activity chart) is a bar chart that shows the different tasks of a project with the time needed. As the project progresses, you should be able to see on the map which tasks have already been completed. You can also choose the person responsible for each task.

When

- To schedule and monitor tasks in a project.

- To communicate the planning and status of a project.

- When the steps, their sequence, and the time schedule in a process or project are known.

- When it is not necessary to show which tasks depend on the completion of the earlier tasks.

Method

1. Identify the tasks:

   - Identify the tasks required to complete a project.

   - Identify the milestones in a project by brainstorming or developing an Ishikawa chart.

   - Decide the time needed for each task.

   - Identify the sequence: which task must be completed before the next one can begin? What can happen at the same time? Which task must be completed before a milestone can be spoken of?

   - Draw a horizontal timeline on the axis from the bottom to the top of the sheet. Create a scale that fits the problem.

2. Plot the tasks and milestones on the X-axis. Mark which tasks are necessary and which are not. On the right side, you indicate when the task must be finished.

3. Verify that each job is indeed on the card.

4. As tasks and activities take place, mark them on the map. Also, indicate to what extent the tasks have already been completed.

5. Draw vertical lines to show where you are on the timeline.

Example

Figure 8.7 shows a Gantt Chart for a benchmarking study. Twelve weeks are indicated on the timeline. Also, two milestones are indicated. The map shows the situation in week 5. The dark-colored parts have been completed; the lighter parts refer to activities that still need to be conducted. The practices have, therefore, been chosen, and the right benchmarking partners are being looked for.

Additions

   - Sometimes, columns can be added that show detailed information, such as the expected time, resources needed, or the person responsible for the activity.

- The process of constructing a Gantt Chart requires group members to clearly understand what is needed and what activities must be performed to conduct a task. Of course, it is necessary to keep the map up to date. Naturally, it is necessary to keep the map updated as a project progresses, making it possible to foresee estimation problems.

- It is useful to indicate important moments or milestones in color.

Figure 8.7. Sample Gantt Chart

ACTIVITY	WEEK											
	1	2	3	4	5	6	7	8	9	10	11	12
Develop a broad plan												
Present the plan to the council												
Form a team												
Train the team												
Develop a detailed plan												
Conduct preliminary research												
Identify practice, indicators, and documentation												
Identify benchmark partners and schedule visits												
Collect public data												
Analyze the data												
Develop the benchmark questions												
Visit the benchmark partners												

8.5.2. Process Decision Program Chart

Description

The Process Decision Program Chart (PDPC) systematically identifies what could go wrong in a plan that is still in development. Measures can then be taken to prevent or reverse the problems. With the help of this tool, you can also possibly revise the plan to avoid future problems or to be ready when a problem does arise.

When

- Before implementing a plan, especially for important and complex plans.

- When the plan must be executed within certain time limits.

- When the price of failure is remarkably high.

Method

- Develop a tree diagram of the proposed plan. It must be a multi-level diagram. After the goal at the first level, the second level holds the most important activities, and the third level is the tasks that are necessary to realize those activities.

- For each of the third-level tasks, there is brainstorming about what could go wrong.

- Examine all potential problems. Cut the problems that are unlikely or whose consequences are meaningless. The problems that then remain are linked to each task at the fourth level.

- Then, there is brainstorming about countermeasures for each of the potential problems. These may include changes to the plan or actions that could counteract the problem if it were to occur. Those countermeasures are then linked to the problems at the fifth level of the tree in a clear layout.

- Then, examine how practical or realistic each countermeasure is. Use criteria such as cost, time, ease of implementation, and effectiveness. The practical countermeasures can then be indicated with an O the unrealistic with an X.

Some questions to identify potential problems

- What input do we need? Are unwanted inputs linked to good input?

- What output do we expect? Can other results also occur?

- What can that problem do? Can something else or something more happen?

- Does it depend on actions, circumstances, or events? Are they controllable or not?

- What cannot be changed, or what is frozen?

- Have we foreseen a margin of error?

- Which assumptions might be wrong?

- What experiences have we had with similar situations in the past?

- How different is this situation from earlier situations?

- If we wanted that failure ourselves, how would we manage it?

Example

A group plans to improve care for patients with chronic conditions, such as diabetes and asthma, with a new chronic disease management program. The group has defined four basic elements and established the basic components for each of those elements. That information is shown in Figure 8.8.

Dashed lines represent the parts of the map that have been omitted. Only some of the possible problems and countermeasures are shown in the figure. For example, one of the potential problems with goal setting is patient relapse. The team believes it makes sense for each patient to have a buddy or sponsor and wants to add that measure to the program. Other aspects of the map help them develop the plan better, such as a visit by all team members to a clinic with a Chronic Illness Management Program (CIMP). Other aspects also allow problems to be taken into account in advance, such as training for CIMP nurses on how to guide patients who choose unrealistic goals.

Figure 8.8. Sample Process Decision Program Chart

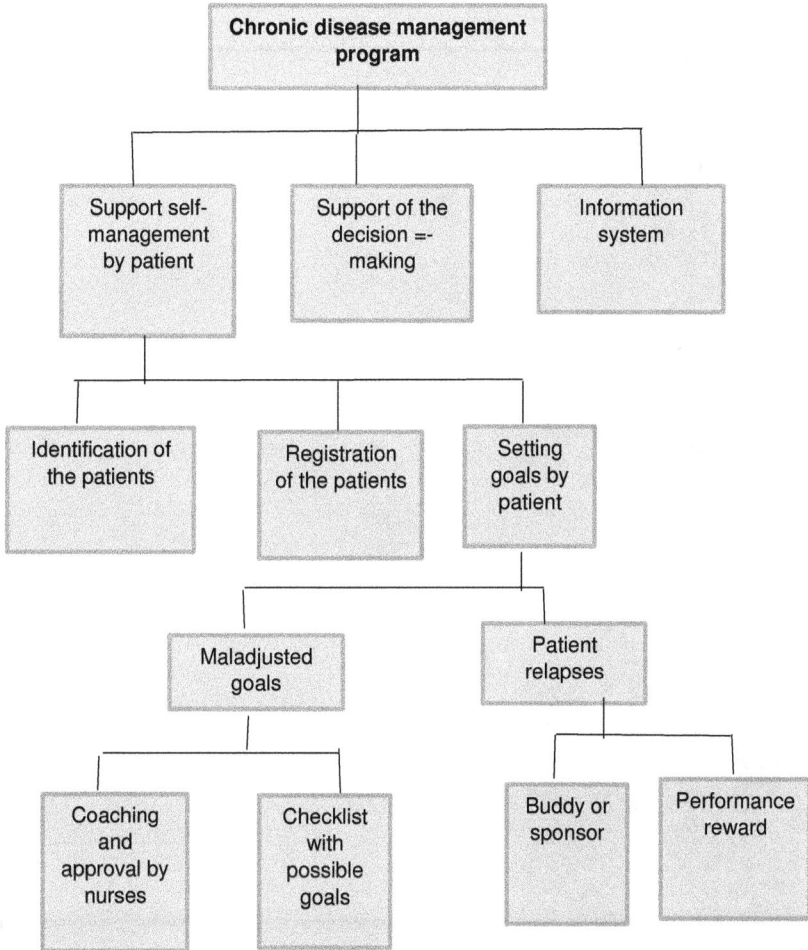

Source: Modified fromTague (2004).

Chapter 9

A new perspective on quality

9.1. The challenges

Although quality assurance has gained a foothold in the West since the 1970s, today, its traditional approach is open to criticism. The result is that employees in organizations often have little enthusiasm for a systematic approach to quality. This is a problem because people have become more aware consumers and have ever higher demands on the quality of services and products. Therefore, it is necessary to bear in mind a few pitfalls before clarifying our own vision of quality development.

First, too often, quality is experienced as an expression of the modern pursuit of controllability, and that arouses resistance, certainly in the nonprofit sector. If quality management is understood as perfect control of the process, it is counterproductive. The illusion of manageability then requires more energy than it yields: more organization, more administration, and more technology in the professional approach. Moreover, it threatens to be at the expense of interpersonal connection and solidarity.

A second issue is the one-sided pursuit of efficiency. The tendency of the government to rely heavily on procedures and protocols that are evidence-based may promote efficiency but not necessarily effectiveness in terms of quality, meaningful care, services, or education. In the nonprofit sector, the core processes are often unpredictable and cannot be calculated in advance in terms of time and resources.

Third, the requirement of objectivity creates the illusion that quality has nothing to do with values but everything to do with objective control of processes and goal orientation. Quality could then be a kind of measurable perfection.

The consequence of these issues is the threat of moral displeasure and the demotivation of the employees working in the nonprofit sector. The requirement to tackle everything more efficiently to still meet the imposed quality indicators causes much stress and less job satisfaction. There is usually little room left for professional dreams, inspiration, or enthusiasm. Therefore, employees experience the formal part of registration and assessment/accreditation as alienating.

Finally, employees too often do not experience quality as an added value for themselves but as a burden that makes it more difficult to perform their core tasks to a high standard. I conclude that there is an urgent need for a different approach to quality.

9.2. Quality development makes the difference

To overcome the issues I reviewed in the previous section, we need an innovative approach to quality. It starts by considering the specific nature of the nonprofit sector.

9.2.1. The specificity of the nonprofit sector

The specificity of the nonprofit sector can be characterized as a set of relational practices that develop between the client, service provider, and other stakeholders. The consequence is that not all relationships and processes are manageable, externally controllable, or objectively measurable. The essence of a process in the nonprofit sector, namely the relationships between people who develop their identities and personalities in the process, is difficult to fit into a traditional control-oriented concept of quality.

Quality always relates to a dimension of a complex process. It can be about the quality of the process, about the characteristics of the product or result, about the satisfaction of customers and other stakeholders, which can be quite different, about the meaningfulness of the vision and the project itself.

The nature of the nonprofit sector advocates integrating the core processes of care, services, education, and culture in quality development. That process must be redesigned repeatedly, considering new social developments, new needs and expectations of stakeholders, and new insights. Neither the goals nor the course itself can be definitively decided. Moreover, it is not a process that can only be conducted according to fixed standards because the actors in the process are constantly faced with the challenge of working together—in interaction with each other—to realize the goals of the nonprofit sector. The process cannot, therefore, be captured in standards or strict, predictable procedures.

Ideally, the organization develops its own system that guarantees internal reflection and critical questioning. In this way, it can adjust during the process and does not have to wait for an external assessment to indicate pain points or shortcomings. When an organization systematically integrates quality into its operations, there is a good chance that it will also remain alert to new developments in its sector. Self-evaluation then becomes a stimulus for innovation.

9.2.2. Quality development

There is a need for consistent involvement of all levels of the organization and external stakeholders in the development of a vision for the organization and its realization. The ability and experience of all stakeholders must be fully recognized and given space. This is accompanied by a different relationship between the management of the organization and the stakeholders.

Quality development is now everyone's business. The conviction prevails that working on quality is not only, and not primarily, a matter of procedures, criteria, and protocols but, above all, of relational practices. Quality development should ultimately be a concrete way of working that ensures that the quality, both of process and of content, can continuously increase during the interaction between the different actors.

Each organization must give shape to its pursuit of quality in its own way. Quality is, therefore, tailor-made and embedded in a specific context.

The development dimension is based on self-management by organizations. Moreover, development permanently challenges organizations to keep reflecting on the vision of care, services, and education and on the process itself. This requires continuous learning and innovation, both on an individual and a collective level. When an organization reaches that stage, one can speak of a quality culture.

Every organization is unique and, to a certain extent, completely different from other organizations, with its own relationships with the world around it. Moreover, the boundaries of an organization are no longer fixed. Modern organizations are members of multiple, often temporary, networks with other organizations.

Because of different visions, experiences, and expectations, it is not easy, but it is necessary to arrive at a common vision of quality. An organization should, therefore, invest sufficient time and energy in a dialogue between all stakeholders and in clarifying what quality means for each of them. In the end, everyone should strive for at least the same organizational goals. The recurring dialogue between parties who are equal and who accept the power of arguments is a precondition for arriving at a relational practice.

Failures of quality projects have much to do with poor or even absent employee participation. If we want to develop quality development as a relational practice, the participation of everyone in all phases of quality development is necessary. Interactive participation is a collection of working methods in which people contribute to the development and implementation of projects through discussions and a joint search for solutions. True participation involves employees at every stage of the process. Joint decision-making implies that interested parties may not only mediate in the planning but may also bear partial responsibility for the implementation and adjustment of the decisions.

Leaders must be adapted to this interactive participation. They must stimulate the mindset that all stakeholders are building quality together. Empowerment of everyone in the organization is therefore an important condition for interactive participation.

9.2.3. Appreciative approach

I opt for an appreciative approach. Traditional quality assurance starts with a problem-solving approach. It is based on the conviction that quality is a problem that must be solved. The appreciative approach, on the other hand, sees quality development as a challenge that can mobilize the energy of everyone in the organization. Thinking from the perspective of problems and weaknesses leads, at most, to the desire to eliminate shortcomings but does not stimulate the ambition to be exceptionally good. The appreciative approach starts from the strengths and possibilities of the organization. It can also be a lever for quality development, fueled by the enthusiasm for an inspiring future perspective and not by the disappointment of shortages. Of course, the appreciative approach also starts from a specific vision of the organization: it sees organizations as centers of human connection. Relationships only really come to life in an organization when there is an appreciative eye. That is, people are willing to see the best in each other. They share their dreams and take care of each other in an appreciative way. Together, they are committed to not only creating a new but a better world.

9.2.4. Values

It is necessary that the critical discussion about what makes a life of high quality be held in the nonprofit sector, and that cannot be a value-free discussion. Choosing solidarity, equal opportunities, human development, independence, sustainability, respect for people and nature, and social self-sufficiency—in short, choosing what makes life humane and of high quality—requires a clear commitment to values.

Any organization that consciously thinks about and is concerned with its place and role in society starts from a value perspective, whether explicitly stated or not. Such a perspective holds the basic values that should guide the behavior of the members of the organization. Examples are integrity, independence, customer focus, freedom, justice, fairness, and trust. Values are, therefore, about the ethical dimension of an organization and reflect what the organization believes in. For nonprofits, the value perspective is typically quite complex. Some organizations start from an ideology--just think of political parties, pillar organizations, or religious and philosophical groups.

Other organizations have a broad social goal in mind. Examples include environmental organizations, movements that strive for a fair distribution of goods or for solidarity, and so on.

9.3. From vision to realization

Every quality development program needs some form of evaluation. For too long, this has been interpreted unilaterally as measuring. This is one of the reasons why the term "quality management" in the nonprofit sector has long been viewed in a less positive light.

Unfortunately, measurement in the practice of traditional quality assurance has been reduced to collecting figures. This way of thinking ignores what really matters in quality development, namely keeping the organization focused on its goals based on information as well as checking whether and how the organization has achieved its goals. Additionally, the organization's policy and approach must be adjusted where necessary. Quality is about valuable information and not numbers in themselves. In addition to figures, qualitative data are also especially important. Employee stories express in their own way how the organization works towards its goals. Moreover, those stories help to discover the meaning behind the pure numbers. Without wanting to deny the importance of meaningful measurements, evaluation can also take place with qualitative methods. Therefore, in our vision of quality development, there must be room for a narrative approach.

A one-sided emphasis on figures also arouses resistance because these practices are quickly linked to control and therefore, to order. Without control, there is no order, no balance, no manageability. However, such a conception of measurement carries the risk of becoming particularly destructive to quality development. The reasoning is that control would make sense only if organizations behaved like machines. However, organizations are organisms that dynamically interact with their environment and constantly develop internally. Processes are more important than fixed structures. Wanting to implement a rigid structure through measurement and control is, therefore, disastrous for an organization's development opportunities. However, we are not advocating a laissez-faire attitude. Again, it is our belief that the core of the processes in the nonprofit sector, what goes on in relational practices, cannot be measured with numbers.

An organization must be willing and able to account for itself internally and externally, among other things, about the realization of its goals, the use of resources, and the deployment of people. However, accountability must take place in interaction with employees, stakeholders, and the environment. Quantitative measurement has a limited value in this context if it is framed in the stories of the organization. Accountability also means investigating how and to what extent the organization dynamically deals with what presents itself from within the organization itself and from the environment.

Quality development also requires the organization to have the creativity to constantly take on new challenges. Where the terms quality care and the associated quality assurance suggest a commitment to safety and stability, the term quality development fits better in a dynamic approach. Of course, this does not mean that an organization floats on the waves like a rudderless ship to an unknown destination. In this context, sustainability means that the organization cherishes the good things and is open to situations that can optimize its quality. At the same time, the perspective of a sustainable future implies that the organization is always aware of the consequences of its actions and of its responsibility to society.

Appendix.
Key thinkers and ideas

It's not enough to just do your best or work hard.
You must know what to work on.

—William Deming

Looking back at the history of quality management, starting after World War II and up to the present, we must recognize the work of several people, each of whom has made specific contributions. Integral quality development has many fathers but no mothers yet. We briefly sketch the lives of each of these fathers and then explain their ideas. Within the scope of this book, that can only be brief.

1. William Edwards Deming

1.1. Life and work

William Edwards Deming was born in Sioux City, Iowa, on October 14, 1900. Edwards was his mother's name. He was trained as an electrical engineer and then studied mathematics, physics, and music (he played various instruments and composed masses and cantatas). He died on December 20, 1993, in Washington (www.asq.org). For 40 years, Deming was a global consultant for railroads, telephone companies, factories, hospitals, government departments, and research organizations. He became best known for his work in Japan, where he started in 1950 and realized a true revolution in quality and economic production. In May 1960, the Japanese Emperor awarded him the Second Order Medal of the Sacred Treasure for this work. Deming is one of the most important authors in the field of quality management. He taught the Japanese the principles of quality management, giving them a major advantage over American and European industries. He stated, among other things, that the inferior quality of American products was not the result of bad labor but of bad management. He did not formulate grand theories, but he did formulate the famous fourteen points for management.

1.2. Fourteen points of attention

1. Set goals for continuous improvement

The will to improve should be a permanent goal. This means that management must supply sufficient resources in the long term to be able to deliver quality work. That is, of course, in contrast with the pursuit of a quick return. Quality management needs time to lead to results. Japan took 25 years (starting in the 1950s and not gaining recognition until the 1970s) to be recognized as a quality leader.

2. Choose a new philosophy

As economic life has changed dramatically, Western industry must rise to the challenge and pay attention to change. Deming suffered from planned lethargy. In this new economy, customers also have other wishes that companies must meet. Customers don't want problems with what they buy. Customer satisfaction, therefore, becomes an important goal.

3. Stop mass inspections

In many organizations and companies, the responsibility for quality lies solely with the quality department. By the time the product arrives at inspection, all is lost: the quality department can only decide whether the product meets the specifications. Quality must be realized at the source. Everyone in the production process is, therefore, jointly responsible for quality work.

4. Stop doing business based on the price tag

The total cost is important. But it is also important to build a long-term relationship with suppliers based on loyalty and trust. This contrasts with the practice of using many suppliers and then having them compete against each other. In practice, this led to an overemphasis on costs and an increase in the variability of raw materials and inventories.

5. Systematically improve the production and service system

The production system includes not only the development process, planning, training, and production but also the after-delivery service. If that system does not function properly, it is usually the result of poor management.

6. Install on-the-job training

To be able to work at a prominent level, employees must be professionally trained.

7. Improve leadership

The purpose of supervision should be to help people perform their duties better. Management supervision is also necessary. Leadership is the basis of quality improvement. It is not enough that only the quality managers are involved with the employees; a clear and real commitment from management is also necessary. Without the support of management, quality projects must fail.

8. Remove fear so that everyone can work effectively for the organization

This concerns employees who do not dare to admit that there are problems or who are afraid of change. Too often, employees who see problems and strive for change are perceived as a nuisance. Often, employees are also afraid that changes will lead to layoffs. Restructuring and re-engineering is often the easiest solution and synonymous with downsizing. After such "solutions," we often must conclude that the organization has not become more creative in finding solutions.

9. Break down the dividing walls between departments

It is important that employees from different departments work together as a team to solve problems. Too often, departments work independently and blame each other for problems. Sometimes, that is simply the result of organizational design, leading to sequential or departmental approaches. This leads to delays and problems. A process approach forces the different departments to work together.

10. Eliminate slogans, exhortations, and goals that impose zero-error standards or new productivity standards

Employees often cannot do much about quality defects. Such incentives, therefore, have a negative effect on relationships. By demanding zero errors or increased productivity, managers are sending the message to employees that they are the cause of the shortages. If structural improvements and better work equipment are not made, these incentives will lead to discouragement and demotivation of the employees. Training and empowerment of employees, on the other hand, can have a motivating effect and thus stimulate quality.

11. Eliminate work standards

Techniques such as management by goals or management by numbers and quantitative goals are counterproductive. Deming was very opposed to measuring all kinds of performance in the workplace. The reason is simple: if quantity is the norm, quality must lose out. If employees realize the high quantitative standards, they are even more difficult to motivate for quality improvement because they already meet the standard.

12. Remove barriers that prevent employees from taking pride in the quality of their work

People who are hired on an hourly basis for physical work often suffer from low morale and low involvement. Managers who are not leaders usually worsen that problem by not trusting those people and believing in their competence and sense of responsibility.

13. Develop an education and self-improvement program

According to Deming, learning in an organization is a matter of using the creativity of the employees and developing the competence to keep what has been learned in the organization. The ISO program, among other things, helps organizations embed their improvements. Quality manuals can be useful to document processes and procedures. It is also necessary that the organization reward and reinforce the learning of employees. That is difficult in an authoritarian organization in which management is convinced that it knows best.

14. Put everyone in the organization to work to help bring about the transformation

Transformation to better quality is a task for everyone in the organization. It is, therefore, necessary that a system of total quality care be developed in the organization.

1.3. "Deadly Diseases"

Deming also identifies several "deadly diseases" that prevent countries from delivering top quality and staying competitive in the global market:

- no stable target.

- too much emphasis on short-term benefits.

- performance measurements.

- management mobility.

- running an organization based on visible numbers alone.

- excessive costs for employee health care.

- excessive costs for warranties.

Deming calls his approach "the theory of deep knowledge." In-depth knowledge implies a broad vision and understanding of the individual, but in fact, truly interdependent elements that together form a broader system: the organization. He believes in the almost unlimited potential of every employee, provided they can work in an environment that supports, develops, and nurtures their sense of pride and responsibility. According to Deming, 85 percent of an employee's effectiveness is decided by his environment and only minimally by his own skills.

A manager who wants to create such an environment must:

- Have a psychological understanding of individuals and groups.

- Remove tools such as production quotas and slogans that only alienate employees from their supervisors and fuel competition among employees.

- Transforming an organization into a large team with sub-teams all working on various aspects of the same goal. Divisions between departments often give rise to rivalry, conflicting goals, and unnecessary competition. It is important that fear, anger, and feelings of revenge are kept out of the work environment. That is why profits should be shared between teams and not between individual employees.

In such organizations, employees will have a better understanding of their jobs, specific tasks and techniques, and higher values. If they are stimulated and empowered in this way, they will perform better.

Finally, we mention the so-called Deming circle. With this figure, Deming shows the four necessary steps that must lead to permanent quality improvement, namely Plan, Do, Check, and Act. Another commonly used term for this figure is the PDCA circle. Later, Deming reformulated the PDCA to PDSA and replaced "Check" with "Study" because the C(heck) could be too strongly associated with control.

2. Joseph Juran

2.1. Life and work

Joseph Juran was born in 1904 into a poor Jewish family in Braila, Romania. Five years later, his father left for America, and after three years, he had earned enough to bring his family to the new country. However, the family also lived in poverty in Minnesota (www.asq.org). From an early age, Joseph proved to be very eager to learn. He got such superior results in math and general science that he skipped four years of school.

At the age of sixteen, he enrolled in university, the first in his family to receive higher education. In 1925, he graduated as an electrical engineer. He went to work in the inspection department of the prestigious Hawthorne Works in Chicago, a complex company with forty thousand employees. In 1926, a team of quality control pioneers introduced a new program at Hawthorne designed to introduce new techniques and tools. In 1937, Juran became head of the engineering division of Western Electric, headquartered in New York. During World War II, he spent four years as an assistant in the Lend-Lease Administration in Washington. He and his team improved process efficiency and eliminated unnecessary paperwork to speed up the transportation of parts to America's overseas allies. In 1945, he left Washington to devote the rest of his life to the study of quality management. At the end of the war, he was a well-known and respected statistician and theoretical engineer. He became head of the Department of Administrative Engineering at New York University, where he taught for many years.

He also built up his own consultancy practice, authored many books and gave many presentations to the American Management Association. During that period, he also developed his management philosophies, which now form the basis of American and Japanese management. His classic *Quality Control Handbook* from 1951, is still a standard work. Juran finds three basic processes essential to quality assurance: planning, improvement, and control (see Table 9.1).

Table 9.1. Basic processes for quality assurance according to Juran

Quality planning	• Identify who the customers are • Determine the needs of the customers • Translate those needs into our language • Develop a product that meets the needs • Optimize the features of the product so that it meets both our needs and the customer's requirements
Quality improvement	• Develop a process to produce the product • Optimize that process
Quality control	• Evidence that the process can produce the product in conditions requiring a minimum of inspection

Source: Adapted from Juran. www.juran.org

3. Philip Crosby

"Do something right the first time."

3.1. Life and work

Philip Crosby was born in West Virginia in 1926. He served in the military during World War II and the Korean War. He then worked for various companies such as Crosley, Martin-Marietta, and ITT (at ITT, he was vice president for fourteen years). Philip Crosby Associates, Inc., founded in 1979, was his management consulting firm. After his retirement in 1991, he founded Career IV, Inc., Philip Crosby Associates II, Inc., and The Quality College. Phil Crosby died in August 2001.

3.2. Thoughts

Deming and Juran are undoubtedly the great minds of the quality revolution. It is to Phil Crosby's credit that he has developed a terminology that mere mortals can understand. His books *Quality Without Tears* and *Quality is Free* are easy to read, and he popularizes the idea of the "cost of poor quality."

His ideas come from his experiences with production lines. He emphasizes the importance of zero defects. Of course, this is not only the responsibility of the production department. To achieve this, management must set the tone and create the right atmosphere. If management does not create the conditions to work with zero defects and does not set zero defects as a clear goal, the employees cannot be held responsible for what goes wrong. The benefit of this approach is less time and fewer materials wasted on things that consumers don't want.

Crosby defines quality as "a conformity to certain specifications set forth by management and not some vague concept of "goodness." These standards are not set arbitrarily but must be derived from the needs of the customers. Four absolute principles of quality management are:

1. Quality should be defined as "meet requirements" and not as "good" or "elegant."

2. The system for achieving quality is prevention, not evaluation afterward.

3. The performance standard should be "zero defects" and not "that's about right."

4. Measuring quality is the price paid for not meeting standards; it is not an indicator.

3.3. Fourteen steps to quality improvement

1. Management should be committed to quality in a way that is visible to all.

2. Create quality improvement teams that include employees from all departments.

3. Measure processes to find any current and future quality issues.

4. Calculate the cost of inferior quality.

5. Stimulate the quality awareness of all employees.

6. Take action to improve quality problems.

7. Monitor progress in quality assurance—set up a zero-defects working group.

8. Train supervisors in quality assurance.

9. Organize zero-defect days.

10. Encourage employees to set their own quality goals.

11. Promote communication between employees and management about obstacles to achieving quality.

12. Recognize employee efforts.

13. Create quality boards.

14. Start again and again—quality improvement never ends.

3.4. Five characteristics of an 'eternally successful organization'

Crosby's ideal was an eternally successful organization. He summarized this ideal in five characteristics:

1. People have a habit of getting things right the first time.

2. Change is anticipated and used to the benefit of the organization.

3. Growth is consistent and profitable.

4. New products and services are developed when necessary.

5. Everyone is happy to work in the organization.

4. Kaoru Ishikawa

4.1. Life and work

Kaoru Ishikawa wanted to change the way people think about work. He urged managers to resist the tendency to be content with improving the quality of the product alone because quality assurance can still go one step further (www.asq.org).

His understanding of company-wide quality control emphasizes the importance of continuous customer service. This means that the customer continues to receive service even after he has already received the product. This service must be present throughout the organization, at all levels (including the management level), and must even permeate the everyday lives of all those involved. According to Ishikawa, quality improvement is a continuous process that can still develop further.

With his cause-effect diagram, also known as the Ishikawa diagram or fishbone diagram, he made an important contribution to quality thinking. This diagram allows the user to see all the causes of a problem and the origin of the process imperfections. This diagram also enables quality improvement from the bottom up. Deming also used the diagram as one of the first tools in the quality assurance process.

Ishikawa also demonstrated the importance of several quality tools, such as the control chart, the histogram, the scatter plot, the Pareto chart, and the flowchart. The concept of "quality circles" also originates from him. Ishikawa was convinced of the need for top management support and leadership. He insisted that the top should also follow quality courses because he knew that without the support of the top, the quality programs would not stand a chance. Ishikawa also emphasized that quality should be checked throughout the process, not just during the production process but also during planning, preparation, and aftercare. He then stated that standards and norms themselves should also be evaluated. Standards are not an end in themselves—customer satisfaction is. He emphasized that managers must constantly adapt to customer needs.

Ishikawa also paid close attention to the principles developed by other quality thinkers, such as Deming's Plan-Do-Check-Act model. Ishikawa expanded Deming's four principles to six:

1. Set goals.

2. Decide methods to achieve those goals.

3. Invest in training.

4. Implement work.

5. Check the effects of the introduction.

6. Take proper action.

4.2. Quality circles

Ishikawa introduced the concept of a quality circle and aimed to:

- support the improvement and development of the organization.

- respect human relations at work and promote job satisfaction.

- unlocking the potential of employees.

He was convinced that the concern for quality should permeate the entire organization and should include the product, the service, the management, and the employees.

Many, such as Juran and Crosby, believe that Ishikawa's teachings are more successful in Japan than in the West. Quality circles are effective if management understands statistical quality assurance techniques and if it is also committed to implementing the recommendations.

5. Genichi Taguchi

5.1. Life and work

Genichi Taguchi was born on January 1, 1924. He studied textile engineering. After World War II, he worked for the Japanese Ministry of Health and Welfare. He conducted the first national survey on health and nutrition. He also applied his quality improvement techniques in the pharmaceutical industry, and he even worked for a caramel manufacturer to reduce the melting of caramels at room temperature.

Taguchi was best known for his "Quality Loss Function" and for methods to optimize quality in the planning phase. He also received recognition for his work, including the Deming Award. (www.asq.org).

5.2. The method

Taguchi sees quality loss throughout the product's journey to the customer, including costs of scrap, reuse, interruptions, warranty requirements, and reduced market share. The increasing customer dissatisfaction can also be expressed in financial terms when the performance of the product drops below the desired performance level. At the same time, he also expresses the increasing costs of a process that reaches a higher level than the desired one. Deciding the target is a guess based on customer surveys and customer feedback.

The quality loss function makes it possible to make financial decisions (at the design stage) about the costs necessary to achieve the desired level of performance.

Quality should be based on robust design, not quality by inspection. According to Taguchi, the design process has three phases:

1. The design of the system, including the development of a prototype.

2. The design of the parameters implies experimentation to find out which factors have the most influence on the performance of the product.

3. The design of the tolerance includes defining strict tolerance limits for critical factors and less strict tolerance limits for minor factors. The designer should focus on reducing the variance in the critical or particularly key factors. Minor factors are those that have a limited or even negligible impact on the performance of the product.

An example

Suppose you are a manufacturer who wants to produce biscuits from raw materials. There are several factors that you can vary in the production process, such as the amount of flour, the number of eggs, the temperature of the butter, the heat of the oven, the baking time, and so on. With the Taguchi method for a powerful design, you first set up experiments to assess the number of combinations of all those factors. For example: working with a low and a high oven temperature, with short and long baking times, with one or more eggs, and so on. The cookies from each experiment are then evaluated for their quality—in other words, they are tasted. A statistical analysis would then tell you the key factors in the process (for example, that the oven temperature influences the quality of the biscuits more than the number of eggs). With that knowledge, you can then develop a process that, for example, ensures that the oven keeps the best temperature and makes it possible to consistently bake good cookies.

After World War II, many Japanese companies struggled to survive with limited resources. It is partly thanks to Taguchi that the country did not continue to struggle but was able to flourish. Taguchi revolutionized the production process by cutting costs. He understood very well that the production process is strongly influenced by external factors. It is to his credit that he developed a method to detect these external factors.

6. Vilfredo Pareto

Vilfredo Pareto was an Italian economist and sociologist. He became well known for his mathematical applications to economic analysis. Pareto was born in 1848 to a Genevan father and a French mother. He studied engineering at the University of Turin. The first two years of that training consisted of mathematics, which strongly influenced his intellectual insights. In 1870, he graduated with a dissertation entitled "The Fundamental Principles of Equilibrium in Solid Bodies." This already reflected his interest in the analyses of equilibrium, which he would later put to effective use in economics and sociology.

Pareto worked as an engineer from 1873 to 1893. While living in Florence, he studied philosophy and politics and authored several articles, being one of the first to analyze economic problems with mathematical tools. In 1893, he became a professor at the University of Lausanne. He died in 1923 in Geneva.

Pareto's first work, *Cours d'économie politique* (1896-1897), contained his well-known law of income distribution, a complicated mathematical formulation in which he tried to prove that the distribution of income and wealth in a society is not a coincidence but a consistent pattern that becomes visible in history, in all societies and countries.

In his *Manuale di Economia Politica* (1906) and *Manuel d'économie politique* (1909)—a translation of the Italian work with a fully mathematical appendix—he laid the foundations for modern welfare economics. He describes the concept of the "pareto optimum," in which he states that the best allocation of resources in a society is not achieved if it is possible for at least one individual to get better, according to his own estimation, while the others still are the same as before.

His most important sociological works deal with the theory of the circulation of elites. Pareto wrote a sociology of the political process, in which history is a succession of elites. Those with superior ability in the lower social groups try to challenge the ruling elite in the higher social groups or even take their places and become a ruling minority themselves. This pattern repeats itself over and over.

7. Masaaki Imai

7.1. Life and work

Masaaki Imai was born in Tokyo in 1930 and studied business administration at the University of Tokyo. He is considered the father of Kaizen, or the Japanese method of continuous improvement. In 1962, he founded Cambridge Corporation, a consultancy firm for the top Japanese companies. In 1986, he founded the Kaizen Institute in Austin, Texas, to introduce the Kaizen principles to Western organizations and companies. He is the author of nine books on Kaizen and related management topics.

Imai laughs at Western managers who forget to use their common sense. In his opinion, Western managers are not so much interested in common sense. (Imai, 2012).

7.2. Principles

Imai took quality thinking a step further with his insights about improvement. According to him, improvement must be continuous. Imai brings an important nuance to the term "improvement": on the one hand, there is Kaizen, and on the other hand, there is innovation (Imai, 1998).

Kaizen is then specifically the implementation of small improvements in an existing situation, and that requires continuous effort. Kaizen is a continuous process, the results of which are visible in the long term.

Innovation is a radical change in an existing situation through major investments in modern technology and/or equipment. In general, innovation is a one-time process where the result is quickly visible. The approach is based on three pillars:

1. Policy deployment: Policy aimed at the implementation of Kaizen.

2. Cross-functional management: In addition to design, production, and sales, attention is paid to aspects of business operations, such as quality, costs, and delivery reliability.

3. Quality function deployment: Puts the customer at the center of quality care thinking. The expectations of the customer form the basis for the product specifications, which are translated into technical properties.

Moreover, Kaizen contrasts process-oriented thinking with result-oriented thinking. Process-oriented thinking values employee characteristics such as diligence, morale, commitment, and fighting spirit as much as the results they achieve. Organizations must, therefore, also measure with process-oriented criteria that are clearly different from result-oriented criteria—for example, the amount of time spent searching for customers (process-oriented) versus the amount of revenue and added value obtained from customer orders (result-oriented). Recognition of efforts should, therefore, not be confused with recognition of results.

7.3. Approach

The Kaizen approach to problem-solving begins with acknowledging that a problem exists. A problem is an opportunity for improvement. Kaizen needs both a top-down and a bottom-up approach. The quality approach takes place at three levels in the organization (Tarlengo, 2023):

1. Management focuses on improving systems and procedures.

2. Groups are formed to focus on improving practices and setting standards in the organization.

3. Individuals focus on workplace improvements.

Kaizen should be introduced from top to bottom. But the ideas for Kaizen must go from the bottom up (a kind of suggestion box). By submitting ideas, all employees can take part in Kaizen in the workplace and play a significant role in an improved way of working. Employees should be encouraged to report minor defects. There is an opportunity for improvement, and this could prevent a severe problem from arising.

Requirements for a Kaizen program to succeed are:

1. Obtaining acceptance from the employees.

2. Removing their resistance to change.

To achieve this, the following is needed:

- Continually improve relationships within the company.

- Emphasize training and education of employees.

- Develop informal leadership among employees.

- Set up small group activities, e.g., improvement teams.

- Support and recognize employee commitment to Kaizen.

- Make the workplace a place where employees can pursue their life purpose.

- Train supervisors and department heads to deal better (and more personally) with their employees.

What Kaizen's efforts are about can be summarized in four words: satisfied internal and external customers!

Most problems related to product or service quality can be solved with a few simple tools that many people are familiar with and that are easy to use. We discussed some of these tools in Chapter 8.

7.4. The Ten Kaizen Rules (Muscad, 2022)

1. Standards: work with and in accordance with regulations.

2. Treasures: see problems as opportunities for improvement.

3. Go to gemba: get information on where it happens.

4. Facts: assume facts.

5. 5 x W and 1 x H: ask Who, What, Where, When, Why and How.

6. PDCA: work systematically.

7. 3xMu: prevent waste (muda), check deviations (mura), control effort (muri).

8. 5 x S: seiri, seiton, seiso, seiketsu, shitsuke: order and tidiness in the workplace.

9. Discipline: keep agreements.

10. Do it: Work by these rules.

Bibliography

Achterhuis, H. (2010). *De utopie van de vrije markt (The utopia of the free market)*. Rotterdam: Lemniscaat.

Alderliesten, H. (2017). Waardenvolle kwaliteitskunde (Valuable quality-management). *Boom Management, 17* February.

Antonacopoulou, E. (2006). The Relationship between Individual and Organizational Learning: New Evidence from Managerial Learning Practices. *ManagementLearning, 37*(4). https://doi.org/10.1177/13505076060702

Argyris, C., & Schön, D. (1978). *Organizational learning. A theory in actionperspective*. Reading (MC): Addison-Wesley.

ASQ. (2006). *Quality Tools*. www.asq.org/ learn-about-quality

Barker, J. (1990). *The power of vision*. Minnesota: Charthouse International.

Basten, D., & Haarmann, T. (2018). Approaches for Organizational Learning: ALiterature *Sage Open*, https://doi.org/10.1177/21582440187942

Beekman, T. (2016). *Macht en onmacht (Power and impotence)*. Amsterdam/ Antwerpen: De Bezige Bij.

Benders, L. (2023). *Reflecteren met het Model van Korthagen (Reflecting with the Korthagen Model)*. Scribbr. https://www.scribbr.nl/stage/model-van-korthagen/

Biebricher, T. (2017). *Onvermoed en onvermijdelijk. De vele gezichten van het neoliberalisme (Unsuspected and inevitable. The Many Faces of Neoliberalism)*. Foundation Critical ethics of care. Nijmegen: Valkhof Pers.

Bouckaert, L. (1999). Kwaliteitszorg en zingeving (Quality care and meaning). *Tijdschrift voor welzijnswerk, 22*, 213, 5-13.

Bouckaert, L., & Zsolnai, L. (2012). Spirituality and business: An interdisciplinary overview, *Society and Economy, 34*(3):489-514. doi:10.1556/SocEc.34.2012.3.8

Bouwen, R. (2016). Werken aan verbondenheid en interafhankelijkheid. Cocreatie van relationele praktijken (Working on connectedness and interdependence. Co-creation of relational practices). *Positieve psychologie*. https://www.professioneelbegeleiden.nl/wefrken-aan-verbondenheid-en-interafhankelijkheid.

Bouwen, R., & Taillieu, T. (2004). Multi-party collaboration as social learning for interdependence: developing relational knowing for sustainable natural resource management. *Journal of Community & Applied Social Psychology, 14*, 137-153.

Bouwen, R., Craps, M., & De Wulf, A. (2005). Knowledge discourses and implications for inclusion and exclusion. In F. Avallone, H. Sinangil, & A. Caetono, Convivence in organisations and society, *Quaderni di Psicologia del lavoro, 12*, 63-72.

Brandt, G. (2003). *Procesmanagement als pijler van uitmuntendheid (Process management as a pillar of excellence)*. Kortrijk: Amelior.

Brown, J. (2002). *From knowledge as substance to knowledge as* participation. (Keynote Lecture on Organizational Knowledge and Learning Conference), Athens, 4-6 July.

Bruggeman, G. (2014). PDCA? No Thanks! *Kwinta,* 27 February.

Bull, B. (1990). The limits of teacher professionalization. In J. Goodlad, R. Soder, & K. Sirotnik, (Eds.), *The moral dimensions of teaching.* San Francisco: Jossey-Bass.

Bullen, P. (1999). Counting and Measuring in Community Services. *Management alternatives.*

Cameron, K. (1995). Downsizing, quality, and performance. In R. Cole, (Ed.), *The Fall and Rise of the American Quality Movement.* New York: Oxford University Press.

Camp, R. (1989). *Benchmarking: The Search for Industry Best Practices That Lead to Superior Performance.* ASQ Quality Press.

Cooperrider, D. (2000). *Appreciative inquiry. A constructive approach to organizational development and social change.* Cleveland: Case Western University.

Cooperrider, D., Ludema, J., & Barrett, F. (2001). The power of unconditional positive question. In P. Reason, & H. Bradbury, Handbook of action research (pp.189-199). New York: Sage.

Cooperrider, D. & Whitney, D. (2005). *Appreciative inquiry. A positive revolution in change.* San Francisco: Berrett-Koehler Publishers.

Cooperrider, D., & Whitney, D. (2017). Appreciative inquiry. Een revolutionaire aanpak van positieve verandering (Appreciative inquiry. A revolutionary approach to positive change). Haarzuilens: Heart Media/Quinter.

Cuyvers, G. (2007). Kwaliteitsvol werken in werkgroepen, teams en raden (Quality work in working groups, teams and councils). Geel: TRIS.

Cuyvers, G. (2019). Zorgen voor kwaliteit. Kwaliteitsontwikkeling voor non-profitorganisaties (Ensuring quality. Quality development for non-profit organizations). Leuven: LannooCampus.

De Dijn, H. (1991). Integrale kwaliteitszorg, een waanidee? (Integral quality assurance, a delusion?). *Streven,* 58(9), 780-786.

De Dijn, H. (2002). *De herontdekking van de ziel. Voor een volwaardige kwaliteitszorg (The rediscovery of the soul. For full quality assurance).* Kapellen: Pelckmans.

De Dijn, H. (2007). Het beheersingssyndroom: Vragen bij de obsessie met evaluaties. In P. Develtere, I. Nicaise, J. Pacolet, & T. Vandenbrande, Werk en Wereld. Confronterende visies op onderzoek en samenleving (Work and world. Confronting views on research and society) (pp. 40-48), Leuven: LannooCampus.

De Dijn, H. (2017). *Drie vormen van weten (Three forms of knowing).* Antwerpen, Polis.

De Moor, W. (1994). Turbulenties en communicatie (Turbulence and communication). *Mens & Organisatie, 48,* 55-71.

De Moor, W. (1995). *Teamwerk en participatief management (Teamwork and participatory management).* Houten: Bohn Stafleu.

De Moor, W. (1996). Interne communicatie en cultuurverandering (Internal communication and culture change). *Mens & Organisatie, 49,* 354-374.

De Saeger, Y. (2014). PDCA is maar een projectmanagement tool (PDCA is just a projectmanagement tool). *Kwinta,* 12 februari.

Devos, G., Verhoeven, J., & Van den Broeck, H. (1999a). *Interne zelfevaluatie-instrumenten voor kwaliteitszorg in het secundair onderwijs (Internal self-evaluation instruments for quality assurance in secondary education).* Leuven/Gent: Vlerick School voor management/K.U. Leuven, Departement Sociologie, OBPWO-project 96.04.

Devos, G., Verhoeven, J., & Van den Broeck, H. (1999b). *Een handboek voor zelfevaluatie in het secundair onderwijs (Handbook for self-evaluation in secondary education).* Leuven/Gent: Vlerick School voor management/K.U. Leuven, Departement Sociologie, OBPWO-project 96.04.

Dillen, R. & Romme, A. (1995). Leren door organisaties (Learning by organizations). *Mens & Organisatie, 49,* 160-182.

Dooley, K., Bush, D., Anderson, J., & Rungtusanatham, M. (2015). The United States' Baldrige Award and Japan's Deming Prize: Two Guidelines for Total Quality Control. *Engineering Management Journal, 2*(3). doi: 10.1080/1042 9247.1990.11414580

Drucker, P. (1980). *Managing in Turbulent Times.* New York: Harper & Row.

Drucker, P. (1993). New Society: *The anatomy of Industrial Order.* Transactional Publishers.

Drucker, P. (2014). *Innovation and entrepreneurship.* New York: Routledge

EFQM. (2021). *The EFQM Model: An Overview.* Brussels: EFQM.

EUPAN, (2020). *Common Assessment Framework The European model for improving public organisations through self-assessment.* Maastricht: European CAF Resource Centre.

Francken, R. (2011). *Birdie leadership.* Kapellen: Witsand.

Franssen, J. (2001). *Accreditatie Hoger Onderwijs; Prikkelen, Presteren, Profileren. Eindrappor (Higher Education Accreditation; Stimulate, Perform, Profil. Final Report).* Amsterdam: Commissie Accreditatie Hoger Onderwijs.

Garvin, D. (1998). The process of organization and management. *Sloan Management Review, 39*(4).

Gergen, K. (1983). *Towards transformation in social knowledge.* London: Sage.

Goubin, J. (2005). Kwaliteitszorg en beleidsplanning. Tussen zegen en boeman (Quality assurance and policy planning. Between blessing and boogeyman). In T. Hardjono, & R. Bakker, *Management van processen. Identificeren, besturen, beheersen en vernieuwen (Management of processes. Identify, manage, control, and innovate).* Deventer: Kluwer/INK.

Haijtema, D. 2010). *Leiderschap is een keuze (Leadership is a choice).* Amsterdam: Business Contact.

Hardjono, T., & Bakker, R. (2006). *Management van processen. Identificeren, besturen, beheersen en vernieuwen (Management of processes. Identify, manage, control, and innovate).* Deventer: Kluwer/INK.

Heron Technologies (2005). *FMEA in 10 stappen (FMEA in 10 steps).* Hengelo, www.heron-technologies.com

Hopkins, D., Ainscow, M., & West, M. (1994). *School improvement in an era of change*. London: Cassell.

Imai, K. (1998). *Kaizen*. Deventer: Kluwer.

Imai, K. (2012). *Gemba Kaizen. A Commonsense Approach to a Continuous Improvement Strategy*. New York: McGraw Hill

Inspectie Secundair Onderwijs (1999). *Bezorgd om kwaliteit (Concerned about quality)*. Brussel: Ministerie van de Vlaamse Gemeenschap, Departement Onderwijs.

Investors in People Nederland. (2005). *Wat is Iip? (What is Lip?)*. www.iipnl.nl

Investors in People (2016). De Standaard (The Standard). Nederland/België.

Ishikawa, K. (1986). *Totale kwaliteitscontrole (Total quality control)*. Amsterdam: Omega Boek.

Juran, J. (1951). *Quality control handbook*. New York: Mcgraw-Hill.

Kelchtermans, G., Vandenberghe, R., De Jaegher, A., & Indenkleef, M. (1991). De professionele ontwikkeling van leerkrachten vanuit biografisch perspectief (The professional development of teachers from a biographical perspective). *Nederlands Tijdschrift voor Opvoeding, Vorming en Onderwijs, 7*, 284-302.

Kelchtermans, G. (1996). Teacher vulnerability. Understanding its moral and political roots. *Cambridge Journal of Education, 26*(3), 307-323.

Kelchtermans, G. (2000). *Reflectief ervaringsleren voor leerkrachten (Reflective experiential learning for teachers)*. Deurne: Wolters Plantyn.

Kelchtermans, G. (2007). Macropolitics caught up in micropolitics: the case of the policy on quality control in Flanders (Belgium). *Journal of educational policy, 22*(4), 471-491. doi.org/10.1080/02680930701390669

Korthagen, F. (1998). Leren reflecteren. Naar systematiek in het leren van je werk als docent (Learning to reflect. Towards systematic learning from your work as a teacher.). In L. Fonderie-Tierie, & J. Hendriksen. (Red.), *Begeleiden van docenten (Guiding teachers)*. Baarn: Nelissen.

Maas, J. (2001). *Koers zetten en houden. Over de kwaliteit van sturen en besturen (Set course and keep it. About the quality of steering and controlling)*. Deventer: Kluwer/ INK.

Mensink, J. (1994). *Zelfmanagement in lerende organisaties (Self-management in learning organizations)*. Deventer: Kluwer.

Mintzberg, H. (1992). *Organisatiestructuren (Organizational structures)*. Schoonhoven: Academic Service.

Misra, G., & Prakash, A. (2012). Kenneth J. Gergen and Social Constructionism. *Psychological Studies, 57*, 121–125. doi.org/10.1007/s12646-012-0151-0.

Morgan, C., & Murgatroyd, S. (1995). *Total quality management in the public sector*. Buckingham: Open University Press.

Moullin, M. (2002). *Delivering excellence in health and social care*. Buckingham: Open University Press.

Moullin, M. (2004). Eight essentials of performance measurement. *International Journal of Health Care Quality Assurance, 17*(3).

Moullin, M. (2007). Performance measurement definitions: Linking performance measurement and organisational excellence. *International journal of health care quality assurance 20*(3), 181-183.

Murgatroyd, S., & Morgan, C. (1993). *Total quality management and the school*. Buckingham: Open University Press.

Muscad, O. (2022). Top ten important Kaizen rules. *Datamyte*, October 30.

Nystrom, D. (2002). *Leadership Summit*. US Navy.

Ovreteit, J. (1990). What is quality in health services? *Health Services management*, 132(3).

Overteit, J. (2009). *Does improving quality save money? A review of evidence of which improvements to quality reduce costs to health service providers*. London: The health foundation.

Panda, I. (2020). *Deming Prize and Malcom Baldrige National Quality Award Essay*. (ivypanda.com)

Parasuraman, A, Zeithamsi, V., & Berry, L. (1985). A conceptual model of service quality and its implications for future research. *Journal of Marketing*, Fall, 41-49.

Pareto, V. (1897). *Cours d'Économie Politique (Political Economy Cours)*. Lausanne: F. Rouge.

Pareto, V. (1906). Manuale di Economia Politica (Political Economy Cours). In A. Montesano, A. Zanni, & L. Bruni, (eds), *Edizione Critica (Critical edition)*. Milan: EGEA, Università Bocconi.

Pareto, V. (1909). *Manuel d'économie politique (Political Economy Cours)*. Paris: V. Giard & E. Brière.

Perspekt. (2017). *Kwaliteitssysteem voor Verantwoorde zorg en Verantwoord ondernemerschap (Quality system for responsible care and responsible entrepreneurship)*. PREZO Verpleging, Verzorging & Thuiszorg 2017. Utrecht: Stichting Perspekt.

Popper, M., & Lipschitz, R. (1998). Organizational learning mechanisms, *The journal of behavioural science, 34*, 161-179.

PREZO(2017). Verpleging, verzorging & thuiszorg (Nursing, care & home care). Utrecht: Stichting Perspekt.

Public Health System Group. (2019). *Quality in public health: a shared responsibility*. qualityframework@phe.gov.uk.

Pupius, M. (2005). An integral approach to achieving organisational effectiveness. In: *Integrating for Excellence*. Sheffield: Sheffield Hallam University.

Quinn, R. (1996). *Deep change*. San Francisco: Jossey-Bass Inc.

Robbins, S., Decenzo, D., & Coulter, M. (2013). *Fundamentals of management*. London: Pearson

Salipante, P., & Bouwen, R. (1995). The social construction of grievances: organizational conflicts as multiple perspectives. In D. Hosking, H. Dachler, & K. Gergen, (Eds), *Management and organizations: Relational alternatives to individualism*. Averbur: Aldershot.

Schein, E., & Schein, P. (2016). *Organizational Culture and Leadership*. Hoboken: Wiley.

Schön, D. (1983). *The reflective practitioner*. New York: Basic Books.

Senge, P. (1990). *The fifth discipline. The art and practice of the learning organization*. London: Century Business.

Socius (2018). *Als balsem, niet als vitriol (As a balm, not as a vitriol)*. https://www.socius.be/als-balsem-niet-als-vitriool/Socius (sd).

Socius. (2015). *Swoart*. socius.be/organisatiebeleid/toolbox-beleidsplanning/werkvormen/werkvorm-swoart/

Staessens, K., & Vandenberghe, R. (1987). De cultuur van een school: omschrijving en betekenis voor onderwijsinnovatie (The culture of a school: description and meaning for educational innovation). *Pedagogisch Tijdschrift, 12(*6), 341-350.

Staessens, K. (1991). *De professionele cultuur van basisscholen in vernieuwing (The professional culture of primary schools in renewal)*. (niet gepubliceerd proefschrift). Leuven: Katholieke Universiteit Leuven, Departement Pedagogische Wetenschappen.

Staessens, K., & Vandenberghe, R. (2006). Vision as a core component in school culture. Taylor&Francis Online. doi.org/10.1080/0022027940260204

Staut, P. (2000). De leidinggevende als voorwaardenschepper voor kwaliteitsontwikkeling (The manager as a facilitator for quality development). In T. Vanwing, *Vormen van Leiderschap*, Brussel: VCVO.

Stelmaszczyk, M. (2016). Relationship between individual and organizational learning: Mediating role of team learning. *Journal of Economics and Management, 26(*4), 107-127. doi: 10.22367/jem.2016.26.06

Swieringa, J., & Wierdsma, A. (1990). *Op weg naar een lerende organisatie (Towards a learning organization)*. Groningen: Wolters Noordhoff Management.

Tague, N. (2004). *The Quality Toolbox*. Milwaukee: ASQ Quality Press.

Tarlengo, J. (2023). Kaizen, continuous improvement. *Safety Culture*, July 31.

Tempelaars, A. (1998). *Padvinder. Deel 1 Leiderschap (Boy Scout. Part 1 Leadership)*. Haarlem: Instituut Nederlandse Kwaliteit.

Than, F., & Olaore, G. (2021). Effect of organizational learning and effectiveness on the operations, employee's productivity and management performance. *XIMB Journal of management, 19(2)*. doi/10.1108/XJM-09-2020-0122/full/html

Van den Berg, R. (1990). *Transformatief vernieuwingsbeleid (Transformative innovation policy)*. Deventer: Van Loghum Slaterus.

Van den Berg, R., & Vandenberhge, R. (1995). *Wegen van betrokkenheid. Reflecties op onderwijsvernieuwing (Ways of involvement. Reflections on educational innovation)*. Tilburg: Zwijsen.

Van den Berg, R., & Vandenberhge, R. (1999). *Succesvol leidinggeven aan onderwijsinnovaties (Successfully leading educational innovations)*. Alphen aan den Rijn: Samsom.

Vandenberghe, J. (2014). *Kwaliteitszorg in de GGZ: ideologie of wetenschap? (Quality care in mental health care: ideology or science?)* Leuven: U.P.C. KU Leuven.

Van de Wetering, A. (2008). Waarderende auditen met behulp van Appreciative Inquiry (Appreciative auditing using Appreciative Inquiry). *Management Issues*. www.managementissues.com.

Van Kemenade, E. (2013). De mythe van de PDCA-cyclus (the myth of the PDCA cycle). *Sigma, 5*, 32-36.

Van Kemenade, E. (2014). Geen PDCA, maar wat dan wel? (No PDCA, but so what?). *Kwinta,* 26 mei.

Vanlaere, L., & Burggraeve, R. (2018). *Gekkenwerk. Kleine ondeugden voor zorgdragers (Madness. Small vices for caretakers).* Leuven: LannooCampus.

Van Nuland, Y. (1999). *Excellent. Een handleiding voor de toepassing van het EFQM-Excellence Model (Excellent. A manual for the application of the EFQM-Excellence Model).* Blanden: Comatec.

Van Petegem, P. (1998). *Vormgeven aan schoolbeleid (Shaping school policy).* Leuven: Acco.

Vanwing, T. (2000). *Vormen van Leiderschap (Forms of Leadership).* Brussel: VCVO.

Verhaeghe, P. (2012). *De neoliberale waanzin (The neoliberal madness).* Brussel: VUB Press.

Verhaeghe, P. (2023). *Onbehagen (Unease).* Amsterdam: De Bezige Bij.

Wenger, E. (1998). *Communities of practice. Learning, meaning and identity.* Cambridge: Cambridge University Press.

Wheatley, M. (1994). *Leadership and the New Science: Discovering Order in a Chaotic World.* San Francisco: Berrett-Koehler Publishers, Inc.

ZBC Consultants. (2006). Procesmanagement: waarom rocessen beschrijven? (Process management: why describe processes?). Ede: www.zcb.nu.

Zorgnet/Perspekt (2013). *PREZO Woonzorg. Kwaliteitssysteem voor excellentie in zorg en beleid* (PREZO residential care. Quality system for excellence in care and policy). Brussel/Utrecht: Zorgnet Vlaanderen/Stichting Perspekt.

Index